QUALITATIVE INQUIRY IN THE PUBLIC SPHERE

D0061265

Qualitative Inquiry in the Public Sphere examines the relationships between pub scholarship, the research marketplace, and the politics of higher education.

It is written from the perspective that higher education is under attack from multiple sides, both political and economic; that academics reside in a precarious position, one fraught with accountability metrics, funding pressures, and spiralling bureaucracy; and that scientific knowledge itself is increasingly contentious in public. These internal and external pressures have fundamentally transformed the public sphere of higher education from one of rational public discourse by and for the public good to one of private market relations and strategic research decisions. In turn, these transformations have fundamentally altered what it means to be a 'productive' scholar within this space—altered what it means to be a public researcher in this space.

Leading international voices from the United States, Canada, Germany, the United Kingdom, and Norway collectively present a forceful rebuke to such developments, raising a clarion call to action on topics ranging from scholarly publishing, audit culture, and the privatization of public knowledge to Indigenous, arts-based, and collaborative research methods.

Qualitative Inquiry in the Public Sphere is a must-read for faculty and students alike interested in the politics of being a public researcher—of conducting research in and influencing dialogue in the public sphere.

Norman K. Denzin is Distinguished Emeritus Professor of Communications, College of Communications Scholar, and Research Professor of Communications, Sociology, and Humanities at the University of Illinois at Urbana-Champaign, USA.

Michael D. Giardina is Professor of Media, Politics, and Physical Culture in the Department of Sport Management at Florida State University, USA.

"The quality of scholarship introduced at the annual International Congress of Qualitative Inquiry is consistently innovative, provocative, and scholarly. This collection of papers represents some of the finest work of international scholars who attended the 13th annual Congress and proposed how to use qualitative inquiry and the different systems of thought that differently shape it to resist the alarming politics of the global right. At once affirmative and urgent, this book serves as inspiration and a call to political action."

Elizabeth Adams St. Pierre, Professor of Critical Studies, Educational Theory and Practice Department, University of Georgia, USA

"The International Congress of Qualitative Inquiry (ICQI) continues to be a major intervention into the ethics and politics of social research. Responding to a felt need for a high quality forum to debate issues of theory, method and social justice, this latest volume of papers from the Congress reflects on the development of the "research-enterprise nexus" in universities and our own complicity in the development of a research marketplace. It calls for a focus on the competition of ideas rather than products, and for wider engagement with communities and constituencies which should benefit from the processes and findings of qualitative research."

Harry Torrance, Professor of Education, Education and Social Research Institute, Manchester Metropolitan University, UK

QUALITATIVE INQUIRY IN THE PUBLIC SPHERE

Edited by Norman K. Denzin and Michael D. Giardina

Routledge
Taylor & Francis Group

NEW YORK AND LONDON

First published 2018
by Routledge
711 Third Avenue, New York, NY 10017

and by Routledge
2 Park Square, Milton Park, Abingdon, Oxon, OX14 4RN

Routledge is an imprint of the Taylor & Francis Group, an informa business

© 2018 Taylor & Francis

The right of Norman K. Denzin and Michael Giardina to be identified as the authors of the editorial material, and of the authors for their individual chapters, has been asserted in accordance with sections 77 and 78 of the Copyright, Designs and Patents Act 1988.

Library of Congress Cataloging-in-Publication Data
A catalog record for this title has been requested

ISBN: 978-1-138-30950-0 (hbk)
ISBN: 978-1-138-30951-7 (pbk)
ISBN: 978-1-315-14338-5 (ebk)

Typeset in Bembo and Stone Sans
by Florence Production Ltd, Stoodleigh, Devon, UK

CONTENTS

Coda: Pedagogy, Civil Rights, and the Project of
Insurrectional Democracy   211
Henry Giroux

ACKNOWLEDGMENTS

We thank Hannah Shakespeare, and Matt Bickerton at Routledge for their support of this volume and the larger ICQI project. Thanks are also due to Quentin Scott for expert copyediting, Natasha Gibbs for production design, and Neal Ternes for assistance in compiling the index. Many of the chapters in this book were presented as plenary or keynote addresses at the Thirteenth International Congress of Qualitative Inquiry, held at the University of Illinois, Urbana-Champaign, in May 2017. We thank the Institute of Communications Research, the College of Media, and the International Institute for Qualitative Inquiry for continued support of the Congress as well as those campus units that contributed time, funds, and/or volunteers to the effort.

The Congress, and by extension this book, would not have materialized without the tireless efforts of Mary Blair, Katia Curbelo, Bryce Henson, Robin Price, and James Salvo (the glue who continues to hold the whole thing together).

For information on future Congresses, please visit www.icqi.org

Norman K. Denzin
Michael D. Giardina
October 2017

INTRODUCTION

Qualitative Inquiry in the Public Sphere

Norman K. Denzin and Michael D. Giardina

Proem

Where to even begin?

Donald Trump. Brexit. Acts of terrorism in Europe. Syrian civil war. Global refugee crises. Gun violence and mass shootings in the United States. Horrifying hurricane damage in Florida, Puerto Rico, and the Virgin Islands. Nuclear threats by North Korea. The ongoing denial of climate change and scientific knowledge. And these are just the above-the-fold storylines that have carried the day over the last 18 months, to say nothing of cyber attacks on critical digital systems and infrastructure, ethnic cleansing in Myanmar, widespread corporate and political corruption, and global economic uncertainty. Without question, we are all—to different degrees and extents—situated within and against a world that is seemingly on edge, crying out for help, unraveling at the seams. It provokes us to ask, once again, about our role in the world—about how as qualitative researchers we might go about effecting change.

To be sure, this is not new ground: debates over the role and place of academics in the discourse of everyday life events have been ongoing since its advent—and in the modern era especially since the 1960s, when Noam Chomsky (1967) passionately argued at the height of the Vietnam War for the responsibility of intellectuals to descend from the proverbial Ivory Tower "to speak truth and to expose lies". Edward Said (1996) similarly inveighed against the dangers of academic 'professionalism', or the condition for which professional prestige and advancement are the end goals, rather than meaningful contribution to the public good. And Michael Burawoy (2005), in his now-famous presidential address to the 2004 American Sociological Association conference, argued forcefully for a public sociology to be the cornerstone of academic work in the discipline: addressing and engaging non-academic audiences with sociological informed analysis and critique. We ourselves have also advocated at length about the need for qualitative researchers to take up research 'outside the academy' (see, e.g., Denzin & Giardina, 2014)—to engage with concerns that align with activist-oriented research and scholarship, or at least that which centers social change as part and parcel of the research act.

Yet while a discourse of activism and social justice has long been privileged in many such calls for more *public* research, the current conditions and logics of the historical present give us pause—force us to ask if we are getting lost among the forest and missing the trees which stand in front of us. In many ways, academics today face a very real war for survival on (at least) two fronts: 1) the market orientation of the neoliberal university (and all of the challenges that come with existing in such a space), and 2) the demonization (or at least, marginalization) of scientific knowledge by politicians and general public alike (and the profound impact this has on civil society). This twinned narrative places academics in a precarious position: on the one hand, evermore professionalizing so as to withstand the imposition of accountability metrics, extramural funding pressures, and the new managerialism rampant in the administrative hierarchies of higher education (see Denzin & Giardina, 2017; see also Spooner & McNinch, 2018); on the other hand, producing knowledge that is itself under assault, politicized, or ignored (as has been the case with climate change data for many years).

Against such a backdrop, perhaps we need to step back and reevaluate the ground on which we stand—reevaluate our engagement with, and indeed place in, the public sphere—and ask how we might be more forceful in producing research that not only matters in the abstract, ephemeral sense of *wanting* to contribute to social justice and social change, but matters in concrete and productive ways for a refashioned *public qualitative inquiry* to take effect. *That is the charge of this volume.*

The Politics of Being a "Public" Researcher

Let's be blunt: things are pretty bleak at the moment in higher education. The numbers paint a dispiriting picture[1]:

- In 1969, tenured and tenure-track positions across all forms of higher education in the United States (public, private, two-year, etc.) accounted for roughly 78.3% of faculty positions; in the intervening 40 years, that percentage had dropped dramatically, to roughly 33.5% (Kezar & Maxey, 2013).
- Federal funding for universities has been consistently declining, and has especially accelerated since the Great Recession in 2008; according to the National Science Foundation, the years 2011 to 2014 saw "the longest multiyear decline in federal funding for academic R&D since the beginning of the annually collected data series in FY 1972" (Simon, 2016, para. 2).

This is especially true with respect to public land-grant research universities, such as those in the Midwest, where the University of Wisconsin saw $250 million cut from its budget between 2015 and 2017, the University of Iowa saw its budget cut by 6%, and the University of Missouri eliminated approximately 400 positions due to budgetary constraints (Marcus, 2017).

- In a similar regard, the Trump administration has proposed cutting between 11 and 18% of the budget for federal agencies that "provide the bulk of government support for university research" (Marcus, 2017, para. 19).

- Public opinion on the necessity of a college degree has changed dramatically in the last ten years: in 2008, 55% of Americans view a college education "as necessary for workforce success", with 43% disagreeing with that statement; by 2016, those numbers had become inverted, with only 42% agreeing that a college education was necessary, and 57% disagreeing (Public Agenda, 2016).

- There has been a decided rise within higher education of audit culture— that is, accountancy, bibliometrics, managerialism, performance indicators, rankings, and the like—which reduces faculty to "depersonalized spread-sheets" in the service of the neoliberal university (Spooner & McNinch, 2018). In this vein, as Gary Rhoades (1998) once lamented in his classic book on the restructuring of academic labor, we have become managed professionals under the control of professional managers.

Clearly, the above-bulleted points are but a few of the major structural issues and transformations facing faculty and students alike in a moment organized in large measure by the neoliberal marketization of higher education—itself an outgrowth of the accelerated marketization of everyday life. To this end, we would argue both internal and external pressures and publics have fundamentally transformed the public sphere of higher education from one of rational public discourse by and for the public good to one of private market relations. In turn, these transformations have fundamentally altered what it means to be a 'productive' subject within this space—altered what it means to be a *public researcher* in this space.

Consider the following example:

Last year (2016), a colleague of ours was invited to interview for a social science faculty position at a leading research university in the United Kingdom. As part of the typical itinerary for such visits, our colleague was tasked with discussing her research focus and plans for the next 3–5 years, as well as addressing what she would "bring to the role in terms of teaching and enterprise". Although discussions of one's research and teaching are of course commonplace in faculty hiring interviews (as are discussions of various forms of service to the profession), the use of the term 'enterprise' was especially instructive, for it *explicitly* hailed the necessity of expressing how one's research would be located in directly working with business, public, or other such organizations to 'create impact'.

Looking more closely at the term and the way it was oriented within this particular institution, it became clear it was being conceived of as a catch-all to frame themes of not only working with business and professional sectors, but also to assert a focus on 'employability', 'entrepreneurship', and 'innovation' (specifically within industry). By all accounts, our colleague deftly navigated this line of questioning, and was able to connect her sociological research to working with public, community, and non-governmental organizations in order to demonstrate how her research would (or at least could) achieve the aims enumerated on the university's 'enterprise' website.

It is important to note that the spirit—or even necessity—of enterprise relations is not singularly located at the afore-anonymized university at which our colleague interviewed. For example, University College London promotes "UCL Innovation and Enterprise" in order to:

> ensure that the economic and societal benefits of our research are fully realized. To achieve this, UCL Innovation and Enterprise brings together academics, the business community and other potential beneficiaries of our research in order to maximize its potential for commercialization and 'real world' use. The goal is to secure our institution's long-term place as a global leader in enterprise and innovation.
>
> (www.ucl.ac.uk/enterprise)

Similarly, at Oxford University, a wholly-owned subsidiary of the university called Oxford University Innovation manages "the University's technology transfer and consulting activities and innovation management services to clients around the world" in order to, among other things, "launch innovative ideas, invest in new ventures, and provide or access consulting services" (innovation.ox.ac.uk).

In the United States, the University of Illinois at Urbana-Champaign's Research Park likewise hosts the EnterpriseWorks Incubator, which

> is owned and operated by the University of Illinois to help launch successful startup companies; the 43,000-square foot facility is at the heart of the Research Park's community building efforts. Its atrium is a hub of activity and its clients span from biotechnology, chemical sciences, software development, to materials sciences. Through the commercialization of leading research from across the University of Illinois, its startups are working to address challenges with transformative results.
>
> (http://researchpark.illinois.edu/enterpriseworks)

And at the University of Michigan, the top public university in research spending in the United States at $1.33 billion, the Fast Forward Medical Innovation program

[is] focused on nurturing commercialization and entrepreneurship, [in which] the U–M Medical School research enterprise offers a holistic approach to biomedical innovation to both faculty and potential external partners.

(https://research.medicine.umich.edu)

This *explicit* focus on the *research–enterprise nexus* is instructive. Moving beyond the singular discussion of (obtaining) extramural grant funding that has long dominated higher education in the United States and elsewhere, the focus on enterprise as framed by and within the 'creation of impact'—through partnership between academic and external publics, be it in the form of research parks, consultancy, licensing, and/or the creation of jobs, patents, or other tangible benefits—is one that is increasingly privileged within the neoliberal university as a means of asserting a positive barometer of research *impact*.[2]

Labor historian Daniel A. Gilbert (2013) notes that quite obviously "research universities in the United States have always shared a close relationship with business" (p. 34). However, he argues it was at the confluence of a number of factors in the 1980s that these public–private partnerships were significantly amplified; namely, the erosion of public funding for higher education and the correlative influx if not outright reliance on external corporate funding dollars to make up for this shortfall. One outcome of thirty or so uninterrupted years of this trend, he continues, is that of the private (rather than public) intellectual; or, the notion of scholars who are "valued to the extent their scholarly work can be commodified and sold on the free market" (p. 36).

This is but one in a number of ongoing developments in which the idea of being a *public* researcher has been reframed within the research marketplace— the way the public sphere of academia itself has been reframed as a *research marketplace* competing not for ideas but for highly valued *products*. As Julianne Cheek (2017, p. 22) makes clear:

> Products highly valued in this research marketplace include outputs such as publications . . . inputs such as monies that are gained externally for research, and throughputs such as the number of students who complete higher education degrees "on time". [. . .] These products provide researchers with currency in the research marketplace—currency that can be used to "buy" goods such as promotion, tenure, and jobs. In this research marketplace, what matters most is the relative position of, or the relative amount of currency held by, a researcher, compared to other researchers who are their market competitors.

Cheek (2017) further argues that 'buyers' in this context include external funders and funding bodies, as well as publishers and editors of scholarly journals; sellers include universities—who compete to sell their degree programs and prestige to student-consumers (through university rankings, such as those by *U.S. News & World Report*)—and private firms (e.g., Thomson Reuters, Google, Scopus, etc.), who construct metrics and rankings that universities become dependent upon. Moreover, she maintains that we as researchers actively support and maintain this marketplace through our very conduct of being academics in this moment—of internalizing if not tacitly agreeing with it in order to exist if not flourish in our careers. This we might surmise, following Gaile S. Canella and Mirka Koro-Ljungberg (2017), is the result of market-driven focus morphing "away from a jurisdictional emphasis (with a potential focus on fairness) to forms of veridiction (neoliberal truth regimes) that legitimate intervention into all aspects of society" (p. 155); in this case, the legitimation of competition among scholars—competition for resources, students, and scholarly worth. It is in this sense that "the conditions and political economy of intellectual work by university-based intellectuals are central terrains of social struggle in the contemporary age of neoliberalism" (Gilbert, 2013, p. 33). Importantly, as Wendy Brown (2015) has argued, neoliberalism as political rationality 'hollows out' democracy and results in the 'undoing' of the liberal democratic state—a state in which "a distinctly public sphere of debate and discussion do not appear as democracy's vital venue (Brown, in Shenk, 2015, para. 25).[3]

Complicating matters is that scientific knowledge is itself under attack from various quarters—from policy makers who often demonstrate a remarkable illiteracy about basic scientific truths; from corporate leviathans who actively lobby against or seek to influence or corrupt the conduct of scientific inquiry; from news media, who often fail to communicate new scientific findings in a way that is accessible to the general public; and the general public itself, which increasingly is found to reject or deny scientific truths when they conflict with their own personally held political beliefs (e.g., evolution or climate change; see Dastigir, 2017). Not only that, but partisan public opinion holds in the United States that "58 percent of Republicans think that colleges and universities have a negative effect on the country" (Fingerhut, 2017), and right-wing media personalities regular decry universities, science, and reason as enemies of the American people. Although this latter assault is a tried and true conservative talking point (see, e.g., Bloom, 1987; Buckley, Jr., 1951), it has been greatly exacerbated by the election of Trump as President—a moment in history when public displays of ignorant provocation are worn as badges of honor, but which have material consequences for the future of higher education (in terms of funding, enrollments, student expectations, and so forth).

And so here we sit; floating in the wind. We have previously addressed the material conditions of qualitative inquiry in neoliberal times—of how audit culture, accountability metrics, rankings, and the like—have come to transform higher education (see Denzin & Giardina, 2017). Yet chronicling these changes— important as it is to do so, calling to light those forces actively shaping our subjectivity as members of a scholarly community—leaves us with a sense of unfinished business. What does it mean to imagine *beyond the boundaries* of the research marketplace? To productively challenge the marketization if not privatization of the (academic) public sphere? What does it mean to *question our own complicity* in the perpetuation of the research marketplace? To reevaluate our approach not only to the research act, but also to the conduct of our scholarly lives? What does it mean to advocate for a *public qualitative inquiry*? What might that look like? And for whom?

These and other questions orient *Qualitative Inquiry in the Public Sphere*. It is in this sense that we join colleagues Canella and Koro-Ljungberg (2017), who call for a "critical counter conduct" (p. 155)—counter narratives to and counter practices of being a qualitative researcher under these conditions. For, as Robyn Dowling (2008) reminds us, "corporatism and neoliberalism are not simply parachuted into contexts like universities; they are enacted, performed, and *contested*" (p. 814, emphasis ours). In the chapters that follow, eighteen scholars turn a klieg light on the scholarly publishing industry, audit culture, research marketplaces, and public expressions of research. They also challenge assumptions about social science research methodology and 'slow science'. And they advocate for new understandings and applications of Indigenous research, arts-based research, collaborative research, and the essence of the research tradition.

The Chapters

Qualitative Inquiry in the Public Sphere is comprised of two sections separated by a one-chapter interlude. Section I begins with Yvonna S. Lincoln's chapter ("Fracking the Faculty: The Privatization of Public Knowledge, the Erosion of Faculty Worklife Quality, the Dimunition of the Liberal Arts"), in which she addresses how knowledge production and scientific discovery are being perverted from their original purpose of improving the lot of humankind, and turned instead to yet another marketable commodity. This rapid marketization of knowledge has led to what may be termed the "fracking" of the faculty—a condition in which knowledge production is less of a journey toward discovery (with many failures along the way permitted or even encouraged, and "dry holes" the expectation), and more of an "extractive industry" similar to mining or oil exploration. Human capital, she posits, thus takes on an entirely new meaning as faculty become the new "natural resource" to be plundered and mined. She further argues that the consequences of this trend similarly result in the fracturing of the collegial university community, and a devaluating of the liberal arts in favor of the science, technology, engineering, and mathematics (STEM) disciplines. The end result, she maintains, is that universities are in danger of losing their original missions for educating the citizenry for democratic participation.

In Chapter 2 ("Pushing Boundaries: Academic De-institutionalization and Our Radical Imagination vs. Ourselves and Audit Culture"), Marc Spooner addresses the "Triple M" crisis in higher education: market, managerialism, and measurement. To this end, he provides an overview of audit culture, followed by an examination of institutionalization and academic programming. He follows this by reimagining the possibilities, products, and processes of legitimate scholarship as it has been repeatedly promulgated from graduate school to tenure. In so doing, he calls on academics to fight against the "increasing pressures to conform to the rigid demands of misconstrued accountability, quality assurance, and/or excellence frameworks, and to further engage with our radical imagination".

In Chapter 3 ("Into the Woods: Scholarly Publishing for a Post-tenure World), Mitch Allen argues that the obsession among academics of publishing in high impact factor journals and with highly rated book publishers is a function of the current market orientation of the tenure and promotion system. When universities assess an academic's worth based on impact factor, he posits, it is a compelling reason to follow certain publication strategies. But what if the tenure system was abolished? What would *that* publishing landscape look like? In this chapter, he thus offers alternative options for scholarly publication in a tenureless ecosystem—open access journals, preprints, data sharing, and public scholarship channels—most of which are already practiced in parts of the academic world. He then addresses the key problem of adopting this system, which is not tenure per se but *publishing economics*—showing how commercial publishers are moving to create vertically integrated publishing monopolies and the difficulty of non-profit channels to compete. He concludes by offering several strategies that scholars can undertake to make the future publishing environment more friendly and responsive to academics.

In Chapter 4 ("The BMJ Debate and What it Tells us about Who Says What, When and Where, about our Qualitative Inquiry"), Julianne Cheek uses recent debates in The BMJ (formerly, *The British Medical Journal*) over the decision to brand publishing qualitative studies as 'an extremely low priority' for the journal to better understand the relations of power that govern the politics of research and publishing in the present moment. In reviewing the timeline of events related to The BMJ dispute, she reveals the private publics and public counter-publics that had a hand in shaping the terms of the debate. In turn, she offers a way forward for qualitative researchers to actively move forward rather than reactively respond to challenges posed by the confluence of audit culture, the research marketplace, and journal publishing.

In Chapter 5 ("Indigenous Qualitative Research in the Neoliberal Public Sphere"), Patrick Lewis makes the case that "everyone should attend to Indigenous inquiry methods because facing neoliberalism is only one more moment in the re-iteration of colonisation that Indigenous people have been resisting. Neoliberalism is just the latest iteration of colonialism and imperialism." To illustrate his argument, Lewis uses the example of how (in Canada) increasingly the recognition of the rights of Indigenous peoples and their land claims are couched in the language of neoliberal governance. As a form of public intervention into this discourse, he then narrates the competing stories that go about constructing and challenging this arrangement, ultimately showing how Indigenous scholars and communities take up and put into practice decolonizing theory to "effectively navigate neoliberal logics in the public sphere."

In Chapter 6 ("Cultivating Critical Reflexivity in the Public Sphere"), Ping-Chun Hsiung chronicles what happened when she stepped out of the academic world to give a public lecture at the Toronto Reference library as part of a lecture series titled "Thought Exchange"—part of the library's program to engage the general public through lectures and discussions in the Toronto area. To this end, she presents four pedagogical strategies she used to engage non-academic audiences. Expertly weaving her research on China's Great Leap Forward with a how-to retelling of her presentation, Hsiung makes it clear that engaging in this form of public sociology—of literally bringing sociology to the public in a non-academic public forum—is more than simply presenting research that is free from jargon or other such academese, but is a skill that needs to be worked at and refined.

Section I comes to a close with Chapter 7 ("Individual Needs, Cultural Barriers, Public Discourses: Taking Qualitative Inquiry into the Public Sphere"), in which Silke Migala and Uwe Flick present four versions of taking qualitative inquiry into the public sphere: 1) as transgressing the original scientific boundaries in which it is located (e.g., sociology, education); 2) identifying and then researching problems that are affected by issues of public relevance (e.g., discrimination, health care, etc.); 3) making the results of our inquiry accessible for public audiences (both in the language that we use and the means through which it is physically made accessible); and 4) adapting our understanding of what 'good' research means. To do so, they present on a qualitative public health research project they undertook into discrimination of specific groups in accessing social support with end-of-life care. Through this example, they aim to illustrate how the processes of doing such research are actively *made public*.

In Chapter 8, Ronald J. Pelias presents us with a performative interlude titled "On Being Awake after the United States 2016 Presidential Election". Calling upon a fragmentary structure in his autoethnographic chapter, he displays the troubling thoughts and incidents that have assailed him since the election, to point toward a frightening right-wing agenda, and to demonstrate why he 'cannot sleep'. Each numbered section offers evidence that the moral core of the United States has been deeply damaged by the election of Donald Trump. In a postscript added a year after Trump took office, he describes a political reality much worse than he—and many of us—had imagined. It is a stark reminder of the troubled times in which we exist as researchers and citizens of the world—of the troubled times that far exceed the sphere of higher education.

Section II opens with James Joseph Scheurich's chapter (Research for Revolutionaries by #JimScheurich"), in which he makes the case that "social science research methodology in general is largely colonialist." The starting point of being critical, he contends, must start with a critique of the dominant U.S. social system and its assumptions, practices, and politics—one that sees it as "based on the exploitation, debasement, deprivation, and devastation of the many worldwide." From there flows his argument that while the purpose and content of critical research may be critical, its methodologies largely bear the imprimatur of this system—a point made clear most recently by the likes of Freire (1970), Anzaldúa (1987), Collins (1990), and Tuhiwai Smith (1999), but which has largely been ignored by white social scientists even as Indigenous, Critical Race Theory and its hybrids (LatCrit, multiracial CRT), and so forth continue to grow. His charge, ultimately, is that we reject the construct of social science research in favor of building new constructions of research, based around critique, resistance, and community—for each alone is not enough to affect change.

In Chapter 10 ("Method ol o gie s . . . that Encounter (Slowness and) Irregular Rhythm"), Mirka Koro-Ljungberg and Timothy Wells follow global slow movements in cities, food, film, travel, medicine, and schools to wonder what happens when qualitative researchers engage in shifting methodological rhythm and varying intensities of scholarly activities (e.g., reading, writing, thinking, inter and intra-acting, interpreting, analyzing, theorizing). Thus, in this chapter, they explore 'experimental' methodological practices that might utilize *slowness* not as a static state but as a shifting rhythm and irregular pattern. They problematize and counter paradoxical neoliberal expectations of speedy yet deregulated, effective yet risky, and progressive yet 'safe' inquiry, methodology, and knowledge production. At the same time, they encourage scholars to approach *slowness* and 'slow scholarship' with critical caution, offering the idea of *irregular rhythm* as alternative and different possibility to respond to the demands for 'speedy' and effective scholarship and qualitative inquiry.

In Chapter 11 ("Collaborative Autoethnography: An Ethical Approach to Inquiry that Makes a Difference"), Judith C. Lapadat focuses on one historical evolution within qualitative inquiry—the rising centrality of ethics—and specifically, the ethics of autoethnography. More specifically, she posits that autoethnography is rooted in ethical intent. Yet, as it has evolved methodologically, some "knotty ethical problems" with autoethnography itself have increasingly become visible. In response, she contends that some of the ethical issues that confound solo autoethnographers diminish when a more collaborative approach to doing autoethnography is adopted, and illustrates an ethical case forward for such research.

In Chapter 12 ("Writing to It: Creative Engagements with Writing Practice in and with the Not Yet Known in Today's Academy"), Jonathan Wyatt and Ken Gale articulate an approach to collaborative-writing-as-inquiry they refer to as 'between the twos'. In offering opportunities for bringing non-totalizing modes of sensing to life within Deleuze and Guattari's experimental and creative originations, and in the multiplicity and the vibrant potentialities of always becoming, they make claims for new, creatively productive writing practices in the university of the future. To do so, they animate rather than simply write about such claims through their back-and-forth, call-and-response performative dialogue—at once challenging and emotive, lyrical and expressive.

In Chapter 13 ("The Future of Critical Arts-based Research: Creating Aesthetic Spaces for Resistance Politics"), Susan Finley recreates her keynote address from the 2017 International Congress of Qualitative Inquiry, one marked by an interweaving of personal history with the resistances politics of a critical arts-based research orientation. She asks: How can critical arts-based research disrupt the flow of history, stem the flow of racist, elitist and nationalist policies? How can critical arts-based research create new spaces for democratic political action?

Section II comes to a close with Chapter 14 ("Musical Chairs: Method, Style, Tradition"), in which James Salvo artfully weaves together the philosophy of the research tradition with a discussion of music, aesthetics, artistry, and mentorship—of how to follow in a tradition not by repeating the already done but by finding one's own way forward. His complex and multi-layered exegesis is as playful and colorful as it is critical of the replication of that which cannot be replicated. He thus calls us to cover different ground in our endeavors, with the knowledge that it is okay—even warranted—to do so.

The volume comes to a close with Henry Giroux's Coda ("Pedagogy, Civil Rights, and the Project of Insurrectional Democracy"), a clarion call to resurrect a radical democratic public sphere through a transformative pedagogy that "relentlessly questions the kinds of labor, practices, and forms of production that are enacted in public and higher education.

By Way of a Conclusion

Staying positive about the state of things—be they in higher education or daily life—is a bit of a strain these days. Almost weekly, it would seem, we are confronted with another front-page story touting university budget cuts, the curtailment of extramural political speech, or other challenges to the conduct of being an academic. We watch as the political process no longer seems to work—that the normal order of things in Congress have simply been reduced to the side with the most votes trying to hurt the other side, the human costs be damned (such as we saw with respect to the Affordable Care Act and the various repeal efforts). We watch as the leader of the free world repeatedly lies live on television, and shake our heads when it doesn't seem to matter anymore.

On a more personal level, we witness shrinking university resources and commodified enterprise cultures impacting our friends and colleagues, especially those with precarious employment as sessional instructors or in continuing but non-tenure-earning lines. We come to terms with mentoring our former students about how to navigate the minefield of higher education, wanting them to be agents of change but acknowledging the harsh realities of what they themselves must negotiate in their current careers in order to stand on firm ground (see Bunds & Giardina, 2017). And we recognize that, as senior faculty, we have a responsibility to use our relative positions of privilege and stability to unsettle the narrative so that change may come about—however small or incremental it may be.

Put more bluntly—more urgently—we need a dignified politics that is open to the possibilities of nonviolent ways of living (Giroux, 2016, p. 219).[4] We need a community centered democracy that promotes civic literacy, and encourages alignments between protest movements led by youth, women, Latinos, Muslims, LGBT persons, the poor. Now, more than ever, we need reasons to believe the citizens can reclaim their voice in the public sphere, where they can speak out, protest, express their outrage, and voice their utopian dreams of peace and justice.

The tools of critical pedagogy are of great importance. We must use our analytical skills to imagine more equitable and just societies, while shaping democratic ideals, and inspiring civic courage (Giroux, 2016, p. 222). We need a public pedagogy that emphasizes an ethics of trust, compassion, care, and solidarity. We need to fight off despair, self-pity and fear. We must model creative resistance. We must forge a banner of solidarity for real ideological and structural change. This would be a discourse willing to unite the fragmented Left around the call for a resurgent insurrectional democracy (see Giroux, this volume). We must encourage the development of critical historical memories. We must mobilize against the violence of organized forgetting. We must stop the willful erasure and distortion of radical discourses that encourage critical thinking (Giroux, 2014, p. 26). We must mobilize students to be critically engaged historical agents, attentive to important social issues. Students must be taught that inquiry is always about power, about what is knowledge, about what is truth; that is, inquiry is always a form of moral intervention in the service of liberation. We cannot separate theories, values, and inquiry from moral and ethical and political being (Giroux, 2016, p. 237). The challenge is to inspire people to become critical inquirers and critically engaged citizens willing to fight for democracy, liberation, and solidarity (Giroux, 2016, p. 241).

What kind of society allows economic injustice, and environmental violence towards its children and persons of color? What kind of society punishes transgender students? What kind of society elects as president a man who mocks the disabled? We seek students and researchers who embrace a politics of emancipation. We seek leaders who will help us enact a pedagogy of educated hope. We need teachers who as public intellectuals will teach students how to be critical historical agents. We need students who are not afraid to raise their voices in solidarity with those who struggle to translate personal troubles into public issues (Giroux, 2016, p. 248; Mills, 1959).

These are not easy times to be a student or professor (though we clearly admit they are easier for some by dint of history, discipline, and privilege). But they do present us with an array of options as to what to do next. The collected authors in this volume point in many directions, and provide poignant examples. But these are not the only options available. We invite you be part of the conversation; to find your way forward.

We still have a job to do; let's get to it.

Notes

1. Although we limit ourselves to a snapshot of the U.S. context specifically in the bullet points below, we acknowledge the overarching concern—that of the changing nature of higher education—is one that is in effect throughout the world and in differing manifestations. This will become clear in a later example in this chapter.
2. This is not to say, of course, that creating impact through one's research is a negative thing; or that public–private research partnerships are inherently problematic. Not by any means. Rather, what we call into question is the material and discursive formations privileging if not (re-)orienting scholarly life around or in the service of the neoliberal university and its attendant *enterprise relations*.
3. We are not suggesting that academics do not engage with the general public. Clearly, they do. In fact, given the rapid proliferation of social media (e.g., Twitter, Facebook, etc.) and online platforms, academics are more public-facing and engaged with the public than ever before. Rather, our point is that the conceptualization of pubic research, within the context of the neoliberal university, is one that privileges specifics *forms* of public engagement.
4. This paragraph, and the three that follow, are adapted with slight modification from Denzin (forthcoming).

References

Bloom, A. (1987). *The closing of the American mind: How higher education has failed democracy and impoverished the souls of today's students.* New York: Simon & Schuster.

Brown, W. (2015). *Undoing the demos: Neoliberalism's stealth revolution.* Cambridge, MA: MIT Press.

Buckley, Jr., W. F. (1951). *God and Man at Yale: The superstitions of 'academic freedom.'* New York: Regnery.

Bunds, K. S. & Giardina, M. D. (2017). Navigating the corporate university: Reflections on the politics of research in neoliberal times. *Cultural Studies ⟺ Critical Methodologies,* 17(3), 227–235.

Burawoy, M. (2005). For public sociology. *American Sociological Review,* 70(1), 4–28.

Canella, G. S. & Koro-Ljungberg, M. (2017). Neoliberalism in higher education: Can we understand? Can we resist and survive? Can we become without neoliberalism? *Cultural Studies ⟺ Critical Methodologies,* 17(3), 155–162.

Cheek, J. (2017). Qualitative inquiry, research marketplaces, and neoliberalism: Adding some +s (pluses) to our thinking about the mess in which we find ourselves. In N. K. Denzin and M. D. Giardina (Eds.), *Qualitative inquiry in neoliberal times.* New York: Routledge.

Chomsky, N. (1967). The responsibility of intellectuals. *The New York Times Review of Books*. Retrieved October 11, 2017 from www.nybooks.com/articles/1967/02/23/a-special-supplement-the-responsibility-of-intelle/

Dastagir, A. E. (2017, April 20). People trust science. So why don't they believe it? *USA Today*. Retrieved October 9, 2017 from www.usatoday.com/story/news/2017/04/20/science-march-war-truth-political-polarization/100636124/

Denzin, N. K. & Giardina, M. D. (Eds.) (2014). *Qualitative inquiry outside the academy*. New York: Routledge.

Denzin, N. K. & Giardina, M. D. (Eds.) (2017). *Qualitative inquiry in neoliberal times*. New York: Routledge.

Dowling, R. (2008). Geographies of identity: Labouring in the 'neoliberal' university. *Progress in Human Geography*, *32*(6), 812–820.

Fingerhut, H. (2017, July 20). Republicans sceptical of colleges' impact on U.S., but most see benefits for workforce preparation. *Pew Research Center*. Retrieved from www.pewresearch.org/fact-tank/2017/07/20/republicans-skeptical-of-colleges-impact-on-u-s-but-most-see-benefits-for-workforce-preparation/

Gilbert, D. A. (2013). The generation of public intellectuals: Corporate universities, graduate employees, and the academic labor movement. *Labor Studies Journal*, *38*(1), 32–46.

Giroux, H. A. (2014). *Zombie politics and culture in the age of casino capitalism*. New York: Peter Lang.

Giroux, H. A. (2016). *America at war with itself*. New York: City Lights.

Kezar, A. & Maxey, D. (2013). *The changing academic workforce*. Association of Governing Boards of Universities and College. Washington, D.C.

Marcus, J. (2017, October 15). The fragile state of the Midwest's public universities. *The Atlantic*. Retrieved October 17, 2017 from www.usnews.com/opinion/knowledge-bank/articles/2016–03–18/why-university-research-and-federal-funding-matters-in-the-2016-election

Mills, C. W. (1959). *The sociological imagination*. New York: Oxford University Press.

Public Agenda (2016, September 12). Public opinion on higher education: Survey results suggest public confidence in higher education is waning. *Public Agenda*. Retrieved October 3, 2017 from www.publicagenda.org/pages/public-opinion-higher-education-2016

Rhoades, G. (1998). *Managed professionals: Unionized faculty and restructuring academic labor*. Albany, NY: SUNY Press.

Said, E. W. (1996). *Representations of the intellectual: The 1993 Reith Lectures*. New York: Vintage Books.

Shenk, T. (2015, April 2). Booked #3: What exactly is neoliberalism (Interview with Wendy Brown). *Dissent Magazine*. Retrieved October 5, 2017 from www.dissentmagazine.org/blog/booked-3-what-exactly-is-neoliberalism-wendy-brown-undoing-the-demos

Simon, L. K. (2016, March 18). The future of America, forgotten in 2016. *US News & World Report*. Retrieved October 3, 2017 from www.usnews.com/opinion/knowledge-bank/articles/2016-03-18/why-university-research-and-federal-funding-matters-in-the-2016-election

Spooner, M. & McNinch, J. (Eds.) (2018). *Dissident knowledge in higher education*. Regina, SK: University of Regina Press.

SECTION I
Private Lives, Public Matters

1

FRACKING THE FACULTY

The Privatization of Public Knowledge,
the Erosion of Faculty Worklife Quality,
the Diminution of the Liberal Arts

Yvonna S. Lincoln

Introduction

University-developed knowledge is rapidly undergoing privatization by virtue of being sequestered into increasingly expensive journals, books, and monographs, all of which are controlled by a burgeoning academic publishing industry (Lincoln, 1998; 1999; 2012, Ohmann, 2003; Pirie, 2009). As a result, it becomes obvious that less well-funded scholars and institutions (with limited library budgets), as well as developing countries, find it harder and harder to access knowledge that might lead to improved life chances for citizens, more democratic forms of government, or more useful scientific knowledge for health, agriculture, clean water and the like. Knowledge production and scientific discovery are being perverted from their original purpose of improving the lot of humankind, and turned instead to yet another marketable commodity. The argument is made that, having marketized virtually everything on the planet, including our privacy and "interiority" (van Manen, 2010, p. 1024), the capitalist concern turned to finding new material that might be commodified and hence, marketized (Pirie, 2009). What better than the steady, rich outflow of information, data, knowledge, and proposed applications (or technology transfer) from elite scholarly knowledge workers? The exceptions are open access journals[1], and U.S. government regulations which force some government-sponsored research to remain open access for a year prior to publication, so that it may be accessed anywhere in the world. The rapid marketization of knowledge, however, has led to what may be metaphorically termed the "fracking" of the faculty.

Fracking

Fracking, or hydraulic fracturing, refers to the process of forcibly driving large volumes of water and chemicals thousands of feet into the ground in order to fracture layers of shale and other rock which contain oil and/or natural gas. The process, which has been around for many decades, is now being employed more widely in what is described publicly as a means to achieve energy independence, particularly independence from the OPEC (Oil Producing and Exporting Consortium) nations. Fracturing permits tapping into the vast reserves of oil and gas trapped deep underground in various shales and reservoirs throughout North America. Unfortunately, fracturing (or "fracking") comes with side effects, including being the suspected cause of increased earthquakes; contamination of ground and aquifer water; the creation of vast sinkholes (particularly in Louisiana; see Murphy, 2013); and property damage from tremors and shaken ground.

Fracking seems like an appropriate metaphor since its roots are in increased oil and gas production, and therefore, the creation of greater capital; in unforeseen environmental damage; in lowering of quality of life near fracking operations; in damage to homes and other buildings; and in genuine health and safety dangers to both humans and livestock. Each of those suspected outcomes seems to have parallels to university life and the technical core's—the faculty's—primary functions: teaching and knowledge production.

The Capitalization and Corporatization of Public Knowledge

Foremost, of course, is the commodification of scholarly production—research—that goes on with the publication apparatus created in the Western world. The transfer of public knowledge into capital production via academic publication—books and journals—is a by-product of the understanding, largely on the part of capitalists, that knowledge is money, is worth money, and that those with money will pay to have current knowledge, data, insights, and implications that proceed from academic publishing. This is not to denigrate the sharing and transfer of scientific and social science knowledge that occurs across the developed world as answers are sought to persistent and troublesome scientific and social issues. Rather, it is to examine with a critical bent who profits from that knowledge in addition to other scholars and policy makers. It is quite clear that money is being made—that is, capital is being produced—from what is tantamount to free labor (Bergstrom, 2001), at least some of which is paid for by the federal government in the United States and United Kingdom.

The labor of knowledge production is a primary reason faculty join research institutions, and sharing of knowledge through teaching another driver undergirding the choice of an academic life. Many faculty undertake research which is externally funded, but many others, having virtually no access to funds not committed to the hard sciences, undertake research simply as a part of their normal workload, and consequently, engage knowledge creation as "free labor" (although time for such work is built into the workload of faculty, typically), with travel, books, many journals, and other expenses related to research borne by the academics themselves. Nor does any faculty member typically grumble about such expenses, simply because the joys of research, learning, and the achievement of discovery and insight provide enormous intellectual and professional pleasure, as well as occasionally recognition beyond one's own work milieu. Further, sound knowledge creation and production, and its publication, are the routes most likely to lead to tenure, to increasing academic freedom, and the more or less permanent employment and employability (McGee, 1992).

The canker in the bark, however, has been the increasing press for knowledge created for immediate application, with a concurrent diminution of focus on basic research. Universities themselves are increasingly interested in turning the products of research into marketable and patentable products, often on a profit-sharing basis with the scholar-inventor. Large universities have frequently created entire departments solely for attending to patent and copyright rights for faculty–university partnerships. As a consequence, faculty work is frequently appraised for its application potential rather than for its actual discovery potential, and for its marketability promise rather than its illuminative value.

That is, knowledge production has become less of a journey toward discovery (with many failures along the way permitted or even encouraged, and "dry holes" the expectation), and more of an "extractive industry" similar to mining or oil exploration. The challenges and delights of the intellectual life are being measured by the applications to which research may be applied, rather than the accumulation added to the body of knowledge. Human capital takes on an entirely new meaning as faculty become the new "natural resource" to be plundered and mined. The "drilling down" into faculty work for commodification and marketization realizability creates a pressure on research work that may ultimately make such work less than pleasurable.

Unforeseen Environmental Damage

The unforeseen environmental damage is less easy to weigh, but far more dangerous to the idea of a university. One consequence of the increasing pressure to publish, and to create marketable products, whether in the form of journal articles and books, or in the form of patentable applications from which capital may be generated, is that competition between faculty—for funding, for publications, for national and international fellowships, and other valued emoluments—increases, while collegiality is subtly and gradually diminished. The collegial community itself is fractured, as faculty are pitted against each other for who can attract the largest number of dollars—what one colleague terms "the dollarocracy" (Capraro & Lincoln, in progress). Competition between and among faculty is abetted, while collegiality and civility become victim to a kind of fiscal race for dollars, prestige, the "branding" of public universities, and rankings around publications, awards, citations, external funding, and other visible "signs" of excellence, such as those proffered by companies such as Academic Analytics— a company that endeavors to track and aggregate research productivity for universities (see Wexler, 2015). Faculty are resisting these measures of productivity, and declare them 'dangerous to higher education'. Faculty cite issues of quality—what is the quality of the work produced?—but also the actual accuracy of Academic Analytics's data (Wexler, 2015).

Other faculty question whether smaller departments and program areas are being evaluated fairly for their contributions, particularly when publications are not in widely recognized journals or other outlets. Faculty are reported as feeling "dispirited," "fragmented," and "devalued" (Bowen & Schuster, 1986, cited in Gonzalez, Martinez, & Ordu, 2014), speaking often of "pressure" and the erosion in the "sheer joy of being a scholar" (Gonzalez, et al., p. 1098). Academic "striving" –that is, an institution's deliberate changes in curriculum, resource allocation and the like in order to enhance prestige—has also resulted in a less diverse pool of institutions, with negative consequences for the faculty, some of whom speak of intent to leave (Morphew, 2009, cited in Gonzalez, et al., 2014). Since diversity in most systems is seen as a sign of system health, decreasing diversity among institutions of higher education can be viewed as an ominous signal for the larger social ecology and environment. The scrabble for prestige known as "mission creep" may eventuate in lowered resources for all institutions, important societal and workforce education and training needs going unmet, and students unable to find the right "fit" of institution to maximize their educational experience.

A Lowering of the Quality of Academic and Personal Life

Faculty are reporting that their worklives have taken on attributes unknown in previous generations. They are being asked to do more, although they have no additional resources with which to carry out these new and expanding responsibilities. For example, interviews with faculty uncovered that they take work home more and more frequently, eating into time with spouses, children and restorative non-work pursuits. Faculty routinely report working 80–90 hours per week, both to obtain external funding, and just to keep even with increased administrative responsibilities, with an enlarged communications network populated largely by email and its demands for instantaneity, and with learning and managing online teaching technologies (Gonzalez, et al., 2014). They describe their lives as having "no boundaries" and "no space" (ibid., pp. 1106–1107), and stating that "it's hard to find time to sit and think" (Bowen & Schuster, 1986, cited in Gonzalez, et al., p. 1098). Time to think is, after all, one of the primary reasons for joining the scholarly life.

Another interruptive force in academic life which faculty nominate as lowering the qualify of worklife is the set of demands associated with accountability (Lincoln, 2011, 2015a, b). The legislative call across the United States for more "transparency" and accountability has generated new forms of reporting every year. Faculty are increasingly asked to self-surveil (Amit, 2000; Strathern, 2000), and to continuously update information as to where their research "stands". The forms grow longer, and the average number of hours spent per week eats away at the time to sit and think, to write, to have the freedom to conjure critically and creatively. The emphasis on productivity—on product, and its contribution to the creation of capital, much like a fracking operation—actually *undermines* faculty productivity of the kind that has fueled great innovation in the West. Until a balance is re-achieved between applied research and basic research, the academies are unlikely to maintain the discoveries that originally made institutions incubators of the kinds of science that leads to whole new industries and applications.

The Slow Diminution of the Arts and Humanities

A third outcome of this bent toward seeing faculty work as a commodity likely to earn money for capitalized publication outlets and universities has been the ill-disguised scorn of academic capitalists for the liberal arts, particularly the arts and humanities. Freeman and Audia (2006) make the point that organizations exist in a social and community context, a kind of organizational ecology of both like organizations and other social institutional forms. Within this social context, or ecology, organizations exhibit reciprocity and interorganizational interdependence, with some kinds of contexts promoting organizational thriving, and others which seem to exhibit "higher rates" of "foundings and failure of organizational forms" (Freeman & Audia, 2006, p. 148). There are two associated premises surrounding the role of context—or ecology. First, "resources are unevenly distributed in both market and geographical space", and second, "social structure channels resources, and therefore, opportunities" (ibid, p. 148). The point to be taken here is twofold: in these interdependent relationships between organizations and social structures, the relationships between them—for instance, between a state university and a legislative higher education funding committee, or a statewide coordinating board—serve the function of "resource partitioning," or channeling of resources (ibid, p. 152). In addition, various resource allocation processes create competition, which "permits winners to choose the most advantageous parts of markets and other resource spaces, forcing competitive losers into less advantageous, specialized niches" (p. 152).

The point of Freeman and Audia's work is a study of interorganizational interdependence (or, as they make clear, interorganizational dependence likewise), and the way relations between organizational and other social structures has both the force and the means to allocate, or partition, resources in specific ways to create both winners and losers. My argument here is that this intellectual vein of research can be viewed at the micro or meso level *intra*-organizationally as well. This is particularly visible in the resource allocation structure between the hard sciences and the humanities. Because the hard sciences are frequently "valued" more highly than the arts and humanities, institutional of higher education tend to "channel" resources closer to scientific, technological, engineering and mathematical (STEM) fields. This is, in reality, a complex set of interwoven issues. Since humanities majors tend to earn lower salaries over time than, say, engineers, external donors in the hard sciences are frequently moved to make substantial donations in support of their disciplines, while donors to the liberal arts and humanities are sometimes unable to make such discipline supporting gifts. It is also the case that substantial funding for the STEM fields flows from both the federal government and corporate sources, whereas arts and humanities fields must rely more heavily on the support of foundations (although monies are also available from the National Endowment for the Arts and the National Endowment for the Humanities, both federally funded). Grants tend to be far smaller, tend to support work for much shorter periods of time, and rarely are programmatic (in the sense of supporting teams of researchers working in a cross- or trans-disciplinary mode). Likewise, organizational and philanthropic "investments" in technological, scientific or medical fields tend to have a return on investment (ROI) that is tangible, translatable, and application-worthy, whether in new scientific applications, new medicines or protocols, or in direct patents, which are frequently shared between faculty and institution.

Institutions of higher education are always already "greedy organizations," in the sense that there is seemingly no limit to the demands which are, or can be, placed upon members, and to which the members feel some responsibility to respond. Globalization has made this characteristic of research universities, in particular, both more visible and more demanding, creating "winners" and "losers" among faculty. The "losers" in the resource channeling competition are frequently going to be arts and humanities faculty, who are both paid less than high-prestige scientific faculty, and who are expected to have far less to commodify for market purposes, except for journal articles and books.

Such resource "starvation" can be related, even indirectly, to the failure of institutions of higher education to fully educate students to their most important task: that of becoming critical thinkers and engaged citizens. And indeed, while the liberal arts have made arguments from Cardinal Newman on regarding the long-term value of a liberal education in bringing an enlarged capacity for tolerance, compassion and democratic commitment—as well as the intellectual skills for rational argument and critical thinking—the continual relegation of the arts and humanities to second-class status within comprehensive universities not only signals the "market value" of the liberal arts, but it increasingly defrauds students of their right to an enlarged, enlightened, moral worldview, necessarily disconnected from market considerations. As well, institutions fail to utilize fully the talents of faculty whose intellectual labor revolves about these critical concerns. The "fracturing" of faculty into resource and prestige "winners" and "losers" sends the unfortunate message to students that the lessons of philosophy, history, the arts, anthropology, comparative religious studies, and foreign languages, for example, are not likely to have any payoff in the market and, consequently, are not worth the credit hour tuition. Career and vocational training and education in the high-paying scientific fields are seen as the most valuable of investments in education, while the classical *raison d'être* for a university education is beggared.

Conclusion

Fracking the faculty, treating both faculty and the intellectual products of their labor as a form of commodity in an extractive industry, has long-term conse-quences for the health of the university—particularly research universities—and the students they prepare for the world those students will inherit. Not only will some excellent Ph.D. graduates choose not to enter the world of higher education, but the larger social fabric may be damaged by this model of human resource usage. As universities become more "corporatized" there are fewer and fewer individuals to ask whether universities should indeed be run like a business. Universities are not businesses, even though some of their necessary processes are, and should be, run like a business (e.g., food service, building maintenance, travel, payroll, and the like). The heart of a university, especially a research university, is its "technical core"—its teaching, discovery, interpretive, cultural conservation and transmission functions, public service, and educating for critical citizenship. To the extent that a university enters into competition either with other members of its ecological context—other universities—or with and among its own faculty, it stands in danger of losing sight of its primary historical missions. To losing sight of these missions is to lose the very heart of a university; its faculty.

Note

1   It is critical to note, however, that "open access" means open only to end users. The largest publisher of social science materials in the world requires well over $500.00 for publishing in their open access journal, and some open access journals require $1,000 or more. Open is not very open to the social scientist looking to make her work more open, since as much as $1,000 must be found to do so. Academic departments are not making such monies available (indeed, may not have such monies to make available), and consequently, open access publishing for the Western scholar may mean self-funding from personal funds. Only those with large grants into which such charges are written are generally able to afford "open access."

References

Amit, V. (2000). The university as panopticon: Moral claims and attacks on academic freedom. In M. Strathern (Ed.) *Audit cultures* (pp. 215–234). New York: Routledge.

Bergstrom, T. (2001). Free labor for costly journals. *Journal of Economic Perspectives, 15*(3), 183–198.

Capraro, R.M. & Lincoln, Y.S. (In progress). Navigating the "dollarocracy": Where did the quality of ideas get lost?

Freeman, J.H. & Audia, P.G. (2006). Community ecology and the sociology of organizations. *Annual Review of Sociology, 32*, 245–269.

Gonzalez, L.D., Martinez, E., & Ordu, C. (2014). Exploring faculty experiences in a striving university through the lens of academic capitalism. *Studies in Higher Education, 39*(7), 1097–1115.

Lincoln, Y.S. (1998). Commodification and contradiction in academic research. *Studies in Cultures, Organizations, and Societies, 5*(1), 1–16.

Lincoln, Y.S. (1999). The postmodern university: Landgrants in the new millennium. *Journal of Curriculum Theorizing, 15*(4, Winter), 113–126.

Lincoln, Y.S. (2011). "A well-regulated *faculty* . . .": The coerciveness of accountability and other measures that abridge faculties' right to teach and research. *Cultural Studies ⟺ Critical Methodologies, 11*(4), 369–372.

Lincoln, Y.S. (2012). The political economy of publication: Marketing, commodification, and qualitative scholarly work. *Qualitative Health Research, 22*(11), 1451–1459.

Lincoln, Y.S. (2015a). Threat Levels: Qualitative Research, Ethics, Power and Neoliberalism's Context. "The Power of/in Academic: Critical Interventions in Knowledge Production and Society", 6th Annual Conference, Goethe University, Frankfurt, Germany, November 13–14.

Lincoln, Y.S. (2015b). A Dangerous Accountability: Neoliberalism's Veer toward Accountancy in Higher Education. "Public Engagement and the Politics of Evidence", Conference, University of Regina, Regina, Saskatchewan, Canada, July 23–25.

McGee, R. (1992). Ideology and political economy: The research publication criterion of academic merit. *Sociological Focus, 25*(2), 97–109.

Murphy, T. (2013). Meet the town that's being swallowed by a sinkhole. *Mother Jones.* Retrieved from www.motherjones.com/environment/2013/08bayou-corne-sinkhole-disaster-louisiana-texas-brine

Ohmann, R. (2003). *Politics of knowledge: The commercialization of the university, the professions, and print culture.* Middletown, CT: Wesleyan University Press.

Pirie, I. (2009). The political economy of academic publishing. *Historical Materialism, 17*, 31–60.

Strathern, M. (Ed.) (2000). *Audit cultures.* New York: Routledge.

van Manen, J. (2010). The pedagogy of Momus technologies: Facebook, privacy and online intimacy. *Qualitative Health Research, 20*(8), 1023–1032.

Wexler, E. (2015). Can data measure faculty productivity? Rutgers professors say no. *Chronicle of Higher Education.* Retrieved May 17, 2016 from http://chronicle.com/article/Can-Data-Measure-Faculty/234595

2

PUSHING BOUNDARIES

Academic De-institutionalization and Our Radical Imagination vs. Ourselves and Audit Culture

Marc Spooner

Elizabeth St. Pierre (2017) dares us towards the radical work of the next generation when she states: "we are limited only by what we cannot yet imagine, by what we cannot think and so do, by difference we cannot bear to embrace" (p. 45). Indeed it is an exciting time of possibility as research approaches continue to be contested, disrupted, and broadened to include a wide variety of promising departures from orthodoxy. What have, in various instances, been termed posthumanism, new materialism, the ontological turn, the affective turn, and/or post-qualitative research (Rosiek, Snyder, & Pratt, 2017), join ongoing developments in community-engaged, participatory, decolonizing, place-based, and Indigenous research approaches and, more broadly speaking, other social justice-oriented work, as these various shifts or turns operate in multiple, simultaneous, and interruptive fashion (Lather, 2017).

Yet, just as these enticing possibilities invite us to expand our research in ways unimagined just a decade ago, a parallel counterbalancing shift towards a ubiquitous neoliberal and accountability-focused culture—both in the academy and in society—imperils these promising developments. As audit culture and governmentality spread, they give rise to a new managerialism set on measuring us against rigid conceptions of research and impact, regardless of how inappropriate, unethical, or deleterious such constricting measures may be to ourselves and our communities. Ultimately, what is at stake is the very notion of what can be considered knowledge itself.

How does all this shape, reinvent, and construct life for faculty when the institutions in which ". . . we function serve as both harbor and tyrant" (Lather, in press)? In this chapter, I call on us as academics to resist, to fight against increasing pressures to conform to the rigid demands of misconstrued accountability, quality assurance, and/or excellence frameworks, and to further engage with our radical imagination; to further push boundaries as we individually and collectively take on our own de-programming and de-institutionalization. Featured first will be an overview of audit culture, followed by an examination of our institutionalization and programming. Next is a call to radically re-imagine the possibilities, products, and processes of legitimate scholarship as the section traces our indoctrination from graduate school to tenure. I conclude this chapter by examining rigour and goodness, as well as a discussion of possible future directions for social science research.

Higher Education's Silent Killer: The New 'Triple M' Crisis

Calls to reconsider both narrow conceptions of scholarship as well as higher education's reward structures are not new. For instance, more than a quarter century ago, Boyer rightly noted that many of the forms of knowledge making that were being marginalized were those that were most communal and collective in nature. Competitive individualism and elite notions of appropriate university research had taken over reward systems to disenfranchise knowledge making that was collaborative, interdisciplinary, engaged with public problems, and in partnership with students. Although Boyer advocated that faculty members be able to engage in all kinds of scholarship, including discovery, he made the argument that the purposes of higher education were not served by a singular individualistic form of scholarship or inequalities in how these different kinds of knowledge making were legitimized, valued, and rewarded (O'Meara, 2016, p. 45).

Since Boyer's (1990) call, the urgency has only increased as a growing number of academics find themselves ranked and benchmarked against rigid research performance indicators and metrics. Included in these metrics and indicators are, at the individual level, publication counts (literally simple additions of yearly journal article output), journal rankings, awarded funding totals, h-indices, various citation impact scores, and a whole host of other simplistically quantified proxies of our worth as scholars. These are also, in various contexts, packaged for unit, department, and university-wide evaluations, funding reviews, comparisons, and rankings. Moreover, in countries where tertiary or post-secondary education is centrally controlled, academics are often subjected to national performance-based research evaluations and funding schemes, such as the *Research Excellence Framework* (REF) in the UK, the *Excellence in Research* (ERA) in Australia, and the *Performance-Based Research Fund* (PBRF) in New Zealand. Additionally, a non-exhaustive list of countries with such exercises includes: Belgium (Flemish), Denmark, Finland, Hong Kong, Italy, Norway, Poland, Portugal, Spain, and Sweden (see Hicks, 2012). As Shore and Wright (2015) note, what is distinctive about performance indicators and audits today is the scale of their diffusion and the extraordinary extent to which society has embraced and endorsed them

(Strathern 2000a). As Michael Power (1994) observed, "we have lost the ability to be publicly skeptical about the fashion for audit and quality assurance" (p. 41) to the extent that "they have come to appear as natural and benign . . . [however] . . . indicators become targets as institutions are reshaped according to the criteria and methods used to measure them; and organizations and people are transformed into 'auditable' entities that focus their energies on doing 'what counts'" (Shore & Wright, 2015, p. 423).

Sometimes the antagonist is not wielding a gun. In this kind of attack, there is no person or event that can be met head-on with a protest or a strike. There is no explosion, no great conflict, no epic battle. Such is the case with higher education's silent killer: the slow, incremental creep of audit culture. Insidious New Public Management technologies first used by the Thatcher regime in the United Kingdom to weaken the public sector are restructuring post-secondary education on a global scale (Hicks, 2012; Wright, Curtis, Lucas, & Robertson, 2014). This enemy has no public face but instead makes its appearance in the banal metrics of automaton-like "bookkeepers" and bookkeeping programs of one form or another. The academy's new "triple M" crisis is of *market*, *managerialism*, and *measurement*.[1]

Market

Caught within the global reach of the neoliberal ethos, the university is rapidly transforming from its former (admittedly contested) role as an accessible institution dedicated to fostering critical, creative, and engaged citizenship, while generating curiosity and public interest research, to being "increasingly defined as a space of consumption, where ideas are validated in instrumental terms and valued for their success in attracting outside funding" (Giroux, 2008–2009, p. 45). Indeed, the university is increasingly being conceived as an entrepreneurial training scheme for knowledge workers while setting its scholarly ambitions no higher than impact factors, university rankings, branding, market share of students, and the wishes and dictates of corporate-styled and -directed research and development.

Managerialism

The university's administrative functionaries—traditionally headed by scholars seconded to act as deans, department heads, and so on—are now reconceptualized as managers (Parker, 2011). Due in part to the requirements of the new accountability regime, there are more of them than ever before and their numbers continue to grow (Ginsberg, 2011; Wright et al., 2014). Corporate shifts in the manner in which universities are governed give rise to a whole class of middle management auditors (accountants in function) who have replaced faculty administrative positions, retaining little of those administrators' collegial academic traditions (other than perhaps their holdover titles, such as associate dean, associate vice president, dean, provost, etc.).

Under New Public Management (NPM), governments transform their public sectors into simulated and competitive quasi-corporate sectors by transposing private-sector-derived accounting, management, and production technologies (Ward, 2012), regardless of how inappropriate and deleterious these may be to the sector's traditional mission (Parker, 2011). Typically, under NPM control universities are coerced to: (a) adopt private-sector management practices; (b) introduce market-style incentives and disincentives; (c) introduce a customer orientation coupled with consumer choice and branding; (d) devolve budget functions while maintaining tight control through auditing and oversight; (e) outsource labor with casual, temporary staff (Ward, 2012); (f) unbundle the public sector into units organized by product; and (g) emphasize greater output performance measures and controls (Lapsley, 2009; Lorenz, 2012). If any of this sounds familiar, you may have NPM infestation at your institution.

Measurement

The confluence of these market, managerialism, and measurement forces is inextricably linked, interdependent, and mutually reinforcing. With this confluence comes the subjugation of universities to neoliberal market logics, which find academics—once conceptualized as partners—conditioned to reposition themselves as employees with students as customers. Next, through NPM and audit technologies, we become auditable subjects as our scholarship is measured against narrowly defined, and often externally imposed, benchmarks. As Ward (2012) describes, "New public management unfolded in public institutions, power and decision-making shifted from the profession's own historically constituted internal and self-administered standards of performance and oversight to 'auditors'" (p. 9).

Institutionalization and Programming

Davies and Bansel (2010) elaborate on the mechanisms and effects of audit culture: "Quality assurance" seems not, then, to ensure "quality" in the academic arena. Rather, "quality assurance" as compliance with audit procedures is more likely to produce a compliant subject, one for whom possibilities for critique and creative innovation are more likely foreclosed than encouraged. Risk management then becomes, for the individual, the management of the risk to oneself of non-compliance, of non-viability within the audited policies and practices of the institution. . . . The practices of accountancy cannot recognize or countenance anyone who sees their job as responsibly working against the grain of dominant discourses, of asking dangerous questions of government, of opening up spaces of difference where new possibilities might emerge from the previously unthought or unknown (p. 12). Through its coercive properties, audit culture renders us as auditable subjects, compelling us to conform to its own (ideological) notions of what counts as scholarship, and especially to, what can be easily quantified, tabulated, and standardized for the purposes of comparable benchmarking. Further teasing out the ideology at play in this process, Shore and Wright (2015) observe,

> the institutionalized processes of measuring and ranking described above and their spread into many domains of organizational and social life reveal the emergence of a new type of governmentality based on a financial calculus—an instrumental, results- and target-driven normative order that governs by numbers and, more importantly, through numbers. . . . In this way, the political technologies of financial cost accounting wedded to the project of management have been highly effective in producing accountable and transparent subjects that are simultaneously docile yet self-managed
>
> (p. 430)

Audit culture or accountability standards are, in practice, thus end-runs that allow states, outside organizations, or university, faculty, or departmental administrations to effectively bypass academic freedom without direct confrontation. Rather, we are left with "the banal herding of our 'selves' through metric funnels onto productivity treadmills" (Spooner, 2018, p. 907).

That is, even when outside agencies and/or administrator-managers are not overtly limiting academic freedom through direct intervention, the audit culture, through a litany of incentives and disincentives leaves little or no time for other forms of "uncounted" work. Furthermore, audit culture, with its narrow conception of what counts, and what can be easily measured, disproportionately disenfranchises knowledge-making that is collaborative, innovative, Indigenous, participatory, interdisciplinary, post-qualitative, or engaged with public concerns and in the public sphere.

Breaking our Assembly Lines

Davies et al. (2017) state, "I am still a work in progress of de-institutionalization" (p. 89). I would join her in saying we, as academics, are all a work in progress towards de-institutionalization. We must all begin, resume, or continue upon such deprogramming work. As revolutionary as the "posts", and the more recent "post-posts and neo-posts" (Lather, in press), have been in stretching boundaries and encouraging us to reconsider, re-imagine, re-cast, and/or cast away traditional social science research assumptions and approaches, a parallel advocacy for similarly decentering conventional academic publishing has perhaps been slower to materialize. Here, with others, for example, Boyer (1990), Gelmon, Jordan, and Seifer (2013a, b), Huber (2005), and Stiegman and Castleden (2015), my entangled "I" is calling for a disruption, as well as a broadening of what counts as an acceptable end-form, product, or output of our academic scholarship. Alternative forms of research products and/or processes (Gelmon et al., 2013b;

Spooner, 2015) must continue to assert their inherent legitimacy in an academic landscape that is increasingly called upon to feature praxis (Guba & Lincoln, 2005) and relationally oriented research outcomes (Lincoln, 1995; Stiegman & Castleden, 2015; Tuck & McKenzie, 2015). It is in some ways reminiscent of Guba and Lincoln's (1989) reflections on their earlier 1985 reformulations of qualitative research validity where they mirrored quantitative criteria; they observed ". . . there remains a feeling of constraint, a feeling of continuing to play 'in the friendly confines' of the opposition's court" (p. 245). Let me be clear, this is in no way to suggest the "post posts" have not been radically innovative, refreshing, and useful for many, but rather to nudge us further in our radical re-imaginations and reformulations of conventional Euro-Western research approaches, processes, and end products. Thus, in the spirit of Boyer (1990), artifacts of our scholarship well beyond the scope of conventional peer-reviewed journal articles and contemporary notions of impact must elbow their way to acceptance at the research, criteria, and peer-evaluation table.

How did we Get Here? From Graduate School to Tenure

How we have permitted "publish or perish" to incrementally creep and morph into "discipline and publish" (Brenneis, Shore, & Wright, 2005, p. 7) must surely be attributable, in part, to the relentless manner and the ubiquity by which we, in the academy, first inculcate new graduate students to believe it. Next, having so deeply imprinted with the ultimatum, it becomes the chief standard by which we restrict and to which we hold ourselves. In fact, the triumph of this detrimental idée fixe is so complete, that it seems we all—as scholars—have adopted a collective fatalism where it is concerned. Journal articles combined with a whole host of arbitrarily superimposed rankings, evaluations, metrics, and impact factors of one sort or another, have crept into becoming the only de facto measure of our academic productivity and merit regardless of their lack of bibliometric validity (Gingras, 2016). In this version of the academic-productivity-meat-grinder, we are only as good as our last journal article ". . . however limited the audience or, truth be told, however repetitive or superficial the scholarship might be as a result of extreme career pressure to produce output quantity ("what counts") over content quality ("what matters")" (Spooner, 2018, p. 902).

So it is that after graduate school, these practices are not extinguished, but rather *strengthened* through the powerful incentive and disincentive schemes and machinations of the audit-university. They persist, partially, through habituation, inculcation, and, frankly, because we, as peers, uncritically hold each other to them. Internal and external, official and unofficial, rankings become effective tools in governing our behaviour. Now add to that pressure, often heavy student debt-loads and fierce competition for shrinking tenure-track employment and we have an almost perfect storm of compliance. Schwalbe (2015) highlights the effects of these conservatizing conditions on students; "under these conditions, it is prudent—as each new cohort of graduate students discovers—to focus one's efforts on publishing in academic journals and avoid rocking any boats, in print or in the classroom."

The SIGJ2 writing collective, comprised of new faculty, further elaborate on how this pressure does not stop once on "the track", but rather carries over:

> We are a group of new academics that value political engagement. We are troubled that activities that venture beyond the university—such as public lectures, workshops in activism, performing collaborative plays, mentoring immigrants, and even writing activist trade publications—do not "count" as serious scholarship. . . . The pressure to publish in defined journals shapes the kind of work we do and the way we re-present it. These pressures lead us to buy into the concept of "relevant" research and other performance criteria that are integral to the governmentality of neoliberal academic institutions. . . . [we] . . . encourage all established academics to accept new forms of scholarship and recognize them officially when it comes to appointments, funding applications, editorial decisions, etc.
>
> (The SIGJ2 Writing Collective, 2012, pp. 1055–1058)

Moreover, even established scholars, like Gelmon et al. (2013a), explain the difficulty in having their non-traditional research count:

> Traditional definitions of scholarship, including rigid interpretations of what counts as a publication and how to define and measure impact, have not served community-engaged scholars well. Academic journals are often not interested in publishing manuscripts about community-engaged activities. In any case, while scholarly journals are critical for communicating with academic audiences, they are poor vehicles for communicating with practitioners, policymakers, community leaders, and the public. Effective CES demands that the scholar produce diverse forms of scholarship in innovative formats—such as documentaries, websites, briefs, or manuals—for non-academic audiences and uses. But work presented in those formats may not be recognized as serious scholarship by academic peers.
>
> (p. 58)

Similarly, scholars involved in Indigenous and community-based research highlight that:

> one of the challenges in (and strengths of) doing community-based participatory research (CBPR), particularly with Indigenous communities as described above, is the length of time needed to build the foundations of a collaborative undertaking, namely building trusting relationships, and a common vision for research that responds to community needs and priorities
>
> (Stiegman & Castleden, 2015, p. 2)

Others, like Wilson (2008), for instance, aptly remind the academic community that:

> the research that we do as Indigenous people is a ceremony that allows us a raised level of consciousness and insight into our world. Let us go forward together with open minds and good hearts as we further take part in this ceremony
>
> (p. 11)

As difficult as it is to break habits and established dogma, in fact, the legitimate outcome or product resulting from research may be no product at all, but rather a change in community practice, a new relational becoming, or some other process-oriented result. No subsequent journal article to justify belonging while playing it safe in the confines of conventional academia. No more working double to justify the non-journal article end goals, processes, or end products of this type of scholarship; a common practice that is often to the great detriment of ourselves and our families (Gill, 2010, in press; Wright, 2014). No longer should we, as academics, obediently fall in line to the publish-at-all-costs dictum of this one-size-fits-all, paint-by-numbers approach to scholarship and judgment. Let us open the doors wide to, and count, other kinds of meaningful scholarship and engagement; including, writing books, developing "slow" science, engaging in community-based research, engaging in ontologies and knowledge creation that is outside of Euro-Western frameworks, providing public policy input, championing changes in community and professional practices, and acting on a variety of citizenship responsibilities.

What Might These Alternatives to Conventional Scholarly Publishing Look Like?

In addition to the alternative products/processes and ceremonies previously discussed, other outcomes could, as McKenzie's (2009) has usefully listed, include: addressing wider audiences through media, op-ed articles, and other popular forms; policy-making and engagement; active participation in struggles and campaigns; collaborating with community-based organizations; participatory research with students, educators, community members, and policy-makers; constituency building: creating social science "literate" and activist communities; workshops on the critical use of research and policy; constructing curriculum documents or guidelines; creating public service announcements from social science research; translating research into practice; theoretical contributions that shift thinking; social criticism; testimony in court; political satire; and public art, museums, parks, photo exhibits as venues for presenting research (p. 219). I would also add to this list, critiques of, and modifications to, university, faculty, and unit policy documents, which themselves go through a rigorous and disciplinary-wide range of peer-review (though often unrecognized for such).

Beyond what McKenzie has listed and what has been previously added, it is vital that the scope of what can be justly considered for assessment ought only to be limited by the boldness of our imagination. After all, what can be conceived of—what can be imagined—has always been the only true limit of intellectual endeavour. In light of that fact, and with new and exciting modalities that offer the potential for scholarly applications and products to be acted upon and disseminated in a greater array of outlets than at any other time in history, surely it is past time for the academy and our peers to eschew outdated and narrow metrics and assess the full complement of our diverse scholarly endeavours. Moreover, even our assumptions about who can act as a peer and who has the authority to grant peer-review must be troubled and expanded to include, among others, Elders, Knowledge Keepers, and other knowledgeable community members.

Discussion: Rigour and Goodness

As I type, I hear echoes of a conversation I had with Patti Lather at the last ICQI in 2017, where upon discussing the rough idea for this chapter, she asked me about rigour and soundness. I am also reminded:

> in general that dominant forms of inquiry are recognizable; taken-for-granted; considered proven, reliable, valid, and good. What Mazzei (in press), following Deleuze and Guattari (1975/1986), recently called "minor inquiry" becomes suspect because it is not recognizable but different, unproven according to the standards of the dominant model, perhaps false, and, hence, not good
>
> (St. Pierre, 2017, pp. 38–39)

Always teaching, in Lather (2017), she similarly shines light on the matter: "From a post-epistemic focus, validity is a boundary line for what is acceptable and not acceptable in research. Validity is, in short, power, the power to determine the demarcation between science and not-science".

Aside from conventional journal article peer-review and publishing, one example of an alternative to it is CES4Health.info. CES4Health "is a free, online mechanism for peer-reviewing, publishing and disseminating products of health-related community-engaged scholarship that are in forms other than journal articles; for example, videos, manuals, curricula and products developed through service-learning, community-based participatory research and other community-engaged work" (www.ces4health.info/). Perhaps, in the future, we will see more of these outlets begin to populate the new "publishing" landscape in a variety of social science disciplines. Others may argue that under a properly functioning collegial governance model, the significance of our scholarship is in some form or another peer-reviewed at committee or in the public domain by fellow faculty members from within and beyond our home disciplines.

Then again, perhaps the future holds something very different, where, as Lather (2017) writes:

> Epistemology is situated as an ethical issue, and objectivism is displaced by linking research as a community project to social action. Key practices are delineated: the use of multiple voices, reflexivity regarding the relationships and contradictions of research processes, reciprocity, sacredness, and sharing royalties as a way to address the cultural and economic capital that academics make out of the lives of others. This includes movement toward action inquiry with attendant validity practices such as "relevance as a criterion for rigor" in policy work where the "mangle of practice" is brought to the forefront in studying the social life of interventions in their messiness and uncertainty via participatory design tools Gutierrez and Penuel, 2014.

Here validity gets recast as a relational becoming that is reviewed by and in the communities in which we work; for example, among others, by knowledgeable members of those communities, Knowledge Keepers, and/or Elders. Here we are now asking, did "your–their" research change a practice? Does the community (or members within the community) in question find it of value? Do community outsiders/marginalized find it of value? Are there alternative tools and mechanisms through which to demonstrate the research processes' or products' soundness? Of the research/er enterprise we are now perhaps asking: Can you make a narrative case for your academic peers to understand the value and rigour of the work- however, this case may take form? Lather (2017) elaborates:

> Here validity has moved from a discourse about quality as normative to a discourse of relational practices that evokes an epistemic disruption, a transgression of set forms. Gesturing toward the future, the "ontological turn" shifts validity from discourse practices to materialities of enfolding, enacting and tracing rhizomatic multiplicities. The science that is about-to-be becomes thinkable with its entanglements, distributed agencies and intra-relationalities (Barad, 2007). Here "matter matters" in evoking a "post-post validity" that is immanent and response-able in moving from canonical to situated practices where science hardly recognizes itself in its affect, force and movement. This is the validity to be developed in the next generation, inexact and yet rigorous, incalculable, flowing along the lines of Deleuzean "transcendental empiricism".

In our pursuit of meaningful scholarly work and critical community engagement that is praxis and relationally-constructed—that includes the human, nonhuman, and greater-than-human—it is time to abandon audit culture's constricting grip. As a near totalizing governing technology, audit culture has become detrimental to the shared radical and ethical possibility so wonderfully imbued in the "post-posts" and always already existing in Indigenous ontologies, methodologies, and axiologies.

Let us not stop halfway, but rather, let us take the "responsible turn" with a diversity of scholarship and action, with reciprocal university–community engagement/s, and with a reinvigorated commitment to fight for greater access to justice, resources, and opportunities for everyone in whatever scholarly form these may take. Bochner (2017) reminds us to keep our head up: "Excessive focus on rigor impedes and distracts from talking about other, more important, problems such as the ethical commitments, moral importance, and artfulness of qualitative inquiry" (p. 1). It is indeed time to poke holes in, resist, play judo with, and jettison harmful notions of quality, productivity, and the increasingly encompassing culture of audit—both in the academy and in society. In reviewing higher education's silent killer: the new "triple M" crisis of market, managerialism, and measurement, and in tracing the manner in which their confluence has acted to curtail our most radical imagination and the kinder parts of our humanity (sans the anthropocentrism), I hope this chapter will act as one tool in our ever-ongoing "work in progress of de-institutionalization" (Davies et al., 2017, p. 89). Time for a renewed "wildness" and disobedience that strives to paint outside the lines, that finds its worth despite pressures to conform to the tired and broken weight-scales of a misguided accountability-calculus; that fully dares take on St. Pierre's (2017) challenge towards that which "we cannot yet imagine" (p. 45).

Note

1   The following brief definitions are based on Spooner (2018, pp. 899–890).

References

Bochner, A. P. (2017). Unfurling rigor: On continuity and change in qualitative inquiry. Qualitative Inquiry, *Qualitative Inquiry*. First published October 5, 2017. DOI: 10.1177/1077800417727766

Boyer, E. L. (1990). *Scholarship reconsidered: Priorities of the professoriate*. Princeton, NJ: Carnegie Foundation for the Advancement of Teaching.

Brenneis, D., Shore, C., & Wright, S. (2005). Getting the measure of academia: Universities and the politics of accountability. *Anthropology in Action, 12*, 1–10.

Davies, B. & Bansel, P. (2010). Governmentality and academic work: Shaping the hearts and minds of academic workers. *Journal of Curriculum Theorizing, 26*, 5–20.

Davies, B., Somerville, M., & Claiborne, L. (2017). Feminist poststructuralisms and the neoliberal university. In N. K. Denzin and M. D. Giardina (Eds.), *Qualitative inquiry in neoliberal times*. London: Routledge.

Deleuze, G. & Guattari, F. (1975/1986). Kafka: Toward a minor literature. Minneapolis, MN: University of Minnesota Press.

Gelmon, S. B., Jordan, C. M., & Seifer, S. D. (2013a). Community-engaged scholarship in the academy: An action agenda. Change. www.csusm.edu/community/facultyengage ment/resources/documents/gelmon-communityengagedscholarship-2013.pdf, accessed October 6, 2017.

Gelmon, S. B., Jordan, C. M., & Seifer, S. D. (2013b). Rethinking peer review: Expanding the boundaries for community-engaged scholarship. International Journal of Research on Service-Learning and Community Engagement, 1, 1–10.

Gill, R. (2010). Breaking the silence: The hidden injuries of the neoliberal university. In R. Ryan- Flood & R. Gill (Eds.), Secrecy and silence in the research process: Feminist reflections (pp. 228–244). New York: Routledge.

Gill, R. (in press). Beyond individualism: The psychosocial life of the neoliberal University. In M. Spooner & J. McNinch (Eds.), Dissident Knowledge in the Higher Education. Regina, SK: University of Regina Press.

Gingras, Y. (2016). Bibliometrics and research evaluation: Uses and abuses. Cambridge, MA: MIT Press.

Ginsberg, B. (2011). The fall of the faculty: The rise of the all-administrative university and why it matters. Toronto, ON: Oxford University Press.

Giroux, H. A. (2008–2009). Academic unfreedom in America: Rethinking the university as a democratic public sphere. Works and Days, 51–52, 45–71.

Guba, E. G. & Lincoln, Y. S. (1989). Fourth Generation Evaluation. Newbury Park, CA: Sage.

Guba, E. G. & Lincoln, Y. S. (2005). Paradigmatic controversies, contradictions, and emerging confluences. In N. K. Denzin and Y. S. Lincoln (Eds.), The SAGE handbook of qualitative research (3rd ed.). Thousand Oaks, CA: SAGE.

Gutierriez, K. D. & Penuel, W. R. (2014). Relevance to practice as a criterion for rigor. Educational Researcher, 43(1), 19–23.Hicks, D. (2012). Performance-based university research funding systems. Research Policy, 41, 251–261.

Huber, M. T. (2005). The movement to recognise and reward different kinds of scholarly work. Anthropology in Action, 12, 48–56.

Lapsley, I. (2009). New Public Management: The cruellest invention of the human spirit? Abacus, 45, 1–21.

Lather, P. (in press). Within and beyond neoliberalism: Doing qualitative research in the afterward. In M. Spooner & J. McNinch (Eds.), Dissident knowledge in higher education. Regina, SK: University of Regina Press.

Lather, P. (2017). Validity, qualitative. The Blackwell Encyclopedia of Sociology. In G. Ritzer and C. Rojek (Eds.). NY: John Wiley.

Lincoln, Y. S. (1995). Emerging criteria for quality in qualitative and interpretive research. Qualitative Inquiry, 1, 275–289.

Lorenz, C. (2012). If you're so smart, why are you under surveillance? Universities, neoliberalism, and New Public Management. Critical Inquiry, 38, 599–629.

McKenzie, M. (2009). Scholarship as intervention: Critique, collaboration and the research imagination. Environmental Education Research, 15, 217–226.

O'Meara, K. (2016). How scholarship reconsidered disrupted the promotion and tenure system. In E.L. Boyer (Ed.), Scholarship reconsidered: Priorities of the professoriate (expanded edition) (pp. 41–47). San Francisco, CA: Jossey-Bass.

Parker, L. (2011). University corporatisation: Driving redefinition. *Critical Perspectives on Accounting, 22,* 434–450.

Power, M. (1994). *The audit explosion.* New York: Demos.

Rosiek, J., Snyder, J., & Pratt, S. (2017). *Posthumanism, Indigenous Philosophy, and Agentially Realist Approaches to Educational Research.* Paper presented in a dedicated session at the 2017 Annual Meeting of the American Educational Research Association, San Antonio, TX. Retrieved September 27, 2017 from the AERA Online Paper Repository.

Schwalbe, M. (2015). Twilight of the Professors. *Counterpunch.*www.counterpunch.org/ 2015/06/05/twilight-of-the-professors/, retrieved October 15,2017.

Shore, C. & Wright, S. (2015). Audit culture revisited: Rankings, ratings, and the reassembling of society. *Current Anthropology, 56,* 421–444.

Spooner, M. (2015). The deleterious personal and societal effects of the "audit culture" and a domesticated academy: Another way is possible. *International Review of Qualitative Research, 8,* 212–228.

Spooner, M. (2018). "Qualitative Research and Global Audit Culture: The politics of productivity, accountability, & possibility." In N. K. Denzin and Y. S. Lincoln, *The SAGE Handbook of qualitative research* (5th ed.) (pp. 894–914). Thousand Oaks, CA: Sage.

Stiegman, M. L. & Castleden, H. (2015). Leashes and lies: Navigating the colonial tensions of institutional ethics of research involving Indigenous peoples in Canada. *The International Indigenous Policy Journal, 6,* 1–10.

St. Pierre, E. A. (2017). Post qualitative inquiry: The next generation. In N. K. Denzin & M. D. Giardina, *Qualitative inquiry in neoliberal times* (pp. 37–47). London: Routledge.

The SIGJ2 Writing Collective (2012). What can we do? The challenge of being new academics new academics in neoliberal universities. *Antipode, 44*(4), 1055–1068.

Tuck, E. & McKenzie, M. (2015). *Place in research: Theory, methodology, and methods.* New York: Routledge.

Ward, S. C. (2012). *Neoliberalism and the global restructuring of knowledge and education.* New York: Routledge.

Wilson, S. (2008). *Research is ceremony: Indigenous research methods.* Winnipeg, MB: F.

Wright, S. (2014). Knowledge that counts: Points systems and the governance of Danish universities. In A. I. Griffith & D. E. Smith (Eds.), *Under new public management: institutional ethnographies of changing front-line work* (pp. 294–337). Toronto, ON: University of Toronto Press.

Wright, S., Curtis, B., Lucas, L., & Robertson, S. (2014). *Research assessment systems and their impacts on academic work in New Zealand, the UK and Denmark* (Summative Working Paper for URGE Work Package 5). Copenhagen, Denmark: EPOKE, Department of Education, Aarhus University.

3

INTO THE WOODS

Scholarly Publishing for a Post-tenure World

Mitch Allen

The obsession among academics of publishing in high-impact factor journals and with highly rated book publishers is a function of the current tenure and promotion system. When universities assess an academic's worth based on impact factor, it is a compelling reason to follow certain publication strategies. But what if the tenure system is abolished? What would that publishing landscape look like? Let's explore that fictional universe.

The genesis of this chapter was the publication of Norman Denzin's book *Qualitative Inquiry under Fire* (Denzin, 2009). As head of Left Coast Press, I was its publisher. Fired up by completion of the volume, Norman asked me for suggestions of what he should write next. The book he had just completed catalogued the threats to qualitative inquiry coming from various compass points—the university, government, institutional review boards (IRBs), granting agencies. It had shades of doom written all over it. My response to Norman, then, was to ask him to show what qualitative researchers could do in the face of so many challenges, to provide them with a path, or paths, forward—to write a vision statement for qualitative researchers. The result was *The Qualitative Manifesto: A Call to Arms* (Denzin, 2010), which was published the following year by Left Coast and one of our publications I'm proudest of.

Move the clock forward seven years. Aitor Gomez asks me to participate in a panel at the 2017 International Congress of Qualitative Inquiry on how qualitative scholars can contest accountability metrics. I had already done a paper on his metrics panel the previous year. In the 2016 paper I had briefly outlined the landscape of accountability metrics, the various systems involved from the Thomson–Reuters Web of Science through Scopus, the h-index, and Google Scholar. I pointed out how these quantitative systems had been developed for established science and technology fields but had been applied to humanities and social sciences without accounting for the differences in citation patterns, timing, or authorship conventions. The result was a systemic bias in traditional metric systems against qualitative research and researchers. I suggested how qualitative scholars could use the existence of multiple measures to ameliorate these biases when going for promotion, grants, or raises. And I pinned the perpetuation of this system on the traditional scholarly tenure/promotion system, which increasingly relied on these metrics and which was not likely to change any time soon.

I had nothing useful to add beyond the contents of the first paper, so I declined Aitor's offer to participate. But then Norman stepped in. "What if the tenure/promotion system went away? What if these restraints no longer existed and the system was open to change? What would you envision?" were Norman's questions to me. What could scholars do if not constrained by a reward system based on journal impact factor? What would scholarly communication look like if academics didn't need to publish in the most prestigious refereed journals or with the most highly ranked book publishers? If playing the metrics game didn't matter? Norman was asking me for my publishing manifesto for qualitative researchers. Given our history, I couldn't refuse. Payback sucks.

While I've been in scholarly publishing for four decades—Sage, AltaMira Press, Left Coast Press—my retirement in 2016 was the first opportunity I had to systematically read about what was going on elsewhere in the scholarly publishing community. Prior to that, my primary attention had been paid to the activities closest to me and their impact on the publishing houses I was trying to keep afloat. I was surprised to discover that there are many initiatives that are already in place that would be welcomed by the qualitative community and would enlarge qualitative publication options in a post-tenure world. Few are currently used by qualitative researchers. The more innovative changes have been taking place in disciplines far beyond our vision and using technology that a small press like mine could not afford. With the benefit of the free time created by not having to worry about corporate budgets, book contracts, or inventory levels, I've looked at some of these experiments and how they might benefit qualitative researchers if given more publication options by the demise of the tenure system.

Open Access Publications

The movement away from the traditional scholarly outlets has been greatly boosted by the growth of electronic publishing and the ease of how this is accomplished through large servers in universities. Frustrated by the byzantine and the time-consuming process of researching and accessing needed material from whichever library held a subscription to a given journal and by the skyrocketing costs of these subscriptions over the past three decades, the open access movement blossomed throughout the university. Any community of scholars who wanted to start an electronic journal needed only to create a website on their university computer and announce themselves open for business. Access to the articles is free to read for anyone with an Internet connection anywhere in the world, subsidized by the university's electronic platform and the volunteer work of the editorial staff. Qualitative authors make their work available to readers in Hungary and Hong Kong, Kenya and Kazakhstan, whether or not the reader is affiliated with a research university possessing a robust journals budget. Some of these experiments, like *The Qualitative Report* (http://nsuworks. nova.edu/tqr/), are highly successful and long lasting. Hosted by Nova Southeast University, at which the journal's editor-in-chief Ronald Chenail is Associate Provost, the journal has benefitted by a herd of volunteer reviewers and editors and by Nova's support over the past twenty years to publish over 1,500 refereed qualitative research articles and provide a weekly qualitative research news service to over 5,000 subscribers to the *Weekly Qualitative Report*. *Forum Sozialforschung* (FQS) provides similar services throughout the world from its German base. The University of Alberta's *International Journal of Qualitative Methodology*, founded by Janice Morse, had a similar business model for two decades until switching to a gold open access (i.e., author pays to publish) model in 2016. While open access journals exist in many fields and number over 10,000 (https://doaj.org/), that is still a fraction of the 40,000 legitimate scholarly journals known (http://journalseek.net/).

Journals have always been designed to last "in perpetuity," being the publication of record for the content area of the journal. But, while a group of scholars may volunteer to run a publication for a limited time frame, it is difficult to sustain this volunteer group for perpetuity. So converting the entire journal publication system to an open access one would require an economic restructuring within universities to create permanent editorial roles to ensure the continuity of open access journals and to fund the platform, production, legal, and publicity costs of hosting large numbers of journals. Potentially, those funds will become available when universities no longer tolerate the high prices of high impact factor journals. Currently, publication in most open access journals does not receive the academic credit that is afforded more longstanding and traditional journals. That, though, is a function of the tenure and promotion system and would not be an issue in a post-tenure world.

Preprints

Qualitative researchers pride themselves on their collaborative stance to research, both with their colleagues and with the people they study. The nature of academic collaboration has been enhanced in recent years by the growth of the scholarly preprint. David Crotty, Editorial Director of Oxford University Press journals, defines preprint as "the author's original manuscript, *before* it has been formally published in a journal. One of the primary purposes of preprints is that they allow authors to collect feedback on their work and improve it before submitting it for formal peer review and publication" (Crotty, 2017).

Preprints have appeared in science, technology, and medicine fields since the early 1990s. What an opportunity for qualitative researchers! Put your roughly hewn draft in a safe public setting that allows peer reviewers to help you find the way from there to a polished product. Responses come organically from colleagues who wish to comment, from those who find your topic of interest and want to help you realize your vision for your work. When you feel you have enough feedback from interested parties, you can submit the revised version to a journal for formal publication. Or not. Just leave it on the preprint server.

By circulating draft publications through the scholarly community at an early stage, by permitting the author to incorporate comments into the final version of the paper before its "official" publication in a journal, authors can take advantage of help without the judgmental sword of formal peer review hanging over their heads. It is a collaborative way forward for research, a path that truly matches the ethos of qualitative inquiry. Access to the work can also be made available to community partners outside the academic realm, who can share their own reactions to a scholar's work. Even if the article's publisher restricts access to the final published paper, access to the original working paper remains open through the preprint services as long as the author decides to keep the paper there.

The oldest of these services, ArXiv, has been in existence over a quarter century and holds over 1.25 million papers in fields as diverse as mathematics, physics, astronomy, computer science, biology, statistics, and finance (https:// arxiv.org/help/general). The service, hosted at Cornell University, claims to add 10,000 papers each month. A similar service, BioRXiv, hosted by the Cold Springs Harbor Laboratory, serves the biological sciences (www.biorxiv.org/ about-biorxiv), and the misnamed Social Science Research Network (SSRN) does the same for economics, law, and sporadically in the other social sciences, none specific to qualitative research. The SSRN website boasts that it holds over 750,000 research papers from 350,000 researchers across 30 disciplines as of August 2017 (www.ssrn.com/en/).

Data-sharing Networks

Another key development of the past decade has been data-sharing networks and repositories. University and disciplinary repositories have existed for some time, though they have continually complained about the unwillingness of scholars to contribute their writings to these archives. Scholars have been more willing to house their work at newer data-sharing networks, many of them founded by groups of academics and available via open access. For example, at Mendeley all scholarly production of a researcher can be stored together in the cloud. Established in 2007 in Germany, and named after pioneer geneticist Gregor

Mendel, the service is free. According to their website, services provided include storage of research data (either private or publicly available) and associated bibliographies, file sharing, article drafts, secure backup of data, and automatic extracting of metadata including assigning digital object identifiers (DOI) to datasets to allow them to be accesses and cited by others (www.elsevier.com/solutions/mendeley). Its openness allows enables collaboration and networking with other scholars.

While Mendeley largely houses natural science collections, *HASTAC* (Humanities, Arts, Science, and Technology Alliance and Collaboratory) was co-founded in 2002 by Cathy N. Davidson at Duke and David Theo Goldberg at the University of California Humanities Research Institute, to provide similar storage and collaboration services for humanities scholars and their output (www.hastac.org/about/history). More recently, the open access Humanities Common was launched. Supported by Mellon Foundation and co-sponsored by the Modern Language Association and several other humanities organizations, the Commons was designed to expand interdisciplinarity in humanities work (https://hcommons.org/). The Open Repository Exchange of the Humanities Commons is designed to hold peer-reviewed journal articles, dissertations and theses, works in progress, conference papers, course syllabi, article abstracts, datasets, white papers, conference presentations, translations, book reviews, maps, charts, images, and multimedia files (https://hcommons.org/core/what-is-core/). The Repository gives each a DOI to allow for citation and copyrighting. Material in the repository carries Creative Commons copyright licenses.

For qualitative scholars, this would allow you to deposit, share, and comment on papers in repository, connect with other researchers on collaborative projects, set up website or blog, create professional profile, or launch a forums or special interest group. No such group on qualitative research existed as of summer 2017.

Public Scholarship

No one seriously questions that universities are under fire. Yet the academic community has traditionally not rewarded presenting the wealth of knowledge generated by contemporary scholarship to those outside the university, to show how knowledge generated through scholarly research can impact individual lives and guide policy. The work of qualitative researchers is particularly accessible to policy makers, community partners, and the general public. Stories have a greater impact than correlation matrixes. Without a tenure system to keep junior scholars focused on churning out articles in high-impact factor journals, more opportunities are afforded to create public scholarship that demonstrate the value of research and research universities and to touch lives of those outside academic circles.

Some of these channels already exist. Some qualitative organizations like IIQM and TQR host blogs, as do qualitative software organizations like Quirkos and MaxQDA, qualitative consultants, and individual researchers including myself (https://scholarlyroadsideservice.com/blog). Their work, though, is generally focused toward the interests of other scholars rather than looking outside the ivory tower. A few exceptions to this exist. The Wenner–Gren Foundation recently funded *Sapiens*, designed specifically to bring anthropological research, mostly qualitative, to the wider conversations on the web. The magazine *Pacific Standard*, founded by Sara Miller McCune of Sage, is another such outlet, providing popularly written summaries of scholarly research projects, as are other older publications like *Psychology Today*.

This is not to underestimate the difficulty of creating effective public scholarship. Scholars are not trained in writing for the public and generally do not do it well. Disciplinary jargon, passive writing, undue attention to the minutiae of data, and caution at overstating findings make scholarly writing ineffective in a world dominated by clickbait headlines and simplified explanations of complex social phenomena. The use of multimedia is also foreign to scholars attached to text. Nor are scholars effective at advertising their works to get attention in the social media dominated by people whose financial and reputational success is largely dependent on that kind of aggressive self-promotion.

While the opportunity exists to enter a wider conversation, it will require a retraining of scholarly mindsets to become central to those conversations. It will also require scholars creating better links with existing news channels to partner in reaching the audiences those channels have created. With the need to churn out yet another refereed article minimized, these opportunities might expand in a post-tenure universe. Scholarly workshops on writing for the public might someday replace those on how to get published in high-impact factor journals.

From Act I to Act II

Stephen Sondheim's operatic musical *Into the Woods*, first produced in 1986, features such well-known European fairy tale characters as Cinderella, Jack and the Beanstalk, Little Red Riding Hood, and Rapunzel. In the first act of the musical, each of these heroes meets their nemesis: a witch, evil step-sisters, a carnivorous giant, a grandma-threatening wolf. Each of the heroes triumphs and the characters sing and dance at the end of Act I about living "happily ever after" (Sondheim 1986).

What a great vision of the future for qualitative publication does this manifesto hold! Publishing our research in sources that the entire world can access, even your internet-savvy mother. Building your ideas with help from interested colleagues without the horrors of formal peer review. Having your data, papers, syllabi, and random thoughts in one place and available, if you choose, for colleagues to pick through and borrow. A renewed focus on getting your important ideas and findings available to the general public. A publishing utopia, constricted only by the tenure system. Don't we all want to be part of it?

In *Into the Woods*, all is not as it seems after intermission. The playwright asks, "What happens after happily ever after?" The opening song of Act II intones, "Wishes may bring problems, such that you regret them." It's a cautionary tale. For the university reward structure and tenure system are only part of the ecosystem of scholarly communication and, even if they change, there's still the problem of publishing economics.

Scholars and their universities are not the only actors in the publishing ecosystem. Publishing houses, commercial and non-commercial, are also actively working in scholarly communication and have much to lose if the tenure system loosens the boundaries of the existing publications hierarchy. "Much" means that a lot of money is invested in the current system. Scholarly publishing is a $25 billion industry, according to a 2015 report, including $10 billion in journals, $5 billion in scholarly books (Ware & Mabe, 2015). Large global media companies have a vested interest in keeping income and profit flowing. The shrinking of the scholarly marketplace by the freezing of academic hires and capping of library budgets has led large companies to swallow up smaller ones as the key strategy in their search for increased market share. This includes my own former publishing house, Left Coast Press, now owned by Routledge, part of $1 billion Informa. Informa is matched or exceeded in size by a handful of other academic publishing competitors: Elsevier ($5 billion in 2016), Wolters Kluwer ($3.4 billion), Wiley ($1.7 billion), and Springer/Nature ($1.7 billion)—all of which rank among the world's largest publishing houses (Milliot, 2017).

These companies have been observing the developing modes of scholarly communication outlined above. They have all seen the shrinking of the pot of traditional scholarly publishing income and have changed their growth strategies, moving from simple providers of content to include many other academic services. In the past two years, Elsevier alone has purchased the preprint service SSRN, the data sharing service Mendeley, and the repository Bepress (Schonfeld, 2017). Each of these organizations was originally launched by groups of scholars as ways to circumvent the traditional commercial publishing infrastructure, of which Elsevier is the most vilified part for its aggressive pricing. Ironically, each of them sold their service to Elsevier for a tidy sum. Elsevier has promised these organizations not to tamper with their existing operation, but the founders of these groups have met with accusations of selling out. In Act II, maybe the Wicked Witch wins after all.

Standard Oil of Academia

Each of these cases raises the spectre of vertically integrated monopolies, like the railroads or oil companies of the heyday of industrial capitalism. Standard Oil provides the model, where oil was prospected, mined, refined, transported, and sold by a single company, each division taking a profit in each step of the process. Its modern counterpart is Amazon. Originally an online retail bookseller, and not a profitable one, Amazon created a self-publishing arm, CreateSpace, to whose authors it could promise preferential marketing through the Amazon website. To help these mostly novice authors produce professional-looking books with attractive covers, Amazon created a production division and sold their services to these authors. Authors who wanted printed copies of their books could use Amazon's print-on-demand capabilities. With enormous amounts of data on what sells and what doesn't, it didn't take long for them to create their own Amazon Publishing business, looking at their spreadsheets of self-published books and offering the most successful authors to become Amazon authors. They also used their mountains of data to lure successful authors away from traditional publishing houses with promises of preferred marketing on the Amazon website. They locked in customers with promise of quick, free shipping through its AmazonPrime service. And, having caused the demise of most bookstores in communities, Amazon began in 2016 to open its own brick-and-mortar stores to replace them. One of their initial stores is located in my own hometown of Walnut Creek, California, opening late in 2017 after having chased off the half dozen traditional downtown bookstores by undercutting their prices. From selecting authors, to production, to printing, to online selling, to bookstores, Amazon has vertically integrated the retail book business in a way the Carnegies and Rockefellers would admire.

Can scholarly communications be monopolized by one or a few players in a similar fashion? Elsevier seems well on its way to accomplishing just that. Its close competitors will not be far behind. Imagine this scenario about a fictional "Carnegie Age Publishers" (called "Carnage" for short). Your grant documents are held by a Carnage repository that also provides a service to help you prepare and store the many supporting documents required by grant agencies. Another Carnage division manages the grant for you at a price lower than your university. You upload all of your data to one of their data services, Carnage's version of Mendeley. When you have drafted your paper, you post it on a preprint service hosted by Carnage. Having already registered with one service, the process is seamless when you decide to submit your article to a Carnage journal. The journal editor has access to the preprint reviews of your work to speed the peer review process. Another Carnage division becomes the official repository for your paper, as demanded by your university and grant agency. Another corporate division automatically adds your published paper to your Carnage-run personal repository and website. The publisher releases the abstract or a press release to a variety of social media and scholarly channels to promote your work. The publisher also includes your article as part of a collection of articles on your topic sold as a Carnage book.

Even if you are not compelled to stay within carefully tailored systems that move you seamlessly from one Carnage research and publishing service to the next, the process of removing it and taking it elsewhere, whether it is to another large-scale commercial competitor or some non-profit collective of scholars, is more troublesome and time consuming than just pushing a button to move your work to the next step. It begins to sound much like Amazon, where it is easier to buy from them not only your summer novels for beach reading, but a six pack of beer to accompany your chips and salsa on the beach and a new refrigerator to keep the beer cold, than it is to scour dozens of websites to find the best deal on each. And shipping is free too! The vertical integration of scholarly communication becomes complete.

How will this publishing monopoly be monetized is still uncertain. Will you be charged for each step in the process? Will you be encouraged, even obligated, to provide funds to Carnage to give your work preferential viewing to those who access any of Carnage's services? The incentive to you will be that those interested viewers will have been carefully identified by the extensive data that the Carnage has on the tens of thousands of scholars who use their services. Will you be one of the tailored subjects for those ads, paid for by other scholars, publishers, grant agencies, and universities? Will their increased share of published work allow Carnage to charge your library more to keep their subscriptions? Will Carnage include ads for other products not related to your scholarship, selling you furniture and vacations to Puerto Vallarta while you conduct a search for a Carnage-published article?

This scenario is well on its way to playing out. Whether it is a dystopia designed to capture and retain every scrap of your scholarly contribution behind some global corporate firewall or whether it is a scholar's utopia to seamlessly move your scholarship from fuzzy idea to permanent archive won't be known for a long time. After all, most of the millions of regular Amazon customers, including many academics, are content with the service they receive. Nor is it known who the key players will be. While Elsevier, Springer, and Wiley seem to be already on the launching pad, there is no reason why an Amazon, Google, Apple, or an as-yet-unknown party will see the opportunity and step in to purchase one of the existing academic media companies—much smaller than the tech giants—or create their own alternate empire.

Is there a non-profit alternative to this system? Non-profit academic organizations are viewed as being more ethical, interested in their constituents, and mission driven, and though not permitted to amass profits, they can hoard surpluses that mimic commercial organizations' profits (Anderson, 2017). It is unlikely, though, that a non-profit group will be able to muster the capital or the organizational skill to operate a system on this scale for the long term, even if infused with grant funds. Consortia of libraries have succeeded in limited ways to provide academic-driven alternatives to the commercial publishing environment, but they are subject to university budget fluctuations and organizational decentralization. Interestingly, the non-profit Chan–Zuckerberg Initiative (CZI) from the founders of Facebook has recently funded the artificial intelligence-powered search engine Meta and the preprint service bioRXiv (Callaway 2017). Can this be the start of a non-commercial information flow chain? And how happy will academics be with it when they know that the costs of this non-profit primarily represent a way of providing a tax write-off for Priscilla and Mark?

Act II: The Finale

Sondheim's play ends with the characters older, wiser, and cautiously optimistic about surviving a future in which wolves, giants, and wicked witches still roam. Following Sondheim, this is not a manifesto in the style of Denzin's *Qualitative Manifesto*. There is little likelihood of a "happily ever after" scenario dancing around the maypole, where qualitative researchers can publish as they wish, expect support from their colleagues along the way, connect deeply with audiences outside the university who can benefit from our insights, and receive kudos from tenure committees and university administrations for their work. Tenure is not going away any time soon, so you can go back to sleep and forget this dream world.

A good night's rest won't change the publishing environment, but a group of committed qualitative scholars can. Some of the ways forward have already been shown in a variety of ways enumerated above and are already in our reach. There have been, and still are, qualitative open access journals not requiring authors to pay for the privilege of publication that can reach any researcher on the globe with an Internet connection. They require intensive volunteer efforts and some level of external funding. They will forego some of the niceties of direct links to other cited articles buried behind firewalls or publicist-driven dramatic announcements of key findings in social media that publishing monopolies can offer. But examples like *The Qualitative Report* and *FQS* show that this kind of journal can be kept in the hands of the qualitative community and still thrive over the span of decades.

Even publications embedded in the corporate portfolios of large media empires are not immune from a committed group of scholars. In the most recent celebrated example, the editor and editorial board of the linguistics journal *Lingua* walked out on their publisher en masse and started an open access alternative, *Glossa*, in protest over the publisher's enormous subscription costs (Jaschik 2015), one of a dozen or more recent instances (http://oad.simmons.edu/oadwiki/Journal_declarations_of_independence). Although the publisher kept the name of the journal and the subscription list, many in the academic community think *Glossa* is now the better journal, having an experienced editorial team at its helm. With some university financial support, the journal can be sustained over the long haul. Without an academic community behind it, a journal is just a name and a shell. Scholars do have the power to effect change in the publications realm.

Some of the newer ways to develop and present research mentioned above should also be in the plan for qualitative researchers to survive in the woods. Preprints and data sharing, described above, are both well-established systems in the STEM world and can be converted to the needs of qualitative researchers. Scholars trying to circumvent the commercial publishing world launched the organizations that created these innovative programs. Qualitative scholars can create their own versions of these or simply join some of the existing ones by adding a qualitative thread to their disciplinary spread. And, of course, they will need to fight hard to avoid having these organizations, run by scholars for scholars, from being snatched up by a rapacious Google or Wiley.

Presenting qualitative research to the broader world should be a less obstructed opportunity. But qualitative scholars interested in this need to learn the rules of that game—how to find the non-academic audiences interested in their work, how to properly promote their work to those people, how to effectively use social media to maintain popular interest, how to build a presence, a brand, a committed audience over the long term, how to groom the long tail. Partnering with your university, professional organizations, and non-profits that have an identical need for public presence can provide qualitative scholars both with the platform and the training to make an impact outside the ivory tower.

Egon Guba's *The Paradigm Dialog* (1990) set out an agenda for qualitative researchers over a quarter century ago. Denzin's *Manifesto*—and the publications and conference he has been instrumental in building—largely follow Guba's blueprint. They each call on scholars to break out of traditional patterns and seek a better path. Resisting corporatization in the university and monopolism in the publishing system requires scholars to create an alternative vision, to retrain themselves and their students toward that vision, and to find key partnerships with other individuals and organizations to build communication systems more morally and politically in tune with the qualitative ethos.

Most important is for qualitative researchers to protect their sense of community. They have survived the obstruction and scorn of more mainstream research traditions because of the mutual support they provide each other. Having now embedded themselves in the academic landscape in a much deeper way than ever before, this sense of community must be what drives the move toward an open publications system that allows qualitative scholars to share with other scholars, students, community partners, policy makers, and the public.

Open access blogger Cameron Neylon (2017), of Curtin University in Australia, points out that we needn't overthrow the entire neoliberal academic system to effect positive change. Collectives, collaborations, and scholarly networks can leave control of publications within a correctly sized community of engaged scholars, even if it is for a small part of the publishing ecosystem. This is especially true given the economic efficiencies in producing and publicizing academic knowledge created by continually improving technologies. The openness of the annual International Congress on Qualitative Inquiry and the publication support networks afforded to those who publish in *The Qualitative Report* and *FQS* are only two examples that can be followed by others. With the support of that community and linking to other communities with the same mindset (Mudditt, 2016), neither the neoliberal university, nor the loaded tenure system, nor vertically integrated publications monopolies can keep qualitative researchers from controlling how their ideas spread into the academy and the broader world.

Does this serve as a publishing manifesto for qualitative researchers? Hardly. But at the end of *Into the Woods*, as the surviving characters are attempting to rebuild their lives, the Baker's Wife reminds them "You are not alone. No one is alone."

There is a way out of the woods, but only if we all hold onto each other along the path.

References

Anderson, K. (2017). Beyond labels—does the type of business matter? *Scholarly Kitchen*. https://scholarlykitchen.sspnet.org/2017/08/08/false-equivalency-are-non-profits-inherently-superior-to-for-profits/?informz=1, retrieved August 6, 2017.

Callaway, E. (2017). BioRxiv preprint server gets boost from Chan Zuckerberg Initiative. *Nature*, April 26. www.nature.com/news/biorxiv-preprint-server-gets-cash-boost-from-chan-zuckerberg-initiative-1.21894

Crotty, D. (2017). When is a preprint server not a preprint server? *Scholarly Kitchen*. April 19. https://scholarlykitchen.sspnet.org/2017/04/19/preprint-server-not-preprint-server

Denzin, N. K. (2000). *The qualitative manifesto*. Walnut Creek, CA: Left Coast Press.

Denzin, N. K. (2009). *Qualitative inquiry under fire*. Walnut Creek, CA: Left Coast Press.

Denzin, N. K. (2010). *The qualitative manifesto: A call to arms*. Walnut Creek, CA: Left Coast Press.

Guba, E. G. 1990. Carrying on the Dialog. In G. Egon & E. G. Guba (Eds.) *The paradigm dialog* (pp. 368–378). Newbury Park, CA: Sage.

Jaschik, S. (2015). Language of protest. *Inside Higher Education*, November 2. www.insidehighered.com/news/2015/11/02/editors-and-editorial-board-quit-top-linguistics-journal-protest-subscription-fees

Milliot, J. (2017). The world's 50 largest publishers 2017. *Publishers Weekly*. August 25. www.publishersweekly.com/pw/by-topic/international/international-book-news/article/74505-the-world-s-50-largest-publishers-2017.html

Mudditt, A. (2016). Humanities common: Networking the Humanities through open access, open source, and not-for-profit. *Scholarly Kitchen*. December 21. https://scholarlykitchen.sspnet.org/2016/12/21/humanities-commons-networking-the-humanities-through-open-access-open-source-and-not-for-profit/

Neylon, C. (2017). Thinking collectively . . . or how to get something out of neoliberal critique without (immediately) overthrowing the capitalist system. *Science in the Open*. July 6. http://cameronneylon.net/blog/thinking-collectively-or-how-to-get-something-out-of-neoliberal-critique-without-immediately-overthrowing-the-capitalist-system/

Schonfeld, R. (2017). Elsevier acquires Bepress. *Scholarly Kitchen*. August 2. https://scholarlykitchen.sspnet.org/2017/08/02/elsevier-acquires-bepress/

Sondheim, S. (1986). *Into the Woods*. http://intothewoodsuhs.tripod.com/id9.html

Ware, M. & Mabe, M. (2015). *The STM Report: An Overview of Scientific and Scholarly Journal Publishing*, 4th ed. International STM Association. www.markwareconsulting.com/the-stm-report/

4

THE BMJ DEBATE AND WHAT IT TELLS US ABOUT WHO SAYS WHAT, WHEN AND WHERE, ABOUT OUR QUALITATIVE INQUIRY

Julianne Cheek

In a Nutshell: What This Chapter is All About

Two questions shape the following discussion:

1. Who says what can be seen and heard, when and where, about our qualitative inquiry?
2. How far we are prepared to go for it to be seen and heard, by whom, and why?

The vehicle that I will use to explore these questions is the decision and statement made in 2015 by the editors of The BMJ[1] (formerly known as the *British Medical Journal*), that publishing qualitative studies was an "extremely low priority" for The BMJ.

The BMJ journal is published by BMJ. BMJ is a company which describes itself as "a global brand with a worldwide audience" designed to assist

> medical organisations and clinicians tackling today's most critical healthcare challenges. We do this by publishing the newest, cutting edge academic research, providing professional development solutions and creating clinical decision support tools. Our expertise extends from publishing and medical education to clinical decision support and quality improvement to enhance day-to-day decision-making and healthcare delivery. BMJ publishes more than 60 medical and allied science journals and one of the foci that it has expanded into beyond publishing is medical education and knowledge at the point of care.
>
> (bmj.com)

One of these 60 medical and allied science journals is The BMJ. The BMJ is a peer-reviewed online publication that also has two weekly, and one monthly, print editions targeting different reader groups (bmj.com). The section of the bmj.com website about the reach and impact of The BMJ states that as of June 2017 The BMJ had an impact factor of 20.7, ranking it fourth among general medical journals. It goes on to state that articles in The BMJ

> make news around the world on a daily basis and are routinely cited in clinical guidelines. Over the years *The BMJ* has received many accolades including Editor of the Year (2014) and Magazine of the Year (2015) at the prestigious Periodical Publishers Association Awards. In June 2014 *The BMJ* received a special received a [sic] Patients Included certificate, to acknowledge and encourage the journal's focus on the involvement of patients in medical publishing.
>
> (bmj.com)

Given its stature and reach in both publishing and education fields, The BMJ editorial policies and decisions have a decided impact on the conduct of research practice. Its statement on publishing qualitative studies is thus an important moment through which to better understand the relations of power that govern the politics of research and publishing in the present moment.

In the Name of our Public(s)/Readers: We, and They, Don't Want to Read Qualitative Inquiry in The BMJ

The rationale given by The BMJ editors for their decision was that qualitative inquiry is of little interest or practical value to readers of The BMJ and therefore unlikely to be cited (Greenhalgh et al., 2016b). The whistle was blown on this decision when certain qualitative inquirers shared, via Twitter, an excerpt from a rejection letter they had received from The BMJ editors. This excerpt read as follows:

> Thank you for sending us your paper. We read it with interest but I am sorry to say that qualitative studies are an extremely low priority for *The BMJ*. Our research shows that they are not as widely accessed, downloaded or cited as other research. We receive over 8000 submissions a year and accept less than 4%. We do therefore have to make hard decisions on just how interesting an article will be to our general clinical readers, how much it adds, and how much practical value it will be.
>
> (Greenhalgh et al., 2016b)

This rejection letter was *actually* saying that, as low priority in a journal where article acceptance rates are less than 4%, no matter how good the qualitative inquiry might be, its methodology, in effect, automatically precluded it from being published in The BMJ. In other words, qualitative inquiry was not going to be seen or heard in that journal. Nor was it going to be seen or heard (or therefore potentially used) by those 'public(s)' who refer to, or consult, the research reported in The BMJ; nor by the 'public(s)' who base their decisions about policy and practices on the research reported in that journal; nor by the 'public(s)' who receive services or procedures based on those policies and practices. Such public(s) include practitioners, administrators, policy makers, and everyday citizens.

The rejection letter from the editors of The BMJ led to an open letter— signed by 76[2] qualitative researchers from 11 countries, all considered experts in health-related qualitative research fields—being sent to them. Among other things, the letter stated:

> We are concerned that *The BMJ* appears to have developed a covert policy of rejecting qualitative research on the grounds that such studies are "low priority", "unlikely to be highly cited", "lacking in practical value" or "not of interest to our readers."
>
> (Greenhalgh et al., 2016a)

The letter was an appeal to The BMJ editors that qualitative inquiry, and inquirers, be seen and heard in The BMJ. It was also a demand that the expertise of the signatories of the letter be seen and heard.

The open letter (Greenhalgh et al., 2016a) challenged the criteria given by the editors for excluding qualitative inquiry from The BMJ. This challenge was based on the fact that premises such as qualitative inquiry being of low priority and interest to their readers did not stand up to scrutiny. The letter pointed out that The BMJ had recently celebrated 20 years of online presence by asking experts to name the most influential paper published in The BMJ during those 20 years. Included in the 20 nominated papers were "11 commentaries or editorials (highlighting the journal's important role in publishing papers that contextualise and interpret research)" (Greenhalgh et al., 2016a), as well as three qualitative studies. So the decisions made by experts about which papers were influential in The BMJ clearly did not match the claim made by The BMJ editors, who maintained that qualitative articles were neither interesting nor of practical value to their readers/public(s) and therefore should be of extremely low priority for the journal.

Reaction to this open letter led to a flurry of responses by The BMJ readership. Additional open letters were submitted supporting the stance taken in the original open letter: for example, Howard et al. (2016) wrote on behalf of three important organizations and "169 individual health policy and systems researchers in 38 countries." Simultaneously, comments in the 'rapid response' section of

The BMJ[3] gave overwhelming support to the original open letter. Ironically, by February 23, 2016 the original open letter had become one of the most highly accessed papers on The BMJ's website. As Greenhalgh (2016) later pointed out in a follow-up response to the editors:

> The open letter on which this editorial was based is currently (by a considerable margin) the most highly accessed paper on the BMJ's website. It has an Altmetric score of 1118 (putting it in the top 20 papers ever published in the BMJ for social media coverage).

Greenhalgh (2016) went on to point out that of the 50 rapid responses received, only one of those considered The BMJ editors' response adequate, the other 99.17% using expressions such as "naïve," "epistemologically blinkered," "incorrect," and "a serious lack of academic proficiency." Such figures somewhat weakened the original rationale/excuse given by the editors for their discrimination against qualitative inquiries; namely, that qualitative inquiry could not be, and was not, of interest to, or a priority of, readers.

The Editors Respond

In spite of public and readership pressure, the editors of The BMJ initially decided not to change their stance in relation to qualitative inquiry. Their first public response, on February10, 2016, was that there would be no change to The BMJ policy. They wrote, "Despite the extensive discussion within and outside *The BMJ* that this letter has provoked, we are not persuaded that we should make the major changes requested . . . the ideal place for publication of many qualitative papers will be journals that are targeted at the specialist audience for whom the findings are especially pertinent" (Loder, Groves, Schroter, Merino, & Weber, 2016a). Further, the editors also responded by contacting Greenhalgh privately "to emphasise that having published our letter and responded to it in the journal, they have delivered what was needed" (Greenhalgh, 2016).

Such responses on the part of The BMJ editors is tantamount to them metaphorically washing their hands and walking away from the debate and the issues raised. Sending qualitative studies elsewhere might seem a convenient, even easy, solution—a type of 'not in my back yard' thinking. However, this simply avoids addressing the issues raised by Greenhalgh et al. (2016a, b). In so doing, the many undeclared, unjustified and connected (+)[4] assumptions embedded in the decision to give low priority to qualitative inquiry are maintained. These include assumptions about which research methodological approaches The BMJ supports and does not support + equally important, should and should not support + method-centric views of what are worthwhile or legitimate or suitable research methods + equally disturbing, what medicine and health is and is not + can and can not be + who can say that. Not acknowledging such assumptions and addressing them merely by shunting qualitative studies somewhere else simply shifts the problem, rather than dealing with it. In so doing, the status quo of not publishing much or, indeed, any qualitative inquiry is maintained by The BMJ.

Also maintained are a series of connected and unsubstantiated assumptions about which 'public(s)' The BMJ is, and is not for + what those public(s) want/need to hear and see + what will be of use to them + normative assumptions about what is, and is not, suitable research for the readership of The BMJ. For as Greenhalgh (2016) asks, drawing attention to such unsubstantiated assumptions by turning them on their head, "By what criteria do the BMJ's editors judge whether they are out of touch with their readership?".

The Response Changes

In light of increasing pressure to respond to questions such as this, The BMJ editors modified their initial response. On February 24, 2016, after the open letter had become one of the most highly accessed papers on The BMJ's website, the editorial response was softened to, ". . . we will be consulting with qualitative researchers to learn more about how we can recognise the very best qualitative work, especially that which is likely to be relevant to our international readers and help doctors make better decisions . . . We are open to and will seek out the very best and most useful qualitative studies and we will continue to publish methodological articles that support good qualitative research." (Loder, Groves, Schroter, Merino & Weber, 2016b).

This was a positive and promising response from the editors. It made public the admission that their previous judgments concerning the publication of qualitative inquiry had been based on, at best, tenuous knowledge about, and limited experience of, its 'quality' and the use to be made of that form of inquiry. It also promised openness on the editors' part to learn further, rather than simply shutting The BMJ door to qualitative inquiry generally.

However, while there were positive aspects to this response, the situation was far from resolved. As is often said about agreements, to some extent the devil is in the detail. Much more thinking was needed about how exactly, for example, the editors would consult "*with qualitative researchers to learn more about how we can recognise the very best qualitative work*" (Loder et al., 2016b, emphasis mine). Questions that arise in relation to such consulting include: What do they need to learn more about, from whom, and how? What does 'the very best qualitative work' mean? How would we know this? Which qualitative inquirers will the editors consult about qualitative inquiry, and why?

Put another way, this cascade of questions is about who will be speaking about, and being heard, in relation to qualitative inquiry, *and*, as a consequence of that, what form(s) or understanding(s) of qualitative inquiry will be seen and heard in The BMJ. Could a consequence of all this consulting be that a particular understanding or type of qualitative inquiry becomes established and normalized as the 'very best' and 'most useful' by The BMJ? Will forms of qualitative inquiry not in keeping with these normalized versions of the 'very best' and 'most useful' qualitative inquiry be automatically precluded from publication? And, as a result, will this lead to more and more of this normalized and specific type of 'very best' and 'most useful' qualitative inquiry being submitted to The BMJ, in turn, leading to more of that type of qualitative inquiry being published in it, in turn, sustaining these journal-specific understandings of what the 'very best' and 'most useful qualitative inquiry is?

Looked at in this way, a response that could be viewed at face value as an inclusive gesture towards qualitative inquiry on the part of the editors of The BMJ, could, in effect, operate as an exclusionary one. It will be a matter of whom they consult with and how. Equally important will be the matter of what they want to achieve at the end of that consultation, and what they will produce as a result of that consultative process. I turn now to explore these matters more fully in the next section.

When One Thing can Become Quite Another—The Subtle (or not so Subtle) Shift in Focus from Significance to Quality

One of the points made in Greenhalgh et al.'s original letter (2016a, b) was that there was no formal policy openly stated on The BMJ's position in relation to qualitative inquiry (or mixed method research), and nor were there appropriate and explicit criteria given for making judgments about the relevance of that inquiry to The BMJ. Greenhalgh et al. (2016a, b) argued that a way forward to address this deficit was that "*The BMJ* should develop and publish a formal policy on qualitative and mixed method research and that this should include appropriate and explicit criteria for judging the relevance of submissions."

This seems a reasonable and sensible request to make. It is a request based on the need for openness and transparency in The BMJ's editorial policy about qualitative studies generally, as well as with respect to assumptions and judgments made about the relevance (or non-relevance) of specific qualitative submissions. However, the response of the editors on February 24, 2016 (Loder et al., 2016b) suggests a possibly unintended but highly significant shift in the potential focus of any such explicit criteria. As we have seen, the editors responded that their goal was to be able to recognise "the very best qualitative work . . . We are open to and will seek out the very best and most useful qualitative studies" (Loder et al., 2016b). This goal extends the potential remit and focus of any explicit criteria developed by The BMJ far beyond judging the *relevance* of qualitative submissions to this journal, as suggested in the open letter. Instead the remit and focus becomes making judgments about what the 'very best' qualitative work *is* and, equally importantly, *is not*.

Does this mean that The BMJ—and other journals grappling with the same issues about qualitative inquiry—might produce some sort of guidelines and/or explicit criteria about what the 'very best' qualitative inquiry is? Could this result in each journal producing its own criteria or guidelines for the 'best' qualitative inquiry? With as many guidelines as journals, could we see a situation where different journals could potentially emphasize different views of what is 'best' in relation to qualitative inquiry; in a worst case scenario, could they even contradict each other?

The idea of having some sort of guidelines or criteria for assessing or making judgments about the quality or 'worthiness' of a qualitative inquiry has long been a fraught and contested one within the field of qualitative inquiry. Nearly a decade ago Hammersley (2008), in a confronting and incisive critique of some of the issues facing qualitative inquiry, wisely argued that qualitative inquiry can not defend not making clear what it does. He observed that those who challenge the quality of qualitative inquiry often complain that "there is no clearly defined set of criteria available for judging it, so that it is of *uncertain* quality" (Hammersley, 2008, p.158, emphasis in the original).

This observation puts the emphasis on problems arising from *uncertainty about* the quality of qualitative inquiry. Such an emphasis has the potential to change the intent of any guidelines or criteria developed, to one that may be more palatable to many qualitative inquirers. This is because the focus is on addressing uncertainty about the quality of a qualitative inquiry, rather than on prescribing ways of being certain about what qualitative inquiry *has* to be to in order to be considered the 'very best' or of good quality.

With such a shift in focus, the goal then becomes not to develop and stipulate rigid criteria about what constitutes absolute or best quality in qualitative inquiry per se. Rather the goal is to provide ways of addressing the uncertainty that others have about how they should think about and make judgments of qualitative inquiry. Therefore, instead of trying to come up with universal generic checklists of criteria that must be complied with (e.g., Tracy's [2010] eight 'big tent' criteria), the task for qualitative inquirers is to make clear, and therefore educate others about, what we do, how we do it and why, *in relation to, and grounded in uncertainty about, aspects of a specific qualitative study*.

Putting emphasis on the need to address uncertainty about a specific aspect of a specific qualitative inquiry, rather than providing ways to be certain about qualitative inquiry per se, is in keeping with the suggestion made by Greenhalgh et al. (2016a, b) in the open letter about the need for an ongoing educational approach to qualitative research in The BMJ. They argue that The BMJ could "provide a forum for methodological commentaries or online discussion" from which "the journal's readership would gain in qualitative research literacy" (Greenhalgh et al, 2016a, b). Such literacy is about knowing what is needed to be known, or taken into consideration, when thinking about the quality of a particular aspect of a specific qualitative study.

A shift of focus towards dealing with uncertainty about how to make decisions about the 'quality' of qualitative inquiry, instead of trying to create certainty about it, might help avoid situations such as the one I found myself in recently. I received a review rejecting a manuscript that we (the research team of which I was part) had submitted for publication to a journal that does not have a history of publishing much qualitative inquiry. As I have discussed this incident in detail elsewhere (Cheek, 2017b), I will not go into the situation in full again here. Instead I want to focus on one of the statements in the review that is particularly pertinent to the discussion here. The reviewer wrote in bold: "I am not an expert at qualitative research, but the methods used in this manuscript do not appear to be rigorously based on any standard qualitative methodology" (Cheek, 2017b, p.26).

Like the editors of The BMJ, this reviewer did not allow their self-acknowledged limited expertise about qualitative inquiry to stop them from making judgments and decisions about that inquiry. Unlike The BMJ editors, who justified their decision by claiming a lack of interest in, and use of, qualitative inquiry by its readers, this reviewer used reference to 'standard qualitative methodology'—*something that simply does not exist, or at the least, would be impossible to have agreement over*—to justify his/her decision. Put another way, the reviewer justified her/his ability to make judgments about qualitative inquiry, not on being an expert in the area, but rather on being certain about what standardized and therefore 'good' and 'rigorous' qualitative inquiry is—presumably (as it is not specified) based on some form of checklist or guideline. It was recourse to this unspecified standardized qualitative methodology that justified this reviewer in assuming an authoritative, actually authoritarian, position as 'an expert nonexpert' (Cheek, 2017b, p.27).

The key point here is that there has been a shift in emphasis from what the standards actually are, or should be (hence the reviewer can comfortably state "I am not an expert in at qualitative inquiry"), to what the standards can be used to do (hence the reviewer can comfortably claim expertise on the basis of some form of standardization of qualitative inquiry). This is why not being an expert did not stop this reviewer from being certain that this was not good or acceptable qualitative inquiry. The decision made by this reviewer to reject the paper was not so much about the qualitative inquiry *itself* as it was about comparing how the qualitative inquiry fitted, or did not fit, with the reviewer's notion of standardized forms of qualitative inquiry.

This is why, as suggested by Greenhalgh et al. (2016a, b), the emphasis in any move to identify the 'very best' or 'most useful' qualitative inquiry by the editors of The BMJ (or anyone else for that matter) must remain on the development of a *qualitative research literacy* that enables judgments to be made about specific aspects of a qualitative study that are in some way uncertain.

An Alternative Suggestion: Why not Simply Shrug our Shoulders and Transfer our Affections Elsewhere?

To this point the discussion has focused primarily on the open letter from Greenhalgh et al. and on the subsequent responses of The BMJ editors when challenged about their decision to effectively exclude qualitative inquiry from The BMJ. In this next section of the chapter I wish briefly to explore two other responses to this decision and the debate that followed it. Each of them sheds new light on, and provides different insights into, the topic of interest in this chapter; namely, in public spheres, who says what can be seen and heard, when and where, about our qualitative inquiry? The first is a rapid response published in The BMJ from J.K. Anand (2016), and the second is an editorial by Clark and Thompson (2016) titled *Five Tips for Writing Qualitative Research in High-Impact Journals: Moving From #BMJnoQUAL*.

In a rapid response dated February 24, 2016, Anand writes, "If The BMJ is out of step with the vast majority of its readership, the majority should stop reading The BMJ . . . The BMJ is what it is. Shrug your shoulders and transfer your affections elsewhere" (Anand, 2016). On the surface, this seems like a reasonable response. Why not simply shrug our shoulders as qualitative inquirers and transfer our affections elsewhere? However, maybe doing this is not quite as simple as Anand suggests. It is not so easy to ignore and walk away from The BMJ because of what The BMJ is connected to, and also because of what the act of publishing in The BMJ is connected to. To explore and develop this point further, we again need to put some pluses (+) into our thinking about research articles in The BMJ, qualitative inquiry and the various publics that they interface with and connect to (Cheek, 2017a, b). I will begin by taking a look at the way in which impact factor, impact and The BMJ connect, and what this, in turn, is connected to.

In the contemporary, all pervasive, audit and accountability culture that researchers find themselves in, publications count + they are part of making oneself calculable (Ball, 2012) + in a competitive research market place, researchers sell their research products, such as publications, to gain market currency (Cheek, 2017a, b; Lincoln, 2012; Spooner, 2017) + this currency can be traded for, among other things, tenure, promotion, jobs and research funding + some publications bring with them (a lot) more marketplace derived currency than others + one type of publication that brings with it a lot of currency is a research article in a high-impact factor journal + this type of publication provides high exchange value and relative ranking, in a research market place driven by supply and demand (Cheek, 2017b), + The BMJ has a relatively high impact factor in its field. Its website (www.bmj.com) advertises that it ranks fourth among general medical journals and that it has a current impact factor (c. 2017) of 20.785 + this makes publishing in The BMJ very attractive to researchers seeking, or needing, to accumulate currency in the research market place they are in.

Thus, although on one level Anand's response (2016) might seem quite reasonable in that of course it is possible simply to ignore the journal—to shrug our shoulders, walk away and publish our qualitative inquiry in other places— at another level, walking away does little to solve the actual problem and in fact, exacerbates it. The BMJ is more than just a journal. It is a journal with a high impact factor. To be seen and heard, and therefore calculable (Ball, 2012) and competitive in the research marketplace, researchers need to be associated with high-impact factor journals. So they keep submitting their work to high-impact factor journals such as The BMJ, thereby sustaining its definitions of research and also ironically its impact factor. Intentionally or otherwise this works to sustain assumptions and understandings of the relative worth/impact/quality of qualitative research approaches and methods. And we could go on. . . .[5]

Compounding the difficulty of simply walking away from The BMJ is a residual carelessness and slurring in much of the writing about the impact factor of a journal and the impact of a specific piece of research in that journal. Erroneously attributing high impact factor/impact/quality to individual articles in a journal based on the impact factor of the journal alone, has worked to sustain such slurring with the terms 'high impact factor', 'impact' and 'quality' at times being used interchangeably. (Cheek, Garnham, & Quan, 2006; Garfield, 1999; Seglen, 1994,1997).

This in turn has worked to create and sustain the assumption that a publication in a high-impact factor journal has higher impact and better reach than one in a low-impact factor journal. Given such slurring, it is in fact possible that an article that has never been cited at all and has had no demonstrable impact can claim to have high impact and quality by association with a journal based metric (impact factor). Conversely it is possible that such carelessness enables an article or piece of research being viewed as having low (or no) impact or quality, not because of what it is, but because of what it is not—published in a journal that has a high impact factor. The starting point for these judgments about quality and impact is the high impact factor journal (i.e., the impact factor score), not the specific piece of research and its impact. In such a view, the primacy given to the "high-impact" journal over the research itself, could result in the task for a qualitative inquirer who wants to publish in this journal having to adapt their qualitative inquiry to the journal and the journal's take on research and qualitative inquiry.

A further consequence of such carelessness and slurring is that excluding qualitative inquiry from, or making it a very low priority in, high-impact factor journals such as The BMJ can be viewed by some of the stakeholders in a research metric driven and obsessed market place as tantamount to declaring (and confirming) qualitative inquiry to be of no/low impact or quality. These are stakeholders, such as funding bodies evaluating and converting publication track records to numerical scores, or promotion committees numerically ranking applicants on the basis of where they have published rather than what they have published. As Blastland and Dilnot observe (2009, p.x), "(n)umbers are today's preeminent public language—and those who speak it rule."

#: Post # BMJnoQual—Putting the Spotlight on Ourselves

While Anand suggested that one response to The BMJ situation was shrugging one's shoulders and walking away from The BMJ, conversely, Clark and Thompson (2016) responded by urging qualitative researchers to metaphorically walk towards what they term "higher impact mainstream journals" (p.1). In an editorial written for the *International Journal of Qualitative Methods*, Clark and Thompson, who are both prominent qualitative researchers, "entreat those seeking to widen access and increase awareness of their qualitative research to be even more determined to meet the challenge of making their work relevant and useful to readers of high-impact mainstream journals" (2016, p.1). Although never explicitly stated in the editorial, it seems as if the specific connection of the editorial to The BMJ debate is the unspoken premise that The BMJ is one such high-impact, mainstream journal.

The editorial offers five considerations or tips, "to help those writing qualitative research for mainstream journals to maximize their chances of publication success" (Clark & Thompson, 2016, p.1). These are: 'try, try, try again'; 'nail your key messages'; 'match messages to audience of targeted journals'; 'tune into the journal'; and, 'remember you are doing community work.' The focus of the tips is on matching, or, put another way, working out and then doing what it takes to match, qualitative inquiry to particular types of journals because of what those journals are connected to or represent. The editorial concludes by reminding readers of their obligation to walk towards, and by implication walk their qualitative inquiry towards, these mainstream higher impact journals. "(M)ainstream journals offer great opportunities for connecting with large and influential communities—as with other forms of community engagement, we don't get to say that we can't, won't, or shouldn't attempt to engage" (Clark and Thompson, 2016, pp.2–3).

Clark and Thomson argue that "(p)erhaps one of the biggest factors explaining the relatively low presence of qualitative research in higher impact journals is that too few articles are submitted" (2016, p.1). Hence, tip one—try, try, try again. However, I am not sure that there is a relatively low presence of qualitative research in higher-impact journals. It depends on what we mean by higher-impact journals. Throughout the editorial, Clark and Thompson use, but do not directly define, the term 'high-impact' mainstream journals (2016, p.1). However, they do state that "(h)igher impact journals tend to have high rejection rates (up to 85–90%) but also potentially greater rewards in terms of visibility and reach due to their larger readership and size" (2016, p.1). Higher impact then seems to be associated with high rejection rates, larger readership and the relative size of a journal. But the question remains, how much higher does the rejection rate need to be *compared to what*, and how much larger does the journal readership need to be *compared to what*, for the journal to be able to claim, and be considered, high impact? And of course who makes these decisions?

In their first tip, Clark and Thompson (2016) also state, "(t)here are many factors that explain why we don't submit to the mainstream enough." The implicit assumption, and slurring between terms here, is that higher-impact journals *are* the mainstream. Their fifth tip—'remember you are doing community work', returns to, and develops, the idea of the mainstream being linked with higher-impact journals and what they term "true community engagement". They state, "When you write for the mainstream, you are enacting true community engagement" (2016, p.2).

But who exactly is this mainstream? Is it the editors of the high(er)-impact journals such as those of The BMJ? The people who read higher-impact and/or larger journals? People who seldom read specialist journals or publish only qualitative work? Further, if writing for the mainstream is true community engagement, then what community are we talking about here, and how far are we prepared to go to engage with it? And what does this mean about writing for the *non-*mainstream? Is it not true community engagement? Does this mean that journals such as *Qualitative Inquiry, Qualitative Research, Qualitative Health Research*, the list could go on, are lower-impact journals and therefore not mainstream journals? And lower impact in comparison to which journals or JCR journal categories? Does this mean that by writing in them we are somehow not enacting true community engagement? While they might be lower-impact *factor* journals than The BMJ, for reasons less related to impact and more to do with metric-related formulae, the case for them having lower impact, not being mainstream, and not enacting true community engagement needs to be made.

However, even in the light of such questions and concerns, on one level it is hard to disagree with Clark and Thompson's five tips (2016) when they are taken at face value. Of course it is important to submit our work to journals that publish work and reach audiences in areas our work is relevant to (tips 3, 5) and to keep trying to do that (tip 1). And of course it is important when considering submitting our research to *any* journal that we nail our key messages (tip 2) and do our homework and tune into the journal (tip 4) (Clark & Thompson, 2016). The problem arises from the refraction of these more generic types of tips when they are applied *specifically* to how we might engage with the process of publishing in what Clark and Thompson (2016) call high(er)-impact journals. It could be that what the refracted tips actually promote is engagement with those journals on their own terms. It is the journal that takes the prior position and thus it is the journal that our qualitative research, and our writing of it, is subordinated to—new forms of the tail wagging the dog Barbour referred to in an article in The BMJ (the then British Medical Journal) close to 20 years ago (Barbour, 2001).

The result of this, as I have discussed in earlier sections of the chapter, can be that, for the qualitative inquirer wanting to publish in such a journal, the task becomes to adapt their qualitative inquiry to the journal's/journal editor's take on research and qualitative inquiry. Engaging with the journal, and being engaged by the journal, can take priority over the types of methods that we use and/or the way that we report our methods and write our research. The question then becomes quite a different one. No longer is it what must we do to get qualitative inquiry published in The BMJ or any other 'higher'-impact journal. Rather, it is more a question of how far, and why, we are prepared to adapt our qualitative inquiry in order for it to be seen and heard in a particular higher-impact journal?

Finishing Up: So Where are We?

The BMJ debate that occurred in 2016 is a useful vehicle for exploring the dilemmas faced by qualitative inquirers when thinking about what public spheres, including what journals, they want or need their research to be seen and heard in and why. Simply shrugging one's shoulders and ignoring high-impact factor journals such as The BMJ in the current research marketplace is not possible. It is The BMJ's position in this research market place—a position sustained by high value market place metrics such as impact factor, *and* the public spheres which this research market place and those metrics connect to—that makes what the editors of The BMJ have said about qualitative inquiry important to qualitative inquirers. It certainly is not the editors' expertise or knowledge about qualitative inquiry. Instead, ironically it is their *lack* of expertise or knowledge about qualitative inquiry, and what they say and do *because* of that lack of expertise, that makes the editors of The BMJ impossible to ignore by qualitative inquirers, and even more important to consider.

Unthinking adaptation of our qualitative inquiry to meet the needs of specific journals and/or editors of those journals can, if we are not careful, sustain certainty about, and standard understandings of, both qualitative research itself and how qualitative research can and must be written. Such certainty and understandings are based not so much on the principles of qualitative research itself, but rather on the principles of qualitative research as suggested and understood by editors and reviewers of specific journals. These are understandings that readers of those journals then come to associate + expect in the reporting of qualitative research + consider as synonymous with a standard qualitative research on which they base their claim to be expert non-experts about qualitative inquiry.

Perhaps, then, a key issue in all this is to see problem(s) for what they are rather than for what others tell us they are. Maybe in this instance the problem is not so much the relatively lower presence and impact of qualitative inquiry in higher-impact journals. Rather, it may be the relatively lower presence and impact of qualitative inquiry in *some specific* higher-impact factor journals such as

The BMJ when compared to others. This then enables qualitative inquiry to put the spotlight on these specific journals and their editorial processes, rather than these journals putting the spotlight on qualitative inquiry and its processes.

In this way the debate is reframed and the onus is placed on the editors and reviewers of journals to justify and provide evidence for the positions they take up and assume about qualitative inquiry. It forces them to confront and justify their own assumptions and the basis for them. This includes the assumptions by The BMJ editors that qualitative inquiry is of low impact *and* that The BMJ has high impact. For, as Adler and Harzing (2009) have pointed out, publishing in so-called high-impact and established journals, conversely, can actually encourage conservative research that asks familiar questions using accepted methodologies rather than research addressing new, often controversial questions that are investigated using innovative methodologies . . . (the result of which is) . . . much academic research . . . (that) . . . is rigorous but irrelevant (p.80) (see also Weingart, 2005).

Reframing The BMJ debate in this way puts qualitative inquiry on the front foot rather than on the back one. It enables qualitative inquirers themselves to work out how far they and their qualitative inquiry will walk away from, or towards, journals such as The BMJ. In so doing it offers the possibility of resisting and unsettling the assumption that opponents of a given quantitative standard such as impact factor or higher impact "have seemingly no choice than to suggest a new one and become standardizers themselves" (Baele & Bettiza, 2017, p.4). By resisting such an assumption and refusing to take up the position of standardizer of our own research, we "acknowledge and discuss the imperfections of what we do, rather than attempt to legislate it out of existence" (Torrance, 2017, p.787). In so doing, we can embrace, rather than attempt to standardize, ignore or eliminate, "uncomfortable spaces", such as those that make up The BMJ debate "that should remain uncomfortable, since this is where learning can happen and a field may be advanced" (Savin-Baden & Howell Major, 2010, p.173).

Notes

1. The BMJ as it is now known was formerly known as the *British Medical Journal*. This name change occurred in 2014. Throughout this chapter I will therefore refer to the journal as The BMJ. However, there is some slippage in the way that the journal name is referred to by others—for example at times some use BMJ, others the BMJ and others *The BMJ*. In this chapter when directly citing other's work I retain the form of the name of The BMJ they used in that writing.
2. A published correction to the original letter added seven additional names that had been accidentally left off the list of signatories to the original letter (Greenhalgh et al., 2016b).
3. The BMJ website (bmj.com) states that rapid responses are electronic letters to the editor. They enable users to debate issues raised in the articles published.
4. The idea of connections is represented by the use of a + in the text. See Cheek (2017a, b) for a more detailed discussion of making such connections by putting some +s into our thinking.

5. See Cheek (2017a, pp. 334–345) for a more detailed example of where the *ands* or the +s can take us when unpacking and exposing the connections in how we think about, and act, in relation to qualitative inquiry in a research market place.

References

Adler, N. & Harzing, A.-W. (2009). When knowledge wins: Transcending the sense and nonsense of academic rankings. *Academy of Management Learning and Education, 8*(1), 72–95.

Anand, J. K. (2016). Re: Qualitative research and the BMJ. A suggestion to Prof Greenhalgh. *BMJ, 352,* doi:10.1136/bmj.i641

Ball, S. J. (2012). Performativity, commodification and commitment: An I-spy guide to the neoliberal university. *British Journal of Educational Studies, 60*(1), 17–28.

Baele, S. J. & Bettiza, G. (2017). What do academic metrics do to political scientists? Theorizing their roots, locating their effects. *Politics,* 1–25. doi:10.1177/026339571 6685727

Barbour, R. S. (2001). Checklists for improving rigour in qualitative research: A case of the tail wagging the dog? *BMJ,* 322, 1115.

Blastland, M. & Dilnot, A. (2009). *The numbers game: The commonsense uide to understanding numbers in the news, in politics, and in life.* London: Penguin.

Cheek, J. (2017a). The marketization of research: Implications for qualitative inquiry. In N. K. Denzin and Y. S. Lincoln (Eds.), *The Sage handbook of qualitative research* 5th ed. (pp. 332–340). Thousand Oaks, CA: Sage.

Cheek, J. (2017b). Qualitative inquiry, research marketplaces, and neoliberalism. Adding some +s (pluses) to our thinking about the mess in which we find ourselves. In N.K. Denzin and M. D. Giardina (Eds.), *Qualitative inquiry in neoliberal times* (pp.19–36). New York: Routledge.

Cheek, J., Garnham, B., & Quan, J. (2006). "What's in a number?": Issues in providing evidence of impact and quality of research(ers). *Qualitative Health Research, 16,* 423–435.

Clark, A. M. & Thompson, D. R. (2016). Five tips for writing qualitative research in high-impact journals: Moving from #BMJnoQUAL. *International Journal of Qualitative Methods, 15*(1), 1–3.

Garfield, E. (1999). Journal impact factor: A brief review. *Canadian Medical Association Journal, 161*(8), 979–980.

Greenhalgh, T. (2016). Response to editors. *BMJ, 352.* doi:10.1136/bmj.i641

Greenhalgh, T., Annandale, E., Ashcroft, R., Barlow, J., Black., Bleakley, A., & Ziebland, S. (2016a). An open letter to The BMJ editors on qualitative research. *BMJ, 352.* doi:10.1136/bmj.i563

Greenhalgh, T., Annandale, E., Ashcroft, R., Barlow, J., Black., Bleakley, A., & Assendelft, W. (2016b). An open letter to The BMJ editors on qualitative research. *BMJ, 352.* doi:10.1136/bmj.i957

Hammersley, M. (2008). *Questioning qualitative inquiry. Critical essays.* London: Sage.

Howard, N., Daniels, K., Gilson, L., Marchal, B., Nambiar, D., & Sacks, E. (2016). BMJ qualitative research policy: a challenge from health policy and systems researchers. *BMJ, 352.* doi:10.1136/bmj.i563

Lincoln, Y. S. (2012). The political economy of publication: Marketing, commodification, and qualitative scholarly work. *Qualitative Health Research, 22,* 1451–1459.

Loder. E., Groves, T., Schroter, S., Merino, J. G., & Weber, W. (2016a). Qualitative Research and The BMJ. *BMJ, 352*. doi:10.1136/bmj.i641

Loder. E., Groves, T., Schroter, S., Merino, J. G., & Weber, W. (2016b). The BMJ editors respond. *BMJ, 352*. doi:10.1136/bmj.i641

Savin-Baden, M. & Howell Major, C. (2010). Afterword. In M. Savin-Baden and C. Howell Major (Eds.). *New approaches to qualitativ research. Wisdom and uncertainty* (pp.172–173). Oxford: Routledge.

Seglen, P.O. (1994). Causal relationship between article citedness and journal impact. *Journal of the American Society for Information Science, 45*(1), 1–11.

Seglen, P. O. (1997). Why the impact factor of journals should not be used for evaluating research. *BMJ, 314*, 498–502.

Spooner, M. (2017). Qualitative research and global audit culture: The politics of productivity, accountablity and possibility. In N. K. Denzin and Y. S. Lincoln (Eds.), *The Sage handbook of qualitative research*, 5th ed. (pp. 894–914). Thousand Oaks, CA: Sage.

Tracey, S.J. (2010) Qualitative quality: Eight "big-tent" criteria for excellent qualitative research. *Qualitative Inquiry, 16* (10), 837–885.

Torrance, H. (2017) Evidence, criteria, policy and politics: The debate about quality and utility in educational and social research. In N. K. Denzin and Y. S. Lincoln (Eds.), *The Sage handbook of qualitative research*, 5th ed. (pp. 766–795). Thousand Oaks, Ca: Sage.

Weingart, P. (2005). Impact of bibliometrics upon the science system: Inadvertent consequences? *Scientometrics, 62*(1), 117–131.

5

INDIGENOUS ~~QUALITATIVE~~ INQUIRY IN THE NEOLIBERAL PUBLIC SPHERE

Patrick Lewis

Everyone needs to attend to Indigenous inquiry methods not just in the current context of neoliberalism, but always and everywhere because Indigenous inquiry methods have resisted 500 years of colonization and oppression. As Sium and Ritskes (2013) noted, decolonization "has been practiced and engaged and theorized in Indigenous communities in ways that have already yielded rich, complex layers of thought" (p. II). It is time to "value the personal as political, to value Indigenous communities as the loci of decolonization theory" (p. II). Storytelling is central to many Indigenous methodologies because the stories of Indigenous peoples centre their research on their communities and ensure that they benefit the community and the people.

Margaret Kovach (2009) reminds non-Indigenous researchers, "the most effective allies are those who are able to respect Indigenous research frameworks on their own terms. This involves a responsibility to know what that means" (p. 12). That being said, probably the best way to convey this responsibility is through the words of Indigenous author Thomas King. In the 2003 Massey Lectures, *The Truth about Stories: A Native Narrative*, King made the now oft-quoted and compelling statement: "The truth about stories is that, that's all we are" (p. 153). It is imperative that non-Indigenous scholars/researchers are sensitive and responsive to the resistance and anti-colonialism that runs through Indigenous methodologies and Indigenous storytelling. "Stories become mediums for Indigenous peoples to both analogize colonial violence and resist it in real ways" (Sium & Ritskes, 2013, p. V). Indigenous storytelling has been a site of resistance and decolonizing theory for centuries. Indigenous storytellers are knowledge keepers who have preserved and strengthened Indigenous epistemologies and ontologies in the face of ongoing colonization. "Stories in Indigenous epistemologies are disruptive, sustaining, knowledge producing, and theory-in-action. Stories are decolonization theory in its most natural form" (p. II).

For Indigenous people decolonization is not a metaphor (Tuck & Yang, 2012); it is a reality lived every day for the past 500 years and at this very moment. That is why everyone should attend to Indigenous inquiry methods because facing neoliberalism is only one more moment in the reiteration of colonization that Indigenous people have been resisting. Neoliberalism is just the latest iteration of colonialism and imperialism with revamped forms of oppression, systemic structures of racism and marginalization veiled in the lexicon of recognizing Indigenous rights and the rhetoric of economic development to benefit all. It is in fact a process that uses such things as the United Nations special rapporteur on the rights of Indigenous peoples to study how to govern Indigenous people. That is, as Lindroth (2014) notes, "expertise and legality function to depoliticise the language of indigenous rights, with states and other actors seemingly governing indigenous peoples less, yet, in recognizing their rights, governing them more cost-effectively" (p. 341), which (cost-efficiencies) is one of the cornerstones of neoliberalism. Consequently, the strange thing is ". . . the UN comes to the rescue and protects Indigenous peoples from states by offering freedom and rights. However, the language of rights works to enhance the image of its proponents" (p. 354)—the states who claim to support the UN Declaration on the Rights of Indigenous Peoples (UNDRIP). Indigenous rights are then 'recognized' by states such as Canada, even going so far as to suggesting implementing UNDRIP during an election campaign (2015 Liberal Party), but then citing existing Canadian laws that preclude that from being actualized; because "indigenous rights are recognised to the extent that they ensure the effectiveness of neoliberal governance" (p. 354). Focus/power of governance appears to shift from the state colonial structures and practices of the past to the rights of Indigenous peoples, their aspirations and desires as everyone can get behind defending rights "because governance through rights is less overt than the earlier desire to civilise indigenous peoples" (p. 355). But it is still couched in Euro-centric notions of freedom and rule of law rather than Indigenous knowledges of natural law, kinship, origin stories and relationality with the land.

How is This any Different than What has been Happening for the Past Four Centuries?

On the surface, it appears the state has taken steps forward in recognizing the rights of Indigenous people and their land claims, but such 'good governance' only recognizes Indigenous rights and claims to "an appropriate cost-effective extent" (Lindroth, 2014, p. 354). It is a shift that comes with a price in that it may afford more protection through legal means for Indigenous peoples in pursuit of rights and claims, but it makes "indigenous peoples, their lands and their rights 'measurable' and thus governable" (p. 354) and thereby puts them under greater surveillance and control of the state through enhanced past practices of who is Indigenous and who is not (Indian Act in Canada, Canadian Supreme Court Rulings: Powley, Daniels), and what constitutes a right or a claim. The government of Canada sidestepped adopting UNDRIP, instead pursuing its own rights systems through the Charter of Rights and Freedoms, the Canadian Human Rights Tribunal, and the courts. "Minimal recognition of rights leads to an increased role by the state in the constitution and regulation of identities through its administrative and technocratic power" (Blackwell, 2012, p. 704). Of course, this is integral to the neoliberal notion of measuring, cost effectiveness, and governability. While the rights and claims of Indigenous people are heightened across the Canadian psyche and generally supported—after all everyone has rights in Canadian law and the Canadian mindset—the forces of globalization and the market march onward across the land, often in devastating ways. The state can say we are addressing Indigenous rights and claims so that Canadians, and some Indigenous nations can believe in such progress, but "the larger rationalities of the market [still] play out on indigenous territories with no radical challenge to the conditions that compel indigenous peoples to seek justice and compensation in the first place" (p. 354). No matter which way things go, Indigenous peoples are constantly having to forfeit something in order to gain something important, but likely less valuable in the long run or so colonial notions of rule of law, rights, freedoms and property law would have it.

Whose Rights and Claims are Really at Stake?

The UNDRIP from the special rapporteur is arguably an improvement in principle upon the way many jurisdictions around the world have previously related or currently relate with Indigenous peoples within the ambit of their nation states. These moves by some states are usually couched in terms of economic benefit or sharing in the growth of markets for Indigenous communities so they too can experience development. However, as Blackwell (2012) points out, "globalisation, an often-elliptical reference to neoliberal economic policies, has brought about increasingly sophisticated forms of exploitation. . ." (p. 703) veiled in the rhetoric of rights, freedoms and recognizing claims. But, at the same time she notes that this has also fostered the growth of "new forms of resistance through the globalisation of human rights" (p. 703). These shifts and moves on the part of states under the aegis of the rights of Indigenous Peoples becomes a double-edged sword, making it increasingly important for Indigenous peoples and communities to carefully navigate a changing landscape (again) while pursuing 'rights' and 'claims'.

The recognition of Indigenous rights and claims by the state appears to be a profound moral and political shift on the part of the colonizing nation state. But as suggested, that is not entirely accurate and has the potential to further the colonising project: the erasure of Indigenous people through assimilation and/or cultural genocide. It is important to remember this has been a centuries-long fight for the right to have rights. As Lindroth (2014) suggests, "those who embrace the language of rights and advocate additional rights for indigenous peoples need to become aware of the power effects these rights entail beyond their stated emancipatory aims" (p. 353).

What's the Story Then?

Stories and storytelling are indeed important and integral to Indigenous resistance, resilience, decolonizing theory and practice, and research methodologies. As Shawn Wilson (2008) wrote, "research is ceremony" and at the heart of that is the ceremonial importance of story which has sustained Indigenous people through the devastating effects of colonization. However, by investing in the state's willingness to recognize and negotiate rights and claims, Indigenous people are "assigned the task of adapting to, rather than challenging, the prevailing conditions that have led to the need for compensations in the first place" (Lindroth, 2014, p. 353). Herein lies the potential danger for undermining Indigenous rights, freedoms and claims as framed by Indigenous epistemologies and ontologies. Because by "invoking the right to remedy and compensation as a tactic, the neoliberal rationality defines a market value for the loss of or damage to indigenous land, culture and life" (Lindroth, p. 353) seemingly doing the morally right thing but actually side stepping the original violations: the repatriation of lands, self-governance, and honouring treaties signed between two nations. The state's willingness to recognize Indigenous rights is not contrary to neoliberal logics; rather it actually furthers the project (read: ongoing colonization) ". . . managed through civil society and the increasingly bureaucratic logic of the state" (Blackwell, 2012, p. 704). Lindroth (2014) makes a compelling evidential argument contrary to those advocating Indigenous rights, because they assume that these rights are self-evident and are only concerned with the technical aspect of Indigenous rights, e.g. "their implementation and how to make sure they are respected" (p. 353). He found that there are power effects pervading this "seemingly 'self-evidently emancipatory' language" (p. 353), highlighting three separate but interrelated power effects being practiced: Indigenous peoples as exceptional; the uncertainty of their rights; and they have a right to remedies— all of which are congruent with neoliberal logics. In Lindroth's assessment, "the practices do not take the form of a coherent power; they are disparate and messy practices with messy consequences" (p. 353).

How Does That Work?

What Lindroth (2014), and many others, note is not new: the neoliberal framework has been toiling away for years constantly moving its project forward through all facets of daily life, including penetrating the governance of Indigenous peoples and what remaining territory they may still have in their possession.

As Blackwell (2012) states, "scholars have increasingly examined how demands for indigenous autonomy fit into the cultural logic of neoliberalism, and feminist scholars have critiqued the selective co-option of women's movement demands" (p. 704), while she has explored how neoliberalism has been exercised through the discourses of gender. However, she also "explores the strategies deployed by indigenous women activists in Mexico to confront new forms of neoliberal governmentality" (p. 705).

Borrowing from Blackwell's study, one can attempt to examine how neoliberal logics work through recent/current Indigenous issues in Canada: in particular, the Canadian Human Rights Tribunal (CHRT) ruling that the federal government of Canada has failed to provide equal funding for social services to Indigenous children on reserve (up to 38% less than provincially). Through that examination, we will return to the opening statement calling on everyone to attend to Indigenous research methods in the neoliberal public sphere.

In February 2007, Cindy Blackstock, executive director of the First Nations and Family Caring Society (FNFCS), along with the Assembly of First Nations (AFN), filed a complaint against the federal government of Canada with the Canadian Human Rights Commission alleging that the federal government discriminates in its funding to social services for Indigenous children and families on reserves through its funding of First Nations Child and Family Services Program (FNCFS Program). A final ruling was not delivered until January 2016, which ruled that the federal government through the department of Indigenous Affairs and Northern Development (INAC) had discriminated and must remedy the issue. However, a great deal has happened between, around, inside, and outside and since that ruling, including the CHRT delivering four non-compliance orders to the federal government of Canada between January 2016 and May 2017; the government of Canada taking the case back to the tribunal claiming a need for more clarification of the ruling; and on August 28, 2017 the government of Canada announced that the department of INAC would be "decolonized" through dissolution and two new departments will be created to more effectively work toward providing services and support to First Nations (Crown-Indigenous Relations and Northern Affairs and Indigenous Services).

The Prime Minister's governing Liberal party received mild praise from some quarters for the latest development of acting on the 1996 recommendation of the Royal Commission on Aboriginal Peoples (RCAP) to dissolve INAC. However, others were wary of having two departments overseeing Indigenous affairs (First Nations, Inuit and Métis). As Veldon Coburn (2017) pointed out, yes this was a recommendation but only if you took a very narrow and two-dimensional view of it from the 4000-page original report! The 1996 RCAP recommendation was actually to:

> . . . split INAC rested on three recurring complaints heard by the commission, outlined in volume 2 of its report: 1) INAC is colonial,

paternalistic, and resistant to change; 2) its performance on Indigenous policy is inadequate; and 3) it has failed to meet treaty and claims obligations. In its report RCAP reasoned that splitting the department would bring the institutional change needed, and the two parts of INAC would address the last two criticisms by "[e]stablishing an Indian Affairs department devoted to policy concerns and reforming the expenditure process (Coburn, 2017).

What the government of Canada actually announced in splitting INAC can be argued to be yet another move to innocence (Tuck & Yang, 2012) through their argument of improving relations with Indigenous people and augmenting services (read governance efficiencies). Furthermore, as Coburn (2017) notes, that recommendation was from the 1990s and stated very clearly that it was time sensitive—late 2017 things are very different now. Such grand announcements also take away attention from the government's ongoing manipulation of the CHRT ruling in favor of the FNFCS and the AFN to equally fund social services for First Nations children.

The neoliberal project of acknowledging rights and claims is borne out through divesting the state of responsibility of social welfare and programming and giving it over to the FNCFS Program. However, their funding mechanisms enables the state to actually control indigeneity—identity, autonomy, governance, and economy. In the case of discriminatory funding inequities to social services we see First Nations take the state to the Human Rights Commission to challenge their funding formulas with the state using the courts, policies, practice, and the Indian Act to try to manipulate that effort, including the government spying on Cindy Blackstock in the middle of the Human Rights complaint (CBC, 2013). As reported, Blackstock, through the Access to Information Act, discovered that the federal government had used 189 staffers to monitor her activity in order to determine whether there were other motives on her part that would then enable them to have the complaint dismissed. But there was "no other motive because there was no other motive," stated Blackstock. She was simply fighting for what was fair (CBC, 2016). The complaint was spurred on by Indigenous peoples because of the crisis of over-representation of First Nation children in the child welfare system of being removed from their homes that was in significant ways caused by the under-funding in the first place. Research shows systemic racism leaving First Nations children four times more likely to be removed from their homes because of institutional structures and practice by social workers on the grounds of neglect and to not ever be returned home (Sinha et al., 2012).

So, Why Doesn't the Government of Canada Just Follow the Ruling and Provide Equal Funding?

Because of neoliberalism's ability to be different in different contexts, it is able to shift and shape its ongoing project which then requires Indigenous people to focus and target rights and claims through a controlled discourse of the state that ostensibly is recognizing and advocating for Indigenous rights, but only to the extent that it fulfils the neoliberal logics of the specific space and place. Although the legal recognition of Indigenous rights and claims may create opportunities for political and economic autonomous participation, there is a consequence of linking rights with economic and political development. Neoliberalism isn't just about economic deregulation and transformation. It is also about governance that implements "practices, knowledge, and ways of inhabiting the world that emphasize the market, individual rationality, and the responsibility of entrepreneurial subjects" (Altamirano-Jiménez, 2013, p. 5), all of which run counter to Indigenous ontologies and epistemologies. As Hale (2005) noted, neoliberal governance also emphasizes affirming basic human rights, including recognition of cultural difference through "compensatory measures to 'disadvantaged' cultural groups" and acknowledging cultural activism so that it articulates a "governance [that] shapes, delimits, and produces cultural difference rather than suppressing it" (p. 13). The state, in taking up the championing of cultural rights in this way "not only pose little challenge to the forward march of the neoliberal project but also induce the bearers of these rights to join the march" (p. 13).

The FNFCS and AFN won the complaint to the Canadian Human Rights Commission after almost 9 years, and the federal government has not complied since the ruling in January 2016 even after four separate non-compliance orders. In the summer of 2017, the Canadian government went to the courts to file "an application for judicial review in respect of the Canadian Human Rights Tribunal's Ruling" (May 2017). Among other things in the application, the Canadian government has made application for "an Order quashing and setting aside certain paragraphs of the Tribunal's Orders for relief . . ." (May 2017). To be clear, the government is using the system to weaponize the very rights, claims and laws it was so eager to acknowledge and recognize for Indigenous peoples of Canada. To wit, the government's application calls for quashing "paragraphs . . . which mandate service provision without allowing for any case conferring, policy review, service navigation or any other similar administrative procedure before funding is provided." The Canadian government through INAC (soon to be two new ministries) continues to work toward the neoliberal project of delimiting, shaping, containing, and controlling Indigenous peoples while recognizing, acknowledging, and articulating their rights and claims.

One of the paramount ways that the state shapes and delimits Indigenous people is through Indigenous identity, which then forces Indigenous people to fall into the state's notion of identity criteria rather than Indigenous practice of relationality through family, community, kinship, and place. By accepting the acknowledgement of rights, claims, and cultural difference, Indigenous peoples then must also accept that it is the state that determines, shapes, delineates, and upholds, or not those rights as created and enacted through the institutional structures of the state. The most recent move by the government of Canada to make application to the courts as mentioned above is demonstrative of the state's willingness to recognize rights while at the same time dictating what those rights will be. Clearly this move is to continue efficiently governing First Nations social services and by consequence First Nations children veiled in the notion of: "case conferring, policy review, service navigation or any similar administrative procedure before funding is provided" (May 2017).

So how have Cindy Blackstock and the FNFCS continued to navigate the maneuvers and machinations of the Canadian government? On first glance one might say it has been and continues to be remarkable perseverance, determination, and patience, but it is much more than that. As mentioned at the beginning of this chapter, Indigenous people have been practicing decolonizing theory and resistance for over 400 years, producing "rich, complex layers of thought" (Sium & Ritskes, 2013, p. II) through story and storytelling in particular. Cindy Blackstock took up the stories of First Nations children receiving inequitable funding, thereby centring her research on their communities and ensures that it benefits the community and the people. Again, the "stories become mediums for Indigenous peoples to both analogize colonial violence and resist it in real ways" (Sium & Ritskes, 2013, p. v).

Similarly, another way is by taking up what Altamirano-Jiménez (2013) calls articulatory practices where by Indigenous peoples can navigate the neoliberal state project to ensure their notion of identity, rights, autonomy, and self-governance:

> Indigeneity is a product of the articulatory practices of Indigenous peoples and different sites, and it constitutes a field where power, social practices, knowledge, governance, and hierarchies are produced, contested, negotiated, and altered in the process of producing the meanings of indigeneity. The concept of articulation is useful in characterizing the diversity of peoples making indigeneity claims and the multiscalar politics of indigeneity production.
>
> (Altamirano-Jiménez, 2013, p. 4)

Cindy Blackstock and the FNFCS seem to have done that. Blackstock and the FNFCS used articulatory practices (story and storytelling) in a few ways. The Caring Society organized several campaigns; *Shannen's Dream, Jordan's Principle*, and *I am a Witness: Have-a-heart-day* through social media and the mainstream media. The campaigns were created to engage students and educators across the country to take up the ideals of good citizenship, social justice, and Canadian values rather than confrontation with the government of Canada. "Engaging students in social justice campaigns provides an opportunity to enhance understanding of community, generosity, and kindness, while practicing problem solving skills" (Blackstock, 2012). How can anyone argue with that? And furthermore these ideas are at the core of the school curriculum and so-called values of

Canadian society. Blackstock, FNFCS and their allies organized children to enunciate (use articulation theory) the idea of children as subjects and as having rights to equal funding to provincial counterparts which grew into a national movement. Through the power of story and storytelling they were able to navigate what one researcher noted was the challenges Indigenous people face with the existence of neoliberal governance that "suggests that Indigenous movements must constantly re-position themselves in response to the state's 'concessions' in order to bring their unresolved concerns out of the de-politicized spheres created through devolution and into public political spaces of contest, debate and accountability" (McDonald, 2011, p. 270). The three campaigns mentioned were/are very successful in that

> The children are standing in solidarity with First Nations children and standing on guard as active citizens for the values that define Canada the most—fairness, justice and respect. Through their engagement in the . . . [three campaigns], children learn how to critically analyze situations and take peaceful and respectful citizenship action for causes they care about. Educators report that children are coming to them wanting to take up the campaigns and integrate them into their learning and educators are finding children are improving their academic, citizenship and personal agency skills in the process.
>
> (Blackstock, 2012)

By using the tools of Canadian citizenship and the school curriculum, but more importantly story/storytelling, and articulatory practices Cindy Blackstock and FNFCS were able to shift the narrative to higher ground by mobilizing children and educators across Canada to take up the stories that embodied the three campaigns while the Human Rights Tribunal case continued. *Shannen's Dream* is a campaign started in memory of the young girl Shannen Koostachin from Attawapiskat First Nation who advocated throughout her childhood from kindergarten to grade eight for a clean, safe school in her community; successive governments promised a new school but never delivered. Shannen was killed in a car accident when she was 15 years old while attending school in a community far from her home. The campaign started shortly after her death and continues today. *Jordan's Principle* was legislation passed in the parliament of Canada on December 12, 2007 that states that "First Nations children have a right to access government services on the same terms as all other children" (Blackstock, 2012). This legislation came about because of arguments over jurisdictional responsibilities for cost between provincial, territorial, and federal levels of government; a very young child, Jordan River Anderson spent over two years in hospital while levels of government argued over who was responsible for paying for his home care. Unfortunately, Jordan died in hospital before ever being able to return to his home. The Trudeau government as of late 2017 has still not fully funded *Jordan's Principle*.

The third campaign is in two parts, *I am a Witness: Have a Heart Day*. The I am a witness is best captured in Cindy Blackstocks own words:

> On Feb. 14, 2012, hundreds of students of all ages gathered at the Federal Court to witness part of the case. The students were not asked to take sides, but simply watch the case and make up their own minds about what was going on. You might wonder how much the younger children really understood while inside the courtroom. In their innocence, children understand the case quite well. They asked questions such as, "why aren't the lawyers talking about the children," and "why isn't the government answering the judge's questions?" Children understand that basic human rights must be accessible to everyone, including First Nations children.
>
> (Blackstock, 2012)

At the same time FNFCS and Blackstock were in court, across Canada thousands of children and supporters were engaged with *Have a Heart Day*, which was sending Valentines to the Prime Minister and Members of Parliament (MP) telling them to provide equitable funding for child welfare and education for First Nations children. Hundreds of children delivered the Valentines in person and thousands more mailed them free because a letter to your MP is free. The work of Blackstock and the FNFCS has been enormously effective in mobilizing children, their families, and educators because they are advocating for First Nations children to receive the same funding and services that any other child in Canada would receive, nothing more, nothing less just equal. As Blackstock noted, many adults respond to the inequities of First Nations funding by suggesting that it is too complicated, however, "to the children, . . . The message was quite simple—First Nations children deserve the chance to grow up safely in their homes, be healthy, get a good education, and be proud of their cultures" (Blackstock, 2012) and one way that happens is through equal funding.

Cindy Blackstock was/is on the speaking circuit too, continually bringing the story(ies) to more and more people across the country and through the media. She has in many ways reshaped the argument with the state around funding (autonomy) through grassroots consultation and mobilization. "This strategy moves from a concept of autonomy as a right granted by the state to a practice of decolonisation that is part of everyday life and community, which is a critical strategy given state recalcitrance" (Blackwell, 2012, p. 705). As McDonald (2011) noted, "there is need to continually theorize articulations of Indigenous demands that can guard against neoliberal co-optation" (p. 269) and the FNFCS and Cindy Blackstock have done just that. However, the Canadian government is still before the court as mentioned and will likely continue to work to ensure that the structures and practice of the neoliberal state (colonialism) continue to be in place. Although the current Trudeau government came into office promising a new relationship with First Nations—Nation to Nation, abiding by and enforcing the Humans Right Tribunal ruling, and implementing UNDRIP—it has yet to do so. These actions or rather absence of action by the Trudeau government is an important reminder "that in addition to aligning with the international discourse on indigenous rights, 'indigenous identity developed political resonance only to the extent that it is employed by the state itself as a marker of inclusion and exclusion" (Jung, as cited in Blackwell, 2012, p. 711). Nevertheless, given the continued effectiveness of Blackstock and FNFCS's articulatory practices and decolonizing theory through story, the federal government of Canada may finally have to provide equal funding.

Blackstock and FNFCS were able to use the neoliberal context to their purpose in that they formed a coalition with children, their families, and educators to re-frame, re-theorize, and re-articulate First Nations children's needs through the highly compelling narrative of so called Canadian values—"fairness, justice and respect"—ideas often woven through neoliberal discourse and governance. But most importantly they were able to reposition the human rights argument into a decolonizing discourse which has moved the autonomy of First Nations child welfare away from the state and into First Nations communities widely supported by non-First Nations communities across the country. The campaigns have interrupted and disrupted the long-running narrative that "indigenous peoples are seen as backward, non-modern subjects who are unable to govern themselves precisely because they are situated temporally always in the past" (Blackwell, 2012, p. 714). Blackstock and the FNFCS utilized the decolonizing stories of First Nations communities and their children to move the issues into the public sphere of Canadian society so that all Canadians see clearly how the government of Canada has been discriminatory and racist in its historical, but most importantly current, relationship with First Nations.

Given the rulings by the Canadian Humans Rights Tribunal, the four non-compliance orders, the federal government's attempt to have the case dismissed through the courts in 2012, the FNFCS's ongoing campaigns, and Cindy Blackstock's tireless work and articulatory practices to reposition the narrative, it is doubtful that the federal government of Canada will be successful in its application to the courts to quash any of the paragraphs in the ruling. Herein lies why it is so important that we attend to the work of Indigenous scholars and communities as they take up decolonizing theory into practice to effectively navigate neoliberal logics in the public sphere.

References

Altamirano-Jiménez, I. (2013). *Indigenous encounters with neoliberalism: Place, women, and the environment in Canada and Mexico*. Vancouver, BC: UBC Press.

Blackwell, M. (2012). The practice of autonomy in the age of neoliberalism: Strategies from Indigenous women's organising in Mexico. *Journal of Latin American Studies, 44*, 703–732.

Blackstock, C. (2012). Reconciliation in action: Educators and students standing in solidarity with First Nations children and Canadian values. *Perspectives, 9.* Ottawa, ON: Canadian Teachers Federation. http://perspectives.ctf-fce.ca/en/article/1998/

CBC (2013). *CBC News.* Snooping on First Nations activist went too far, privacy commissioner says. www.cbc.ca/news/canada/snooping-on-first-nations-activist-went-too-far-privacy-commissioner-says-1.1364426

CBC (2016). *CBC Radio Day 6.* Alanis Obomsawin documents Cindy Blackstock's fight for equality for Aboriginal children. www.cbc.ca/radio/day6/episode-301-human-rights-in-china-u-s-open-getting-schooled-in-comedy-cindy-blackstock-and-more-1.3743693/alanis-obomsawin-documents-cindy-blackstock-s-fight-for-equality-for-abor iginal-children-1.3743703

Coburn, V. (2017). The dismantling of INAC. *Policy Options Politiques: The Public Forum for the Public Good.* http://policyoptions.irpp.org/magazines/september-2017/the-dismantling-of-indigenous-and-northern-affairs-canada/. Retrieved September 6, 2017.

Hale, C. (2005). Neoliberal multiculturalism: The remaking of cultural rights and racial dominance in Central America. *PoLAR, 28*(1) 10–28.

King, T. (2003). *The truth about stories. A native narrative.* Toronto, ON: House of Anansi Press.

Kovach, M. (2009). *Indigenous methodologies: Characteristics, conversations, and contexts.* Toronto, ON: Anchor Canada.

Lindroth, M. (2014). Indigenous rights as tactics of neoliberal governance: Practices of expertise in the United Nations. *Social & Legal Studies, 23*(3), 341–360.

McDonald, F. (2011). Indigenous peoples and neoliberal "privatization" in Canada: Opportunitie, cautions and constraints. *Canadian Journal of Political Science/Revue canadienne de science politique, 44*(2), 257–273.

Sinha, V., Trocmé, N., Fallon, B., MacLaurin, B., Fast, E., Prokop, S., et al. (2011). *Kiskisik Awasisak: Remember the children. Understanding the overrepresentation of First Nations children in the child welfare system.* Ontario: Assembly of First Nations.

Sium, A. & Ritskes, E. (2013). Speaking truth to power: Indigenous storytelling as an act of living resistance. *Decolonization: Indigeneity, Education & Society, 2*(1), i–x.

Tuck, E. & Yang, K. W. (2012). Decolonization is not a metaphor. *Decolonization: Indigeneity, Education & Society, 1*(1), 1–40.

Wilson, S. (2008). *Research is ceremony: Indigenous research methods.* Black Point, NS. Fernwood.

6

CULTIVATING CRITICAL REFLEXIVITY IN THE PUBLIC SPHERE

Ping-Chun Hsiung

I should begin by situating myself as a member of the Taiwanese/Chinese diaspora, a trained feminist activist, and a practitioner of critical qualitative research in a Canadian university.[1] This helps explain what it meant to me when I stepped out of the academic world to deliver a public lecture at the Toronto Reference library as part of its lecture series entitled "Thought Exchange" in October 2016. As I prepared my lecture, I focused on specific challenges I had encountered and the guiding principles I use to develop my pedagogical approach. This chapter presents on four of the pedagogical strategies I use to engage non-academic audiences in the politics and practices of truth-telling.

My Intellectual Journey

Over the last two decades, I have carried out ethnographic fieldwork, interviews, and archival research to advance knowledge and theory in gender studies and qualitative research at local and international levels. In the field of gender studies, I have focused on family change, gender relations, and community organizing in Chinese societies. I worked in factories that produced wooden jewelry boxes to understand how Taiwan's 'economic miracle' came about in a local and daily way through the work and family life of married women. In the early 1990s, I began collaborating with feminist scholars and activists in women's NGOs in China, which has led to more than two decades of fruitful exchange and intellectual engagement.

My interest in qualitative research has compelled me to examine the practices and development of qualitative research as a means of social science inquiry *in* and *from the perspectives of* the global South, and its relation to the dominance of the global North. I advocate for locally grounded, globally informed qualitative research from the global South to bridge the North–South divide. I used China as a case study to derive a history of social science inquiry from the global South. Specifically, I conceptualized the 'investigative research' developed by Mao Zedong as a unique research tradition by examining its practices during China's 'Great Leap Forward' (1958–1962) and its effects on the re-establishment of Chinese sociology in the 1980s (Hsiung, 2017a) and on social science inquiry in contemporary China (Hsiung, 2015).

Putting abstract concepts into practice has been an essential part of my intellectual activism. I have incorporated my research findings and intellectual interests into my graduate and undergraduate teaching at the University of Toronto. I have also engaged with academic audiences through publications, teaching/lectures, and presentations at conferences in North America and Europe.

However, I was apprehensive when I was invited to give a public lecture at the Toronto Reference Library. On one hand, I welcomed the opportunity to reach out to a non-academic audience, because the series was part of the library's program to engage the general public through lectures and discussions across the greater Toronto area.[2] On the other hand, I was not sure how to reach out to a non-academic audience whose exposure to the non-Western world is often filtered through a lens that objectifies non-Western subjects as inferior 'Others.' It reminded me of belligerent remarks directed toward my intellectual pursuit. For example, I, and the graduate student I supervise, must justify a research program that is situated outside of Canada when faced with questions such as "Why do you study China?" "Communism is dead! Why should we care about China?" "Why should Canadian taxpayers pay for your work in China?" "How would the general public benefit from your work?" and "Why should non-academics care about your historical study of China?"

I decided to use my research on China's Great Leap Forward (GLF) and Great Famine as a starting point to discuss the politics of knowledge production and ignorance perpetuation with the non-academic audience. My goal was to bridge the divide between the academic and non-academic worlds, bring China studies to the West, and insert criticality into the public sphere. My ultimate objective is to advance civil engagement among the general public by discussing what it takes to 'speak the truth' in everyday life, how to adjudicate a fine line between truth, white lies, and defiance, and why it is essential to safeguard whistleblowing in civil society.

As I began to prepare my lecture, I remembered the perennial calls by public sociologists, who urged academic sociologists to engage in public debates and/or contribute to policymaking (Burawoy, 2005). Heath (2012) and Stacey (2004) wrote about the institutional and ideological barriers that have prevented them from realizing the potential of public sociology. The societal, transformative effects of their research on poverty and gay marriage in public sphere were diminished by public beliefs and institutionalized practices. It became very clear that if I wanted to meaningfully engage the non-academic audience in Canada,

I needed to problematize the pervasive, yet often unspoken, simplistic dichotomy that simultaneously upholds the West as a democratic, advanced society and projects China as an authoritarian, backward 'Other.' To me, engaging in public sociology as a diasporic practitioner of qualitative research means cultivating critical reflexivity in the public sphere. This can open up a space, even if only temporarily, where it is possible to recognize the vulnerability of the democratic system of the West, dissent within an oppressive context, and the necessity of criticality in everyday practices across the East–West dichotomy.

Cultivating Critical Reflexivity in the Public Sphere

Over time, I have developed four pedagogical strategies to cultivate critical reflexivity in the public sphere: (1) using images to capture the politics of knowledge production and ignorance perpetuation during China's GLF and Great Famine; (2) calling upon personal stories to illustrate agency and dissent in the Chinese context; (3) situating 'truth construction' in comparative contexts; and (4) connecting 'truth construction' to daily practices at a personal level.

Examining the Politics of Knowledge Production and Ignorance Perpetuation through Images

I began my presentation by providing a general background about China's GLF, which was a massive social, political, and economic experiment launched by the Chinese Communist Party (CCP). It was intended to use China's vast population to rapidly transform the country from an agrarian economy to a modern, industrial, communist utopia. The experiment was a dramatic public policy failure that led to steep economic decline and fuelled the Great Famine, in which an estimated 33–55 million people died. During the GLF, the CCP state launched nationwide campaigns such as steel production, irrigation projects, crop and grain production experiments, collectivization, communes, and public canteens. I used several archival photos to help the audience relate to my presentation.[3]

For example, a photograph of backyard furnaces for steel production shows the shape and size of clay furnaces and tools, as well as the physical labour of workers in the field.[4] The image reveals the extremely low level of industrial technology used for steel production at the time. To fuel the furnaces, trees and forests were cut down, and doors and furniture were taken from peasants' homes. I also noted that pots, pans, hinges, and other artifacts that were donated (or confiscated) from peasant households as 'scrap' for the furnaces. I also included an image of pig irons produced by the backyard furnaces.[5]

By combining these images with my oral presentation, I was able to demonstrate how far-fetched it was for the CCP to claim that the GLF would allow China to catch up and even surpass technology in the UK and US. For example, the image of pig irons produced by the backyard furnaces demonstrates the disparity between reality and the CCP's textual-based rhetorical campaign. Even with no previous knowledge about China and the GLF, the audience was able to understand the failure of the experiment as well as the indoctrination involved in the campaign.

I then used the image of public canteens to discuss collectivization, one of major feature of the GLF[6]. The public canteens were proclaimed as providing unlimited supplies of meals and taking women out of kitchens and into the agricultural production. Top down pressure from the CCP pushed local communes to organize, or to claim records in organizing, public canteens. I also presented images to illustrate how 'truth' about agricultural production was systematically fabricated and disseminated.

For example, I presented a mural painted in a village wall. It depicts an adult male riding an oversize hog with a little girl sitting behind him, with the following caption (Chen & Wen, 2010)[7]:

Raising a pig as big as an elephant, 肥猪像大象
Although its nose is not as long as an elephant's, 就是鼻子短
When it's slaughtered, 全社杀一口
An entire commune can feast on it for half a year. 足够吃半年

I treated the mural as 'constructed' archival data and spoke about the institutional mechanisms that had been used to produce it. The CCP had established an infrastructure down to the village level to disseminate its discursive message, and activated human resources, such as writers and artists, to produce tailor-made mass-media images. This ensured that commands from the top would be implemented through the bureaucratic chain, so images occupied prominent physical spaces at individual locales.

I showed the audience a map of crop production in Beijing and its surrounding areas. The top arrow marks a commune in the Tianjin area that had presumably produced 120,000 kilograms of rice per mu (roughly 666 square meters or 797 square yards)[8]. The bottom arrow marks another commune where 5,000 kilograms of cotton were allegedly harvested in one mu. These figures are in blatant deviation from the actual production figures: the most productive crop yields were actually 200 kilograms for rice and 50 kilograms for cotton per mu (Wang, 2005). I also included an infamous photo that exaggerated rice production. It shows four laughing children jumping on thick, dense rice stocks.[9] Although the image was doctored, it was presented as the truth and was very powerful and effective at the time.

My presentation went beyond the conventional 'show-and-tell' approach. By examining the mechanisms behind the images, I provided a *sociological analysis of knowledge production*. My discussion of the objectives of those images explored how the CCP's experiment led to the establishment of a rhetoric regime that sanctioned the production of fabrication and falsehood. Media outlets were appropriated to broadcast visual images that supported official claims. By moving beyond a predominately text-based mode of academic presentation and incorporating images, I made it easier for the non-academic audience to relate to the underlying arguments deeply rooted in the disciplinary sub-field of 'sociology of knowledge.'

Calling upon Personal Stories to Illustrate Agency and Dissent in the Chinese Context

Another strategy I used was calling upon personal stories to challenge the stereotypical notion of an all-encompassing effect of the authoritarian Chinese regime. Although the GLF was a policy failure with catastrophic consequences for the population, the CCP did change course after two years. To understand this change in policy after such a short time, it is necessary to explore dissent within the CCP state. To illustrate this kind of defiance, I discussed petition letters written by soldiers, villagers, low-ranking bureaucrats, and elementary school-teachers that informed their superiors about the grim realities of food shortages, massive death rates in the countryside, and corruption, cruelty, and abuse among local officials. I explained the personal risk individuals assumed when expressing their dissent: their grievances were ignored and/or systematically suppressed. I used the legacy of Lufong Zou (1910–1959) to underscore my argument.

As the vice-president of Peking University, Zou was in charge of three research teams from Peking and People's Universities. They were instructed to investigate public canteens, one of the signature features of the GLF. The research teams were made up of 162 senior and junior faculty members, graduate students, and undergraduates; they were sent to three counties in Hebei and Henan provinces. After spending months in the countryside, the research teams found huge gaps between the political objectives of the CCP state and real-world practices. Their observations and data collected in the agricultural sector and public canteens were particularly troubling. After weeks of deliberation and debate, the research teams concluded that the public canteens had failed to increase women's participation in the agricultural sector, and that the canteens had not effectively met the dietary needs of families. In their reports, the research teams cautiously raised concerns over the utility of the public canteens. Although their final report was approved by political leaders at the universities, members of the research teams were denounced when Chairman Mao (the leader of the CCP) questioned the findings. As the leader of the research project, Lufeng Zou personally shouldered the blame and eventually committed suicide.

While Zou's photo was projected on the screen, I used stories about him and others who raised dissenting voices during the GLF to demonstrate that although the CCP was an authoritarian state, its power was not all-encompassing. It is true that policymaking in China was not based on democratic processes (Li, 1999) and that the collective was promoted over individual interests (Dong & Jia, 1958).

However, in various ways, critical perspectives were asserted (Hsiung 2015), individual interests were negotiated (Gao, 2013), and dissenting positions were incorporated into policymaking (Li, 1999).

When presenting these various types of dissent to my non-academic audience, I was careful not to refer too much to academic scholarship and my own interest in the institutional and discursive practices of 'remonstrators' (*jianguan*) in the Chinese context. However, I believe that academics have a duty to encourage the public to challenge ignorance perpetuated through stereotypes and misconceptions. Therefore, I drew from little-known information to bridge the academic and non-academic divide. I introduced the traditional Chinese practice of 'remonstration,' which dates back to 200 BC (Ch'ien, 1982; McMullen, 2012). The term refers to a moral and political expectation that intellectuals and civil servants will voice their remonstration (objection) to the state/ruler, even if it means sacrificing their lives (Ch'ien 1982; McMullen 2012).

Remonstration is intended to render a ruler 'corrigible' (capable of being reformed). Historically, it has been used by Chinese bureaucrats and common people to voice injustice or oppression (Guy, 1987). In the CCP, a few critical intellectuals drew upon the tradition of remonstration by bringing incompetence, corruption, and popular grievances to the attention of the authorities (Goldman, Cheek, & Hamrin, 1987). Some local bureaucrats also experimented with remonstration during periods characterized by a relaxed political climate (Heilmann, 2011). In both types of cases, the tradition of remonstration carries with it the expectation that the ruling authorities will listen to, and rectify, the problems presented by those remonstrating. I explained to my audience that because of the tradition of remonstration, many low-ranking bureaucrats felt it was their duty to write to Mao about abuses and cruelty among administrative officials and the widespread famine (Yu, 2005). I also explained that Zhou's suicide should be understood within the Chinese tradition of remonstration. My hope was to encourage the Western, non-academic audience to go beyond a simplistic/stereotypical perception of China and its authoritarian political landscape, which inadvertently objectifies the non-Western subject into an inferior 'Other.'

Situating 'Truth Construction' in Comparative Contexts

The third pedagogical technique I used in my presentation was to argue that 'truth' is not always clearly defined and/or permanent: it is often contested. It is therefore important to examine how 'truth' is constructed, and by whom, and to accomplish what objectives. For example, scholars have documented institutions, mechanisms, and political objectives that continue to cast doubt about the health effects of cigarette smoking. Another example is the orchestrations by industry and politicians that are behind the so-called 'controversy' over climate change. In my discussion, I referred to three well-known scandals in the auto industry to illustrate how statistics may be falsified for financial purposes.

First, I discussed how in 2015, Toshiba's chief executive and president resigned after the company was found by an independent panel to have overstated its operating profit by a total of $1.22 billion over a six-year period. This amount was roughly three times the company's initial estimate. According to the report delivered by the independent investigators, the misreporting of profits started when senior managers began to impose unrealistic performance targets after the financial crash in 2008. The report stated, "within Toshiba, there was a corporate culture in which one could not go against the wishes of superiors. . . . When top management presented 'challenges,' division presidents, line managers and employees below them continually carried out inappropriate accounting practices to meet targets in line with the wishes of their superiors" (News, 2015).

Second, I discussed how in April 2016, Mitsubishi, Japan's sixth-largest automaker, admitted that its four domestic mini-vehicle models had not met Japan's fuel economy regulations. The company also admitted that the period of deception was much longer than it had previously revealed. Over the last 25 years, Mitsubishi had manipulated its fuel economy testing methods to conceal its failure. After this announcement, the automaker's market value plunged 50%, with a loss of $3.9 billion in one week (Tajitsu, 2016).

After presenting these two cases, I noted that misrepresentation is not unique to the Asian context. In 2017, Volkswagen, a German company and the world's second-largest automaker, pled guilty to three counts of felony criminal charges (conspiracy to commit fraud, obstruction of justice, and entry of goods by false statement) in the US for cheating on diesel emissions tests for a decade. The company accepted to pay $1.5 billion in civil fines and $2.8 billion in criminal fines. Six supervisors admitted that they had misled regulators and consumers by installing secret software to cheat on exhaust emissions tests and make engines appear cleaner than they were. Such software was installed on 500,000 vehicles in the US and 11 million vehicles worldwide. Furthermore, Volkswagen officials told their engineers to destroy a document that detailed the cheating, and their lawyers encouraged employees to destroy other documents. The company's senior management team, including its chief executive, resigned following the scandal (Shepardson, 2017).

Based on these examples, I pointed out similarities between malpractice in China and the auto industry, even though they were decades apart. In both cases, the objectives of the state/company were communicated through bureaucratic/managerial channels to the lower levels. These objectives were translated into performing measurements/indicators that bureaucrats/employees were expected to fulfill. Pressure to perform or outperform unrealistic expectations not only provides incentive to widespread deceiving practices, it also sanctions epidemic complicity. The immediate forms of fallout from the malpractice differed slightly. Zhou took his own life to repudiate the actions of the state, even though his dissent was very much muted at the time by the CCP. It has taken decades for the CCP to admit that the GLF was a policy error. In contrast, executives from the auto industries were forced to apologize and/or resign after the fraud was exposed. The companies took a financial loss in term of stock prices and fines, and it will take some time for their tarnished reputations to recover. Unlike the nationwide famine in China, the auto industry examples did not lead to tangible human costs, but there are many examples where lives were lost due to systematic institutional failure. The space shuttle disasters are infamous examples.

In 1986, the US space shuttle Challenger broke apart 73 seconds into its flight, killing all seven crew members. Vaughan used historical ethnography to delineate the incremental development of NASA's organizational culture and practices that normalized risk. Engineering reports of mechanical failure became routinely interpreted as 'acceptable risk' (Vaughan, 1996). With an increasing range and degree of acceptability, material and structural malfunctioning of the shuttle became defined as a 'maintenance problem' rather than a 'safety to flight issue' (Vaughan, 1996). In her book, Vaughan clearly demonstrated that the organizational culture and the normalization of deviance were the cause of the Challenger disaster, rather than the commonly accepted theory about technical failure and managerial wrongdoing.

Seventeen years later, in 2003, the space shuttle Columbia disintegrated as it entered Earth's atmosphere, killing all seven crewmembers. The causes were analogous to those of the Challenger disaster. Vaughan was called as an expert witness to testify before the US Congress. When she was asked whether she had been consulted by NASA since her book's publication, she replied, "It seemed like everybody called—my high school boyfriend even called—but NASA never called" (Vaughan, 2006, p. 367). Although her reply was widely quoted, Vaughan was slammed by a top administrator at NASA as using a "cheap shot" for instant fame (Vaughan, 2006, p. 367).

The shuttle disasters served as good examples, helping my audience better understand the GLF and Great Famine. They were familiar and less foreign. Although the space shuttle disasters and China's Great Famine differed exponentially in terms of loss of human life, stories of both astronauts and farmers who were fathers and teachers brought home the human cost of the disasters, helping my Western audience relate emotionally to the Great Famine. One audience member commented, "You talked about an estimated 3.5 million Chinese [who] died. These were not just numbers. They were real people. It was like 90% of the Canadian population got wiped out."

Connecting 'Truth Construction' to Daily Practices at the Personal Level

The fourth and final strategy involved exploring how each of us engages in 'truth construction' in our daily lives. Specifically, I focused on the practice and function of 'white lies.' My examples of benign excuses (e.g., calling in sick at work to attend personal matter, using a 'prior commitment' to skip a social gathering, saying 'someone is at the door' to end a phone call) were met with smiles and laughter. I then displayed an image of a candy machine you might find in a grocery store.

I shared an embarrassing white lie I had repeatedly told my daughter while grocery shopping when she was about two. To avoid hassle and stay in control in public, I told her the colorful candies in the machine were medicine for really sick kids. From time to time, my daughter would innocently point at the candies and say, "mom, these are for the sick kids. We don't need them, right?" I admitted that I felt terrible about her innocent comments. For a long time, I wondered how I could 'confess' to her to assuage my guilt. I was also concerned that my white lie might compromise my daughter's trust and even irreversibly undermine our mother–daughter bond. I was very relieved when my daughter got older and stopped noticing the candy machine. I was also relieved when, as a teenager, she told me she did not remember that I had told her the candies were medicine for sick kids. A huge cloud was lifted as I realized my white lie did not cause any lasting psychological damage.

This anecdote illustrates that 'truth-telling' is personal. Everyone engages in various forms of truth-telling, which involves seldom-analyzed norms and practices that involve an interactive process of decision-making shaped by individual objectives and societal expectations. Truth-telling also involves a political component: it can denounce injustice, inequality, and abuses of power. The actions of three activists can help illustrate this point.

In 1955, Rosa Parks 'spoke the truth' by refusing to give up her seat to a White passenger on a bus in Montgomery, Alabama. Her act of defiance and the ensuing Montgomery bus boycott became signature symbols of the Civil Rights movement in the US. After Candace Lightner's 13-year-old daughter was killed by a drunk driver, she turned her loss into action by denouncing drunk driving and founding the Mothers against Drunk Driving (MADD) campaign. After having his leg amputated, Terry Fox started a cross-country marathon in Canada in 1980 to raise awareness and funds for cancer research. Since then, the Terry Fox Run has grown into an international event. These examples share several attributes related to truth-telling. First, they demonstrate how an action of individual truth-telling can grow into a national outcry with lasting effects. Second, they reveal that this kind of truth-telling is not new: it has always occurred in everyday life. As whistle-blowers, the actions of these individuals could have been suppressed, so it is vital to discuss ways to cultivate a mechanism that not only protects whistle-blowers but also compels others to join the truth-telling action.

Concluding Remarks

In this chapter, I presented four pedagogical strategies that I used to present a public lecture on the politics of truth-telling to a Western non-academic audience.

My objective was to cultivate critical reflexivity in the public sphere and cultivate truth-telling by identifying related incentives, practices, and mechanisms. Individuals must be willing to challenge injustice and/or put forward alternative visions. They may lack formal status or official position; their power in remaking the societal landscape arises from their incentive to act. Truth-telling practices can eventually turn individual voices into collective activism, through the encouragement of norms and mechanisms that give individual actions a chance to snowball into collective undertakings. An essential aspect of this mechanism is to protect whistle-blowers, through either clandestine or public means.

My first engagement with a non-academic audience turned out to be non-eventful. During the question-and-answer section, some members of the audience asked for clarification and/or additional information, especially regarding the GLF and Great Famine. Some criticized the CCP state, while others commented that its failure was inevitable given the size of the country and the low levels of industrial technology and agricultural development. I found it disappointing but informative that my efforts to cultivate critical reflexivity did not seem to resonate. None of the audience picked up the thread on the vulnerability of the Western democratic system. The examples I used to destabilize the West–China dichotomy did not seem to gain any traction, even though the audience did break out in laughter when I told the story of the candy machine.

After the host thanked me and the audience slowly cleared the room, I started to pack up my things, feeling unheard and unfulfilled. As if to reinforce this feeling, a gentleman from the audience approached me. He said he had spent years teaching English as a second language in Asia and Toronto. He said my presentation was very good and my pronunciation was much better than some of his students. However, he said I had not pronounced the word 'memoirs' correctly. He said it for me and asked me to repeat it for him. I was amazed and a bit taken aback at the time. In retrospect, this exchange not only reveals the symbolic meaning, power dynamic, and dismissiveness of the West. It also encapsulates the politics and challenges of cultivating critical reflexivity in the public sphere.

Notes

1. The theme of the 2017 International Congress on Qualitative Inquiry was "Qualitative Inquiry in the Public Sphere." The Congress provided a gathering space for qualitative practitioners from around the world to reflect and strategize on individual and collective resistance. In his welcome address, Denzin invited participants to "[advance] the causes of social justice, while addressing racial, ethnic, gender and environmental disparities in education, welfare, and healthcare" (Denzin, 2017). In a panel called "Coalition for Critical Qualitative Inquiry," I joined other panelists to share my praxis as a critical qualitative practitioner. This chapter is based upon my presentation, called "Practicing Critical Reflexivity in the Public Sphere" (Hsiung, 2017b).
2. The invitation was the result of efforts by Lucy Gan, a special librarian at the East Asian Library at the University of Toronto, in an attempt to bridge the divide between scholars focusing on China and the general public.

3. For my presentation, I selected archival images from websites that included posters, photos, and drawings of the Great Leap Forward. None of the websites provided original sources, even though many of the images have become iconic of that era. For this chapter, Lucy Gan, a trained Chinese librarian, called upon her professional expertise to help identify the sources. For some images, she was able to locate their original sources, for others it was only possible to locate them in publication or photographic collection. Given these issues with copyrights, the images in this chapter will be narratively described without including a visual presentation. When possible, however, a link to the URL from where I gathered the image for my presentation will be included.

4. Image of backyard furnaces available at http://alphahistory.com/chineserevolution/wp-content/uploads/2013/05/backyardfurnaces.jpg

5. Image of pig irons available at https://sites.google.com/site/lewisfry/smelter02.jpg, retrieved October 1, 2017.

6. This photo was taken at Yanziji Commune, Nanjing City, Jiangsu province, depicting dinner of the Chinese New Year Eve at the public canteen in 1959. The caption of its original publication states, "Eat as much as one wants. Endeavor as the best as one can" (放开肚皮吃饭，鼓足干劲生产).

7. Image of the mural was originally published by Shashan Bao, a local pamphlet in 1959. The image is included in an online collection of photographic images of the Great Leap Forward at www.360doc.com/content/09/1128/18/62878_9950087.shtml, Retrieved October 1, 2017.

8. For the image of this poster, see www.sciencenets.com/data/attachment/album/201508/04/120125c06ohd68142q4cqd.jpg, Retrieved October 1, 2017.

9. This photo was originally published in the *People's Daily* in the summer of 1958 and subsequently republished nationwide. It is available at http://images2.china.com/news/zh_cn/history/11066805/20130813/17993810_831385.jpg

References

Burawoy, M. (2005). For public sociology. *American Sociological Review, 70*(1), 4–28.

Chen, G. & Wen, J. (2010). *Zhongguo Xuanchuanhua Shihua* [A historical study of propaganda posters in China). Guiyang: Guizhou jioayu chubanshe.

Ch'ien, M. (1982). *Traditional government in Imperial China: A critical analysis.* Hong Kong: The Chinese University Press.

Denzin, N. K. (2017). *Qualitative inquiry in the public sphere.* Paper presented at the The 13th International Congress of Qualitative Inquiry, University of Illinois at Urbana-Champaign.

Dong, D. & Jia, Y. (1958). *Gongchan zhuyi sixiang fangguanmang* [Advancing the Communist Ideology)]. Baoding: Hebei renmin chubanshe.

Gao, W. (2013). *Zhongguo Nongmin fanxingwei yanjiu* [Counteraction of Chinese Peasants, 1950–1980]. Hong Kong: The Chinese University Press.

Goldman, M., Cheek, T., & Hamrin, C. L. (Eds.) (1987). *China's intellectuals and the State: In search of a new relationship.* Cambridge, MA: Harvard University Press.

Guy, R. K. (1987). *The Emperor's four treasuries: Scholars and the State in the late Ch'ien-lung era.* Cambridge, MA: Harvard University Press.

Heath, M. (2012). Making marriage promotion into public policy: The epistemic culture of a statewide initiative. *Qualitative Sociology, 35*(4), 385–406.

Heilmann, S. (2011). Policy-making through experimentation: The formation of a distinctive policy process. In S. Heilmann & E. J. Perry (Eds.), *Mao's invisible hand: The political foundations of adaptive governance in China* (pp. 62–101). Cambridge, MA: Harvard University Press.

Hsiung, P.-C. (2015). Doing (Critical) qualitative research in China in a global era. *International Sociology, 30*(1), 86–102.

Hsiung, P.-C. (2017a). The politics of rebuilding Chinese sociology in the 1980s. *Qualitative Inquiry, 23*(1), 89–101.

Hsiung, P.-C. (2017b). *Practicing critical reflexivity in the public sphere.* Paper presented at the the 13th International Congress of Qualitative Inquiry, University of Illinois, Urbana/Champaign.

Li, R. (1999). *Lushang Huiyi Shilu* [A documentary account of the Lushan Conference). Zhengzhou: Henan Renmin Chubanshe.

McMullen, D. (2012). Memorials and essays: Political protest in late medieval China. *International Journal of China Studies, 3*(3), 239–269.

News, B. (Producer). (2015, July 21). Toshiba chief executive resigns over scandal. [Business] Retrieved from www.bbc.com/news/business-33605638

Shepardson, D. (Producer). (2017, January 11). U.S. indicts six as Volkswagen agrees to $4.3 bln diesel settlement. Retrieved from www.reuters.com/article/us-volkswagen-emissions-epa/u-s-indicts-six-as-volkswagen-agrees-to-4-3-billion-diesel-settlement-idUSKBN14V1T0

Stacey, J. (2004). Marital suitors court social science spinsters: The unwittingly conservative effects of public sociology. *Social Problems, 51*(1), 131–145.

Tajitsu, N. (Producer). (2016, April 26). Mitsubishi Motors says cheated on mileage tests for 25 years. Retrieved from www.reuters.com/article/us-mitsubishimotors-regulations/mitsubishi-motors-says-cheated-on-mileage-tests-for-25-years-idUSKCN0XN0DV

Vaughan, D. (1996). *The Challenger launch decision: Risky technology, culture, and deviance at NASA.* Chicago, IL: University of Chicago Press.

Vaughan, D. (2006). NASA revisited: Theory, analogy, and public sociology. *The American Journal of Sociology, 112*(2), pp. 353–393.

Wang, Z. (2005). 1959 nian "fan you qing" yundong zhong de yijian ge an [A case of the 1959 anti-rightist campaign]. *Zongheng, 11.*

Yu, X. (2005). *Dayuejin, Kurizi Shangshuji* [Collection of grieving letters] Hong Kong: Shida Chaoliu Chubanshe.

7

INDIVIDUAL NEEDS, CULTURAL BARRIERS, PUBLIC DISCOURSES

Taking Qualitative Inquiry into the
Public Sphere

Silke Migala and Uwe Flick

Introduction

Current politics in Western European countries, as well as in the US under Trump, try to work with symbolic and social barriers between majority populations and migrant communities. In this context, discrimination of cultural communities in areas such as health and welfare, social justice, and accessibility of institutional support can intensify feelings of disadvantage and being excluded or treated in unequal, unjust, or unfair ways. This can lead to or intensify social conflicts and tensions. In this situation, it becomes relevant to understand where and how such feelings of being disadvantaged are produced and where real disadvantage happens in institutional routines for example.

What does it mean in such a situation to take qualitative inquiry into the public sphere? What are public spheres for qualitative inquiry? In answering such questions, we can distinguish four versions of taking qualitative inquiry into the public sphere:

1. To transgress the disciplinary boundaries of the original scientific contexts in which qualitative inquiry was and is traditionally located, such as sociology and education: What happens, when qualitative inquiry is transferred to other contexts beyond sociology, for example medical and health sciences or engineering and architectural sciences? How far is this transfer still referring to our understanding of qualitative inquiry?
2. Public sphere can mean to identify research problems and target groups that are affected by issues of public (societal) relevance. In current times, for example, discriminations of cultural groups in the context of health care services can become a wider issue of societal schism.

3. Taking qualitative inquiry into public spheres will also mean that we should make our results accessible for public audiences—in the way we write about our research and how and where we publish our findings, when we bring our results to audiences which can be located themselves as in the public sphere.
4. Finally, this can mean that we need to adapt our understanding of what good research means. This can be realized by extending our quality criteria to those of relevance and impact of our research for public contexts.

In what follows, such issues will be discussed on a more general level and illustrated by an example of subsequent research projects. These projects address an issue of public relevance—discrimination of specific groups in accessing social support. They address this issue in a context, which is relevant in the public sphere—the context of integration, exclusion and confrontation of social majorities and cultural minorities. The concrete case is the access to professional support in the area of end of life care and in particular palliative services.

The Initial Project: Users' and Professionals' Views of Access to Palliative Care for Russian-speaking Migrants

The initial project addressed the palliative quality of life and, more concretely, the utilization of services by Russian-speaking migrants in Germany. We received funding from the German Ministry for Education and Research (2013–2017) and aim at providing results for improving the practices in health services.[1]

Starting points for this first study were twofold: First, reports from practitioners show that Russian-speaking migrants' (RSM) utilization of palliative home care services and hospices is lower than expected. One reason for this could be barriers that prevent them from finding the adequate support and services at the end of life. Second, earlier research showed that migrants from the Russian language area are one of the largest migrant groups and communities in Germany. They are mainly late repatriates or Jewish immigrants from the countries of the former Soviet Union. After the collapse of the Soviet Union, in Germany the legal conditions for a wider immigration of Jewish people with German roots were improved in 1991, also with the aim of strengthening the Jewish communities in the reunited Germany. This allowed about 220,000 Jewish immigrants—including their sometimes non-Jewish family members (spouses and underage, unmarried children)—to come to Germany. They were distributed across Germany and its Federal States (Bundesländer) according to quotas and contingents. In regard to their situation vis-à-vis health care, studies by Schenk (2011) and Vogel (2012) showed that similar to the Russian late repatriates, the family and in particular female relatives have a key function in any kind of nursing, which also includes palliative nursing. They also described a high risk of distrust with public services and professionals with whom the clients were not familiar. The main challenge is to build up trust and relations for good care. Other challenges are how to take religious prescriptions, such as kosher nutrition and access to native language services, into account.

For the group of late repatriates, a double experience of exclusion has often been described: After they were discriminated in the Soviet Union because of their German descent, they are now perceived as Russians by the indigenous population in Germany (Schönhuth and Kaiser, 2015). Because of the mostly secular socialization of Jewish immigrants, their integration occurred with tension between mainstream society and the Jewish communities on the one hand and the immigrants' individual definitions of being Jewish on the other. The immigrants saw themselves as being confronted with the expectation to profess their Jewish culture and religion, although the foundation of both was unfamiliar to them (Körber, 2009). The few studies addressing this target group from a health care angle show how a family orientation and traces of a collectivist attitude of values impede a more individualist active utilization of health care services (e.g., Schenk, 2011). This may explain why RSM have more trouble in finding, accessing, and utilizing services than the German majority population.

Research Design: Addressing a Public Issue in a Wider Disciplinary Context

Also in other fields of health care, a structurally identified undersupply of a specific subpopulation can become a structural problem. In the case of untreated drug and addiction problems this may lead to subsequent diseases such as hepatitis C (see Flick and Röhnsch, 2014). In case of migrant subpopulations such an undersupply with specific support can be, in particular, related to limited integration in the new societal context: Lack of support can be a result of a lack of integration and it can intensify the limitations in the integration and, in particular, in the feeling of being part of the new societal context. Such a lack of support and its relation to feeling/being integrated is something that is produced, increased, or reduced in the interaction (or lack of interaction) between people in need of help and those who represent institutions that could provide such help.

Research Questions

To understand the perceived barriers involved in this process in more detail, it seemed necessary to reconstruct the experiences of the two sides involved in this social problem (see Holstein and Miller, 2003 and Flick, 2015). Thus, the main research questions in this study were:

- What are Russian-speaking migrants' ideas of a peaceful death and of quality of life at the end of their life?

- What are the requirements of palliative and hospice care for Russian-speaking migrants according to the professional groups involved?
- What are subjective needs of Russian-speaking migrants in palliative care?
- What are the barriers to utilizing adequate forms of palliative care, such as barriers against using hospices, for example?

Research Design

These questions were the starting point for constructing a research design addressing both views by triangulating data coming from both sides of the (working, possible, or failing) interaction—(potential) clients and professionals.

Sampling of Participants

On the clients' side, palliative cases were the sampling units. This means that cases of RSM in which treatment in a hospice or in palliative care was currently experienced or, in the case of relatives, had been experienced recently. The original idea was to interview mainly the patients and also to conduct interviews with their relatives. Access to the participants was organized via palliative institutions and their staff or self-help groups for RSM in general, or such groups in the context of palliative care. Social media were also used for getting in touch. However, it proved difficult to include patients in the sample for several reasons: First, and not surprisingly, given the practitioners' reports we took as a starting point, there were few cases with a RSM background in palliative treatment during the period of data collection. Another reason was the reluctance of palliative staff to support contact to patients—mainly with the argument that interviews would over-challenge them. Finally some of the patients we contacted refused to take part in the study. One potential interviewee died before being interviewed. In other cases, relatives of patients withdrew their agreement of participation shortly before the interview. In the end this means that we reached the intended sample of 29 RSM palliative cases, mainly consisting of interviews with (27) relatives and only a few interviews with (4) patients. In two cases we conducted two interviews concerning one patient (see Table 7.1).

Data Collection

We applied episodic interviews (Flick, 2014, 2018b) with the patients and relatives. This type of interview is based on the basic assumption that life experiences are stored and retrieved either as semantic knowledge (e.g., concepts such as the meaning of family care) or as narrative-episodic knowledge (e.g., concrete situations and descriptions of how family care is provided). Targeted, direct questions were formulated to elicit semantic knowledge or relations between concepts (e.g., 'What helped you decide to use palliative care services?'

or 'Which palliative services have helped you the most?'). Questions aiming at episodic knowledge were formulated as narrative stimuli to encourage respondents to elaborate upon their experiences (e.g., 'Can you tell me more about the role of the family in caring for the terminally ill patient? How did you help the patient? Can you give me an example?'). The interview schedule covered several topical areas:

1. Access to the palliative care system and hospices in Germany and experiences with it.
2. Needs and expectations regarding the quality of life.
3. The role of the family.
4. Coping with fears.
5. Representations of good quality care at the end of life.

Interviewees could decide whether to be interviewed in German or Russian. Most participants preferred to be interviewed in Russian (see also Flick and Röhnsch, 2014 on issues related to language use in interviews). The place where the interview took place could be chosen by the participants as well (e.g., at home, in a café, the palliative station, etc.).

On the complementary side of service providers we conducted 61 expert interviews (see Bogner et al., 2018) with various professions working in hospices and palliative care. Here the sample includes:

1. Professionals in this context (currently) working specifically with RSM.
2. Staff from palliative and nursing care in general.
3. A number of professionals working in these fields in Russia.

Triangulation of Perspectives

This first study is based on a triangulation of perspectives (of both clients and professionals) by using and triangulating several methodological approaches in a comprehensive comparative design (see Table 7.1).

Data Analysis

The data were analyzed by applying thematic coding (see Flick, 2014) in a multi-stage fashion. First, interviews were addressed as a series of case studies. A short description was produced for each case (i.e., each interviewee). This description comprised a motto of the case (a typical statement), demographic information about the interviewee, and central topics mentioned in the interview. Statements were initially open-coded concerning a selected thematic field (i.e., caregiving representations) for each individual case (i.e., each interview). Second, a thematic structure of the interviews was developed, which comprised the topics of the

TABLE 7.1 Design and methods

Method	Episodic interviews (n = 31)			Expert interviews (n = 61)		
		F	M		In Germany	In Russia
					51	10
Sample	Patients	3	1	With migration back-ground	17	
	Relatives	24	3			
	Total	31				
	Reasons for migration	(Late-) repatriates Jewish immigrants Others		Various professions in hospices and palliative care		

interviews across the cases. Comparative dimensions were identified across cases and used as a starting point to elaborate common aspects and differences. For example, dimensions of comparison included how relatives perceived and negotiated their role during the caregiving process. Such dimensions were used to classify cases and to identify interpretative patterns as specific combinations of features.

Some Findings

The results include a wide range of statements and narratives about finding access to and support by palliative services, and even more about reservations and barriers to professional support on the clients' side. For the present article, we chose examples of how identity-establishing affinities and heterogeneities in the study group affect the possible use of palliative support. Here we can only refer to a limited excerpt of the panorama of experiences in this respect.

Clients' Views

In the results we find a number of discriminations against RSM clients in need of palliative support. These vary in the views of the clients (patients and relatives) but even more between clients and professionals. In the clients' views, we find several types of discrimination.

First, discrimination due to lack of comprehensible information (content and language). Examples refer to situations in which the doctor had given information too late or information was missing. Complaints about missing information materials in their native (Russian) language are also mentioned, as well as barriers of access to palliative care for RSM because of the lack of information, of resources, and of adequate transfer in the health care system. The following excerpt from an interview with a relative who cared for a patient as a friend illustrates this lack of information:

And then she was told that it is pointless and she does not need it to become hospitalized. But nothing was explained to her.

(Relative 3, friend)

Potential clients' misunderstanding of treatment practices (e.g., palliative sedation as 'lethal injection') can produce existential fears, which make RSM clients refrain from using palliative care.

Second, discrimination due to language deficits. This becomes more concrete in the danger of patients' social isolation in stationary institutions, also because of lack of access to media such as Russian-language radio, TV, and journals:

It is important that someone talks to the patient, is simply able to ask him, how he is doing or how the weather is today. Everyone needs someone to talk to until the end

(Relative 25, daughter)

That relatives are employed as translators and are over-challenged and stressed by this task is mentioned here as well. Another problem is that hospital staff accept the decisions of patients, which are not really based on information, when it comes to administration of treatments or not. Such lack of communication and the resulting isolation are also mentioned in the following example:

He was completely alone there and I know that was suffering from having no-one to talk to and from not understanding what was happening to him.

(Relative 25, friend)

Third, discrimination because of specific religious affiliations is also mentioned. Clients report the absent structures of cooperation of palliative institutions with the Jewish community or to the Russian Orthodox community. The institutions delegate to the patients' relatives how to take the patients' spiritual needs into account.

Fourth, discrimination due to contradictory expectations of good and successful care (or good and well-managed dying). To 'send' a relative to a hospice contradicts some interviewees' understanding of family care and is related to fears of a familial or societal isolation when mutual commitments are not fulfilled:

I don't want him to be brought somewhere, that strangers care for him. We are not used to that because we . . . yes we come from Russia and are used to care an ill person with one's own love and one's whole soul.

(Relative 21, sister)

Other issues in this context are the use of pain medication and the fear of opiates. Because of the expectation of curative treatment until the last moment, hospices are rejected as places for dying: "There you even smell death. There is no other smell there at all" (relative 7, wife).

Fifth, family paternalism leads to restrictions in the patients' right of self-determination and of autonomy by concealing a diagnosis:

> Well it is a fortune if you do not have to be concerned with such issues. Then you are not so stressed as if you knew everything and build up more pressure. Stress accelerates such a process.
>
> (Relative 11, daughter-in-law)

The consequence is often that the relatives make decisions the patients should take themselves:

> No, I did not only support him but I took the decision. Because the decisions are taken from the closest people, they know what their closest relative needs. That was always like this in our family.
>
> (Relative 8, daughter)

In sum, the results of this first study from of the clients' perspective demonstrate a range of identity-establishing affinities and heterogeneities in the study group and give insights into the subjective needs and expectations of the study group. They show that membership in the group of RSM cannot be equated with specific socio-cultural or religious understandings and rituals that may be relevant for end-of-life care. The relatives we interviewed, for example, share their understanding of familial connectedness. However, that does not result in a shared understanding of their roles as accompanying and caring relatives. Perceived barriers to access are seen in palliative and hospice services because of language problems and information deficits. Rejections result from negative representations of hospices as 'locations of dread' and from hope for healing until the last moment. Finally these services are not used because of lack of resources and information that is given too late or is lacking. The allocation of palliative services is often not working efficiently in the health care system. The experiences presented by both the patients and their relatives are complemented, sometimes contradicted, but often supported by the professionals we interviewed.

Professionals' Views

On the side of the professionals we also find a number of discriminations regarding RSM as a target group of palliative care mentioned in the interviews.

First, in light of the limited structural and time resources it is often problematic when medical colleagues recognize the need for palliative care too late and a transfer in due course does not happen. The interviewees see information deficits mainly on the side of colleagues in other areas of health care as the reason for this failure:

> And sometimes I wish that the information for patients by the media and the doctors in charge would be better. [. . .] Well this idea of the patients, of the colleagues that palliative is rather a medicine of dying is rather obstructive.
>
> (Doctor 6)

They rarely experience patients' proactiveness, which seems even more limited in people with a migration background. Even if this is not a migration-specific problem, information material in migrants' native languages is lacking. This could prevent misunderstandings about the definition and meanings of terminologies or certain treatments in hospice and palliative services:

> Well the information about the service structures [. . .] Don't know if there is much [. . .] that you say more purposefully in their own language: What does exist? What is a hospice? What is a palliative ward? What is palliative home-care nursing, what does a palliative home-care doctor? I think this would make sense.
>
> (Doctor 8)

Second, few staff members emphasize that, beyond language barriers, they do not perceive any differences in communication due to the Russian migration background of their patients. They mention that "there actually are always relatives who master the German language." Other professionals problematize the stress which is linked to "using" relatives for translating. At the same time, they refer to additional challenges resulting in cases where only the relatives are available as dialog partners, because in these cases, family paternalism seems particularly problematic. Service providers also see family paternalism as a limitation of the patients' rights of self-determination. Examples refer to cases when patients who are still capable of acting are patronized by their relatives or by their family:

> And that is the crucial point: if the family decides the patient should not know anything about his state, this of course is a limitation of self-determination.
>
> (Doctor 8)

This family paternalism not only becomes manifest in that relatives decide that the patients should not be informed about their state, their limited chances of treatment, and thus their life expectancies because of some misunderstood protection. It also results from the wishes of families and of patients to be told what is best and what to do. They also see themselves as not being able, or as not expected, to take their own and autonomous decisions for their situation:

> Russian speaking migrants, [. . .] because of their history in the Soviet Union are used to manage this differently. It is simply—they always want all to be stipulated how to do it and they have to learn that they also can decide something for themselves.
>
> (Nurse 1)

Third, many palliative care institutions in general have to work with waiting lists. Some professionals mention the limited chances of RSM being accepted for treatment and that native German patients are sometimes preferred. In particular, the limited resources available in institutions (places, beds, etc.) are mentioned as reasons for turning down (more) RSM.

In general, most staff members see a very limited number of Russian-speaking patients utilizing their services. Despite a generally open attitude towards individual needs, service providers are often insecure about how to act with this target group because of their lack of experience with it. When in their own institution or for their own services no solutions can be identified for the problems they see in the work with this target group, service providers tend to call for external culture-specific services.

Taking Qualitative Inquiry into the Public Sphere in This Example

These results are only a small and exemplary sample from the findings in this project. Coming back to our topic of qualitative inquiry in the public sphere, we can identify several meanings of this topic so far in our example:

1. We took qualitative inquiry to a field beyond the original disciplines of qualitative inquiry and studied practices in this field—palliative care at the intersection of medicine and nursing.
2. We revealed views and experiences in that field—those of potential clients (patients, relatives) with a different social and cultural background and those of practitioners in that field about this target group. This allows the uncovering of cultural differences and discriminations (referring to a specific sub-culture).
3. We took these insights back to the field to practitioners working there who perhaps may be less aware of the cultural differences that turn into discrimination and barriers when it comes to accessing palliative support for RSM. For this purpose we organized feedback rounds and seminars for practitioners and health care managers in the field.

So far and with this first project, we remain in a general framework of qualitative inquiry—trying to understand individual experiences or practices, identifying patterns or typologies against the background of such experiences or practices and feeding such insights back to practitioners and institutions in the field under study. In this example, however, we are also confronted with a more general level of relevance. The problems mentioned in the interviews are not only individual problems but are related to the more general issue of integration and exclusion of cultural—migrant—subgroups of our society. This means the problems are part of a wider and more complex issue—that of social justice. They are also part of potential societal conflicts in times when immigration, fear of social disintegration, and discrimination become the major issues of general politics in countries such as Germany—at least in the public perception and discourse. Then we reach the fourth level of taking qualitative inquiry to the public, when we explore such problems as access, cultural discrimination, and social justice in a wider societal context and as an issue of (organizational) ethics.

The Follow-up Project: Intercultural Concept of End-of-life Care—Ambitions and Reality from a Perspective of Organizational Ethics

This extension of research perspectives is implemented in a second project building on the first study and in parts of the data from this first study. The funding for this study comes from the German Ministry of Health for three years (2017–2019)[2]. The study aims at reconstructing the significance of cultural diversity of the aging society in scientific and health policy discourses from a critical perspective on power relations from a perspective of organizational ethics. The project is part of a wider program of research addressing ethical issues of social justice in an aging society. Our problem—justice in the access to and accessibility of health care services against the background of migration—is a specific issue of intergenerational justice in the health care system.

Backgrounds

Cultural diversity in health care and the resulting conflicts are increasingly recognized and problematized in the context of the demographic development in Germany (Grützmann, Rose, and Peters, 2012; Ilkilic, 2008). Claims of justice and equality emphasize all people's dignity and entitlement to a healthy life. This entitlement should be independent from people's origin, first language, religion, or nationality. Here, inequalities and possible injustice in the health care system become relevant in particular for vulnerable groups such as people with a migration background (Wenner and Razum, 2016). Barriers such as insufficient verbal communication in regard to treatments, lack of information about legal entitlements for provisions of care, and differences in ideas about principles of self-determination (for example, individual vs. collective processes of decision) are mentioned. These barriers obstruct equal chances in accessing health services at the end of life for people with migration backgrounds as well (Grützmann et al., 2012; Kohls, 2012). Furthermore, it becomes evident that care for an aging population can no longer be provided purely through familial care and general nursing. The area of hospices has a long tradition of voluntary work. In nursing, a voluntary engagement is called for and supported by developing the funding for informal aid networks. Currently families carry the main burden of care at the end of life. In particular, people with a migration background are at specific risk of undertaking this burden (Nationale Akademie der Wissenschaften Leopoldina & Union der deutschen Akademien der Wissenschaften, 2015), although not all older migrants can draw on help by their families (Kohls, 2012).

Against these backgrounds, the follow-up project moves on from the RSMs' somewhat private views and experiences with accessing and using palliative care and professionals' day-to-day estimations. Now the focus is on the public side of the problem by addressing discourses about the issue with an ethical perspective. The main conceptual interest is on interculturality in care, how it is spelled out and informs practices and related discourses. We will now pursue this focus in a number of central research questions and more specific sub-questions.

Main Research Questions

The main research questions address the conceptual framework of interculturality and the practical consequences:

- Can interculturality as a normative concept contribute to a good and just care at the end of life in a society that is aging in diversity?
- Which interventions can be derived from interculturality for alternative solutions to health policy discourses, taking ethical approaches into account?

These main research interests are spelled out more concretely in a number of sub-questions:

1. How far is cultural diversity, as a challenge for designing end of life care, a relevant part of the current health care discourse about demographic change?
2. How far are relevant ethical principles, such as social justice, health-related equality of chances, and the avoidance of discrimination for vulnerable groups, taken into account in juridical rules, funding, and organization of health care structures?
3. Which normative ideas do patients and relatives have of a good and fair end of life care? Which expectations do they link to this care, and which (positive and negative) experiences do they express about it?

4. How do organizations in the health care system and the protagonists in these organizations perceive their responsibility for implementing an interculturally sensitive end of life care? Which concepts of care in hospices and nursing prove as relevant in this context? What are the expectations regarding the users of their organizations in such concepts?

5. Which possibilities and limitations are evident regarding attempts at producing successful interculturality in the caring practice at the end of life? How do the responsible actors deal with resulting challenges (e.g., conflicts of values)?

6. Which causes for the (still) existing lack of stabilization of intercultural care are evident? Which limitations can be traced back to conflicting values? Which consequences can be derived from analyzing them?

Triangulation of Perspectives

Answering this range of research questions calls again for a triangulation of perspectives, which will materialize in several methodological approaches to the phenomenon:

1. The first step will be a secondary analysis of interview data with palliative patients and their relatives from the previous study. This reanalysis of qualitative data (see Corti, 2018 and Wästerfors et al., 2014) aims to explore the interviewees' normative concepts and expectations of caregiving. These data are re-analyzed with a new focus on ethical issues shining through or mentioned explicitly.

2. A critical discourse analysis of scientific publications (Rau et al., 2018; Willig, 2014) and health policy documents aims at reconstructing the impact of normative concepts and discursive practices in recent discussions about health policy. This discourse analysis focuses especially on the legal and structural frameworks of nursing and hospice care at the end of life.

3. New expert interviews (Bogner et al., 2018) are conducted with various actors in the health care system. The interviews focus on the social representations (Flick, 1998) of ethical responsibility shared by the experts and on their role within the organization of care.

4. Round table discussions with external experts of ethics derived from philosophies and humanities support the framing of the data collection in these three steps from ethical and philosophical perspectives. Later these round tables will contextualize findings from the first three approaches.

Discourse Analysis

For the discourse analysis, various data formats, such as texts, audiovisual data, artifacts, and observable social practices, can be used as material in a defined field of study. In the case of textual documents, we include more than simply single documents. According to the specific research question and the type and context of the document, we select and construct a corpus of documents (Bauer and Gaskell, 2000). In our case (as in many other studies), officially published materials such as press releases or scientific publications are included. These textual documents are complemented by interviews with experts from the field. The structure of the material and what can count as complete selection have to be reflected and justified in the research process (Keller, 2012).

Sampling of Materials

The construction of our material corpus for the discourse analysis is oriented on principles of purposive sampling (Patton, 2015; Schreier, 2018). Which data are selected for the more detailed analysis will be determined according to the principles of theoretical sampling (see Flick 2018a), using the criteria of content and theoretical relevance. Maximal contrasting will focus on heterogeneous parts of the discourse and will be complemented by minimal contrasting in the areas that are included in the analysis. Similarities and differences will be analyzed with the aim of reaching a theoretical saturation. The selection of materials for the discourse analysis will be oriented on sampling criteria such as:

1. Relevant scientific publications and documents from health politics discussions that represent the discourse in the light of demographic change and the challenges linked to it.
2. To analyze the health policy discourse, particularly relevant political documents from decision processes will be included.
3. We will construct a material corpus of publicly accessible statements and position papers concerning legal revisions and their drafts in the process.
4. The following actors, institutions, and organizations in the health care system who are involved in shaping the discourses about palliative care, intercultural aspects, and justice will be included in the purposive sampling (see Figure 7.1).

At the (micro) level of the individual, the focus is on subjective views of patients, relatives, and service providers. On the structural (macro) level, the effects of health policy discourse and of collective symbolic representations are analyzed. In between, we address the (meso) level of the collective and symbolic representations of organizations in their position papers and claims.

The first results of such a discourse analysis will be the starting points for the subsequent analysis of individual and collective representations of ethical norms on the side of responsible actors in organizations of end of life care. In the further progress of the research, we will discuss how far an intersectional perspective allows the study of the interdependencies of relevant categories of differentiation between the structural and representational levels. This aims at identifying starting

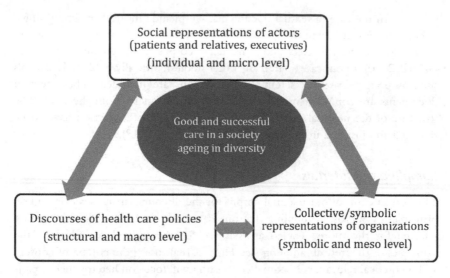

FIGURE 7.1 Levels of discourse on health and palliative care and justice

points for processes of change and for developing adequate interventions. The expert round tables will discuss and contextualize the results/findings in an ethical perspective.

Qualitative Inquiry Understood as Audience-oriented Endeavor Based on a Division of Labor

In the last part of this chapter we locate the described projects and approaches in a broader theoretical and methodological framework. Regarding the background for considerations about taking qualitative inquiry, and more generally, social sciences into the public sphere, suggestions by Michael Burawoy (e.g., 2005) about the various functions of sociology in public and academic discourses are a starting point:

> The social sciences distinguish themselves from the humanities and the natural sciences by their combination of both instrumental and reflexive knowledge—a combination that is itself variable, and thereby giving different opportunities for public and policy interventions.
>
> (Burawoy, 2005, p. 22)

In 'dissecting professional sociology,' Burawoy sees '*public sociology*' as a part of a broader division of sociological labor and distinguishes between *policy sociology*, *professional sociology*, and *critical sociology*. Sociology is providing instrumental and reflexive knowledge for academic and extra-academic audiences. *Professional* sociology is concerned with research conducted within research programs that define assumptions, theories, concepts, and questions, for example, whereas critical sociology fuels critical debates of the discipline within and between research programs. Burawoy locates both forms of sociology in the academic realm. *Policy sociology* is concerned with defense of sociological research, human subjects, funding, congressional briefings. *Public sociology* finally is concerned with the public image of sociology, presenting findings in an accessible manner, teaching basics of sociology, and writing textbooks. Critical, reflexive qualitative inquiry is addressing social problems from the viewpoint of affected individuals in groups, aiming at improving their situation.

Conclusion

The two projects briefly discussed here aim at understanding how the processes of dealing with social problems in this concrete realm are either working or failing, by analyzing the experiences and contributions of the parties involved in these processes. Therefore the help-seeking client with a specific (cultural) background and the service providers were included in the first study. The providers in this field are offering that help but are confronted with the experience that (too) few potential clients reach their institutions or are reached by them. According to Burawoy's model, the first project intended to provide *instrumental* and *reflexive* knowledge that could be fed back into the practical realm in order to change routines and to increase sensitivities and reflexivity among professionals. To take these new insights into the public sphere means that we go back to patients' organizations and representatives to provide more information about adequate services. And this also means that we go to practitioners to provide more culture-sensitive services in this field. To make such a feedback process more successful, it seems important to take into account Sandelowski and Leeman's (2012) reflections about how to write usable qualitative research findings, and Murray's (2014) suggestions for the implementation of qualitative research findings in practice. The impact of potential 'opportunities for public and policy interventions', mentioned by Burawoy (2005), becomes much more likely by adding and completing the second project we discussed here. It transfers the individual experiences and conflicts that became visible in the interviews to a more fundamental level by addressing the ethical issues linked to such experiences and conflicts. It transfers them also to a more general level by analyzing the public, institutional, and political discourses around an organizational ethics of distributional justice in aging, and at the same time culturally proliferating societies.

Notes

1. Funding for this study was obtained from the German Ministry ofResearch and Education (Funding Reference No: 01GY1312).
2. Funding for this study was obtained from the German Ministry of Health (Funding Reference No: 2516 FSB 003).

References

Bauer, M. & Gaskell, G. (Eds.) (2000). *Qualitative researching with text, image and sound. A practical handbook for social research.* London/Thousand Oaks, CA: Sage.

Bogner, A., Littig, B., & Wolfgang, M. (2018). Generating qualitative data with experts and elites. In U. Flick (Ed.), *The SAGE handbook of qualitative data collection.* London/Thousand Oaks, CA: Sage, pp. 652–667.

Burawoy, M. (2005). For public sociology. *American Sociological Review, 70,* 4–28.

Corti, L. (2018). Data collection in secondary analysis. In U. Flick (Ed.), *The SAGE handbook of qualitative data collection.* London/Thousand Oaks, CA: Sage, pp. 164–181.

Flick, U. (Ed.) (1998). *Psychology of the social.* Cambridge, MA: Cambridge University Press.

Flick, U. (2014). *An introduction to qualitative research* (5th ed.). London/Thousand Oaks, CA/Dehli: Sage.

Flick, U. (2015). Qualitative inquiry—2.0 at 20?: Developments, trends, and challenges for the politics of research. *Qualitative Inquiry, 21*(7), 599–608.

Flick, U. (2018a). *Doing grounded theory* (Book 8 of *The SAGE Qualitative Research* Kit, 2nd ed.). London: Sage.

Flick, U. (2018b). *Doing triangulation and mixed methods* (Book 9 of *The SAGE Qualitative Research Kit,* 2nd ed.). London: Sage.

Flick, U. & Röhnsch, G. (2014). Migrating diseases: Triangulating approaches—applying qualitative inquiry as a global endeavor. *Qualitative Inquiry, 20,* 1096–1109.

Grützmann, T., Rose, C., & Peters, T. (2012). Interkulturelle Kompetenz in der medizinischen Praxis. *Ethik in der Medizin, 24*(4), 323–334.

Holstein, J. A. & Miller, G. (2003). Social constructionism and social problems work. In J. A. Holstein & G. Miller, (Eds.), *Challenges and choices. Constructionist perspectives on social problems.* New York: Aldine de Gruyter, pp. 70–91.

Ilkilic, I. (2008). Kulturelle Aspekte bei ethischen Entscheidungen am Lebensende und interkulturelle Kompetenz. *Bundesgesundheitsblatt—Gesundheitsforschung—Gesundheitsschutz, 51*(8), 857–864.

Keller, R. (2012). *Doing discourse research—an introduction for social scientists.* London/Thousand Oaks, CA: Sage.

Kohls, M. (2012). *Pflegebedürftigkeit und Nachfrage nach Pflegeleistungen von Migrantinnen und Migranten im demographischen Wandel—Forschungsbericht 12* [Bundesamt für Migration und Flüchtlinge, Hrsg.]. Nürnberg.

Körber, K. (2009). Puschkin oder Thora? Jüdisches Leben in Deutschland. In J. Brunner and S. Lavi (Eds.), *Juden und Muslime in Deutschland. Recht, Religion, Identität.* Göttingen: Wallstein, pp. 233–254.

Murray, M. (2014). Implementation: Putting analyses into practice. In U. Flick (Ed.), *The SAGE handbook of qualitative data analysis.* London/Thousand Oaks, CA: Sage, pp. 585–599.

Nationale Akademie der Wissenschaften Leopoldina & Union der deutschen Akademien der Wissenschaften (2015). *Palliativversorgung in Deutschland. Perspektiven für Praxis und Forschung* [Schriftenreihe zur wissenschaftsbasierten Politikberatung]. Stellungnahme. Halle (Saale).

Patton, M. Q. (2015). *Qualitative research & evaluation methods—integrating theory and practice* (4th. ed.). London/Thousand Oaks, CA: Sage.

Rau, A. Elliker, F., & Coetzee, J. K. (2018). Collecting data for analyzing discourses. In U. Flick (Ed.), *The SAGE handbook of qualitative data collection*. London/Thousand Oaks, CA: Sage, pp. 297–313.

Sandelowski, M. & Leeman, J. (2012). Writing usable qualitative health research findings. *Qualitative Health Research*, *10*, 1404–1413.

Schenk, L. (2011). *Rekonstruktion der Vorstellungen vom Altern und von Einstellungen zur (stationären) Pflege bei Personen mit Migrationshintergrund*. Endbericht. Unter Mitarbeit von Roger Meyer, Andrea-Sophie Maier, Polina Aronson und Kübra Gül. Hg. v. Charité und Zentrum für Qualität in der Pflege. Zentrum für Qualität in der Lehre. Berlin.

Schönhuth, M. & Kaiser, M. (2015). Zuhause? Fremd? Eine Bestandsaufnahme. In M. Kaiser and M. Schönhuth (Eds.), *Zuhause? Fremd? Migrations- und Beheimatungsstrategien zwischen Deutschland und Eurasien*. Bielefeld: transcript, pp. 9–24.

Schreier, M. (2018). Sampling and generalization. In U. Flick (Ed.), *The SAGE handbook of qualitative data collection*. London/Thousand Oaks, CA: Sage, pp. 84–98.

Vogel, C. (2012). Generationenbeziehungen der (Spät-)Aussiedler. Forschungsstand und exemplarische Befunde zu Einstellungen. In H. Baykara-Krumme, P. Schimany & A. Motel-Klingebiel (Eds.), *Viele Welten des Alterns. Ältere Migranten im alternden Deutschland*. Wiesbaden: VS Verlag für Sozialwissenschaften, pp.289–313.

Wästerfors, D., Åkerström, M., & Jacobsson, K. (2014). Reanalysis of qualitative data. In U. Flick (Ed.), *The SAGE handbook of qualitative data analysis*. London/Thousand Oaks, Ca: Sage, pp. 167–180.

Wenner, J. & Razum, O. (2016). Ethische Fragen der Migrantinnen- und Migrantengesundheit. In P. Schröder-Bäck and J. Kuhn (Eds.), *Ethik in den Gesundheitswissenschaften. Eine Einführung*. Weinheim, Bergstr: Beltz Juventa, pp. 182–191.

Willig, C. (2014) Discourses and discourse analysis. In U. Flick (Ed.), *The SAGE handbook of qualitative data analysis*. London/Thousand Oaks, Ca: Sage, pp. 341–353.

INTERLUDE

INTERLUDE

8

ON BEING AWAKE AFTER THE UNITED STATES 2016 PRESIDENTIAL ELECTION

Ronald J. Pelias[1]

I am trying to hold the pieces together, trying to discover a narrative that will let me sleep, let me put my anxiety to rest. The 2016 election is over and the citizens of the United States have elected Donald Trump. I find myself reduced to fragments that chart my emotional landscape since the election results were reported. I want to make sense of it all, to believe that the damage to the United States and the world will be minimal, to know that the United States can withstand this assault on its values. I want to sleep again, but I don't think I can.

Trying to Sleep Again

1

I can't sleep. As the election results roll in, it becomes clear that Hillary Rodham Clinton will lose the election. I sit there watching the TV, stunned, angry, fearful. Mostly though, I feel a growing agitation and despair collecting in the bottom of my stomach. I was sure this would be a good night for Democrats, sure that the American people could not possibly vote for a man like Trump, sure that the United States would be taking a step forward rather than a step backward. I tell myself there is nothing I can do tonight. Go to bed. You have to catch an early fight in the morning. I get in bed, but I can't sleep. I keep wondering if there was some error, if the projections were wrong, if the Republicans or Russians tampered with the vote. I keep thinking of the millions of people, including those who voted for him, who will suffer if Trump's inchoate and preposterous policies are enacted. I keep thinking of the millions of people who have been thrown into a state of fear because they are not white, straight, Christians. I keep thinking of the millions of women, including those who did not and those who did vote for Trump, who will lose their hard-fought reproductive rights and who are now at greater risk of sexual assault and violence. I keep thinking such thoughts and I cannot sleep. I keep checking the news, each time feeling my anxiety and sorrow grow.

Now, weeks after the election, I am still not sleeping well, cannot assuage my apprehension in anything I hear or read. When I nod off, my mind insists I not forget. I wake up, shaking. I keep checking the news. I want to sleep, but see nothing that gives me solace. I can't sleep.

2

I leave for Philadelphia the Wednesday morning after the election for the annual meeting of the National Communication Association. It feels as if I am abandoning my wife in the middle of a crisis, but she tells me to stay with my plans, that she intends to keep her plans to leave the country on Friday to attend a conference in Spain, that it will be good for us both to get away. I agree, but I'm not sure if I want to be in public space while I'm processing what I'm feeling. As I get closer to Philadelphia, the city with the cracked liberty bell, it occurs to me what a fitting metaphor that is. I wonder if the bell will now break apart, shatter into pieces. I allow myself, though, to remember the pleasure I have in seeing so many of my friends and professional colleagues, people who I only get a chance to see once or twice a year.

I walk into the lobby of the hotel and the first person I see is a long-time friend and colleague, Keith Berry. I open my arms for a hug in a greeting ritual and say, with all the expressiveness of seeing someone you're truly glad to see, "Hi Keith, how are you?" He returns my hug but, with sorrowful despair, says, "Not well. Not well."

"What's wrong?" I say, worried about him.
"You know. Trump."

I had not made the connection between his mood and the election. In my joy of seeing him, I had forgotten, forgotten for just a moment in twenty-four hours. Keith brought me back to my sorrow, back to where I didn't want to be, but also to a place where I knew I was with like-minded friends. As the convention went on, most of us adopted a new greeting ritual, one that demonstrated the pleasure in seeing old friends, but also signaled the pain we were in. To the familiar question, "How are you?" we would work our talk to do double tasks with the precision of a skilled performer, "Great," we would say, "except for. . . ." I thought that might help me sleep, but it didn't.

3

Being with Hillary Rodham Clinton keeps me awake. I keep thinking where we would be going as a country if she had been elected: the policies that would actually help those who voted against her; the millions of people of color who could more easily sleep at night; the survival of our planet. And I keep returning to her, the injustice done to her for over thirty years of public service; she, standing strong against the vicious personal attacks, based in lies and driven by sexism; she, getting up each day and fighting for us all. And I keep hearing her concession speech, given with such grace in a moment of such pain. I say similar words as these over lunch to my colleague and friend, Carolyn Ellis, and as I speak, I begin to cry. I cannot stop.

4

I try my best to exercise about five days a week. Usually, I spend about an hour and a half walking the treadmill and doing some light lifting at the gym, followed by thirty minutes of floor exercises at home. When I exercise at the gym, I face two televisions, one carrying FOX news and the other CNN. I become angry watching both. I saw FOX, day after day, spend countless hours talking about Hillary Rodham Clinton's emails, working as hard as they could to suggest some great crime had been created, while they minimized Trump's actual crimes (e.g., sexual assault, fraud) and likely crimes (e.g., calling for armed violence, inciting hate crimes, tax evasion, treason). I saw the ongoing construction of news to serve their base market, feeding them a constant maelstrom of lies in the service of a bankrupt ideology. I saw how they abused any guest who might present any information at odds with their propaganda. I saw how they became a twenty-four-hours-a-day commercial for Trump. For years now, I've come to expect such problematic practices from FOX news, the network that creates viewers, study after study demonstrates, who are the least informed. And I've come to expect that CNN believes it is doing its job if it lets a few talking heads of opposing views yell at each other without ever reporting the facts; if it allows false arguments to stand (e.g., "both candidates are flawed" as if their flaws are equivalent; "the economy is failing" as if there is evidence to support such a claim; "global warming is still an open question" as if legitimate scientists are still debating this); and if it accepts the spin of political pundits and campaign operatives without bothering to challenge or correct their lies. When I return home to continue my exercises, I usually flip on MSNBC. Despite having the reputation of being an ideological balance to FOX, they, like FOX, gave Trump extensive coverage because it was good for ratings; they, like FOX, offered limited coverage to the candidates' policies and the likely consequences of their enactment; they, like FOX, allowed invalid arguments to stand without interrogation or correction.

As the Trump administration begins, the media coverage continues seemingly unreflective about how they fail to meet fundamental journalistic standards, how they daily do a disservice to the American people, how they have succumbed to and become complicit in corporate greed. The liberal bias of the news, as the Republicans and FOX news would have us believe, is yet another lie too many American have come to accept.

I toss and turn throughout the night after listening to televised news. It has abandoned striving to be objective and fact-based. It has dropped investigative reporting. News is not news when it reports from a stance of post-truth. It's a propaganda machine spewing verbal garbage. It's letting the American people down.

5

As the Trump administration takes shape, I watch appointment after appointment being filled with sycophants who have ingratiated themselves to Trump rather than with people who have qualifications for the job. I listen as name after name is announced; I hear the names of people who have already earned my disdain. Known racists, known misogynists, known xenophobes, known liars, known global warming deniers, known warmongers, known individuals with vested corporate interests, and known failed and criminal politicians. Trump is creating his own swamp, one with a putrid smell. His appointments become evidence that there will be no productive change under Trump. They become another reason I can't sleep.

6

I am currently teaching a theatre class at the University of Louisiana aimed at education majors using performance theory and practices as a potential basis for creating a more engaging classroom. The book for the class, *Breaking the Learning Barrier for Underachieving Students* by George D. Nelson, concludes with a chapter on discipline and punishment. Reading the chapter again in preparation for class, it occurs to me that the principles Nelson outlines for appropriate behavior in the classroom are based in standard values most teachers would support. To cover the chapter, I decide to start the period class by asking the students to identify three rules they would adopt as the most important for their classroom. I ask the students to read their list and all but a few students put "respect for others" as a fundamental principle. To offer a summary, I find myself saying:

> I'm glad so many of you value respect for others. Most of us would not allow a child in our class to make fun of another child with a disability, would not allow one child to bully another, would not allow one child to use hateful speech in regard to another, would not allow a child to talk

about another child using vulgar language, would not allow one child to disparage another child's religion or sexual identity, would not allow one child to grope another child, would not allow a child to keep another child from joining a group because of his or her home of origin, ethnicity, or race, would not allow a child to ridicule another child's cultural beliefs, would not allow one child to have all the toys in the classroom in the hope that some might fall from his or her hands for others to have. And we surely wouldn't want the child who did all those things to be elected class president, much less the President of United States.

The class falls silent, tense. Students are looking down. "No one cares to respond to what I just said?" I ask. More silence. Finally, a student speaks up. "I think you're trying to make us feel bad for voting for Trump. I know many of us made that decision because we believe his election will be good for the country." Several heads nod in agreement. A few say that former Secretary of State Hillary Rodham Clinton wasn't a good choice. A few say they couldn't trust her. A few say they were both bad choices.

"I appreciate the bravery of those of you who shared your perspective," I say back, after noting that no one stood in support of what I had said. After all, I say to myself, this is Louisiana. "My point was to suggest that when you teach students to respect others, I believe it matters. What values do you want your students to hold as they leave your classroom after a year with you? What moral principles will be in your classroom and to what extent will you model those principles for your students? Will you stand behind your own beliefs? Classroom space is political space, from what you teach to how you ask your students to behave. Each of you will put on display, day after day, your ethical values. I think this should matter to you." My tone has become scolding and the students only want to get through the period now. "Let's move on," I say, but the tension is too thick for much more to be accomplished. We make it to the end of class and everyone is relieved. I leave the classroom feeling disappointed in my students, all of whom are women. I am angry and in my anger I imagine myself saying to them: If you voted for Trump, I hope you never have a chance to teach children. I wouldn't want you teaching my child. You are a hypocrite. You will do damage. You do not have a sufficient moral compass to be around children. That night I try to convince myself to restore my faith in my students. I struggle and I cannot sleep.

7

The images I have of Trump before and after the election differ. Before the election, he had a swagger, carried himself like an arrogant bully, ready to fight with anyone who got in his way or who didn't like him. Even those who supported his campaign knew he was churlish, petulant, narcissistic, and dangerous. After the election, he still behaves in the same way, except now he seems like a spoiled, bratty child who is lost. Now, he is more dangerous than ever. Now, there are greater consequences when he throws a fit. I wish this was a bad dream.

8

Following the election, many of the sidewalks on the University of Louisiana campus were chalked with messages of love instead of hate. As I walked from the parking garage to the building where I teach, I read: "All people are welcome on this campus," "Black lives matter here," "Love, not hate," "We are here for you," "Hugs for all in need." "Love whoever you want, just so long as you love." Message after loving message appeared in red, white, and blue chalk. After walking a block or so, I stopped and looked back, overwhelmed. I just stood there, taking in all these messages of care. I wanted to fall into those words, to let them swallow me, to live in that safe space.

These are the words that persons of faith would embrace, not the words of hate that come from so many of our so-called Christian leaders. "If you don't vote for Trump, you will go to hell," a priest told his parishioners. "We must stop the sodomites from ruining the sanctity of marriage," a preacher sermonized to his congregation. "Clinton is a sinner, the devil incarnate," a minister informed his followers. How easily religions based in love settle into a rhetoric of hate, establish their faith group as the only truth, use their ideology as a weapon against others! How often Christians fail Jesus' primary message to love one another! How similar they are to ISIS! How quickly they become hypocrites!

Perhaps, if I think of the words on the sidewalk, I can get some sleep.

9

How could people be indifferent to the fact that in Republican-governed state after Republican-governed state a strategy was deployed to keep persons of color from voting? False claims of voter fraud was one of the many lies the Republicans told. They shut down the hours for early voting, they shut down polling places, they shut down people, all so they might be elected.

How could people be indifferent to the fact that during the entire Barrack Obama presidency the Republicans' only objective was to undermine any initiative he put forward so that they might be able to argue that Obama and the Democrats failed the American people when election time came?

How could people be indifferent to the fact that Russia intervened in an American election on behalf of Trump, that people with close links to Russia worked inside Trump's election campaign?

How could people be indifferent to the fact that the FBI, with either strategic intent or gross incompetence, influenced the election?

How could people be indifferent to the fact that senate committees were established and spent millions of taxpayer dollars for the singular purpose of undermining Hillary Rodham Clinton's bid for the presidency?

How could people be indifferent to the fact that Trump's strategy for dealing with the opposition is to accuse them of doing what he does? If you are constantly lying, call your opponent "the biggest liar ever." If you are engaged in criminal activity, claim your opponent should be locked up? If you sexually assault women, claim your opponent doesn't treat women with respect. If you are a racist, claim your opponent has done nothing to fight for civil rights and is exploiting people of color just to get their vote.

How could people be indifferent to such strategies? How can anyone sleep?

10

Before my acting class is scheduled to start, I begin chatting with the students who have arrived early. I, a White instructor, approach a Black student I don't know very well, even though we are near the end of the semester. The student has been a quiet presence in class, seldom speaking unless required to do so. Her performance work has been unremarkable. She has been the kind of student who fades into background, one that a teacher might forget soon after the semester is over. I glance down and notice a large button attached to her book bag. The button reads: Black Lives Matter. She sees me reading the message and I offer a thumbs-up gesture and a smile. When my signal registers with her, she rises from her desk and throws her arms around me in embrace. I am surprised and manage only to utter, "They do matter." No other words are spoken, neither by me nor her. Her performance after this incident was by far her best. I will not forget her.

That small gesture seemed to me the correct political statement; it was a simple acknowledgment that injustices are being carried out on Black bodies and that solutions need to be found. It was a straightforward act of sensitivity to another. It would have been inappropriate to say in response, as right wing conservatives often do, all lives matter. If I had, I would have minimized her legitimate concern, would have provided further evidence for her that White people don't think Black lives matter. I would have been racist.

As I try to fall asleep, I wonder how being sensitive to others has become dismissed under the label "political correctness," how basic human decency has been discarded so that some might feel more comfortable in their own morally corrupt views, how Trump has given permission for people to make America hate again.

Trying to Stay Awake

Now, as I go about my day, I look at people differently. I can't stop wondering if each person I encounter is a Trump supporter. If I identify someone who I believe fits that category, I assume he or she is deeply uninformed and/or unethical. That is the only explanation for his or her behavior that makes sense to me. I am not proud of this way of thinking, not proud of how I am moving in the world, not proud of the contempt I hold for Trump supporters. I've been told I need to reach out to these voters and try to understand where they are coming from. I believe I do understand them and I do not want to be around them. I do not want to live in the presence of their hate, of their unethical practices, of their ignorance. I know this is a problematic way of being, but I am unwilling to bend to what I see as their fascist ideology.

I am sure comments like the ones in the above paragraph are not productive. Such remarks only reify the divide, make people more entrenched in their views. A November 22 CNN poll found that 53% of the American people believe that Trump will do a very or fairly good job as president. Perhaps I'm wrong. I surely hope so. But right now, I am frightened by the beliefs of half of the U.S. population. I am frightened by what they might do. I am frightened by what a Republican-controlled House and Senate might do. I am frightened by Trump and the people he has placed in his administration.

Given the election results, I don't know what might move us toward a better America, might place us on higher ethical ground, might gather us together in a collective sensibility that truly believes in justice for all. Should I protest in the streets? Should I put aside my own convictions in an effort to find common ground? Should I try to create dialogue or would I be just a fool for thinking dialogue is possible, suckered once again by uncompromising right wing agenda? Should I, as Hillary Rodham Clinton in her concession speech advised, give Trump "an open mind and the chance to lead" or should I act on my belief that he has already demonstrated he is not worthy of our trust?

I do not know what is best to say or do. I do not have a narrative that will let me sleep. I live in a fragmented, cruel world, one that imploded on the day Trump was elected. I cannot make sense of it all. But here is what I do know: All progressives must stay awake, be vigilant, try to minimize the damage to our collective soul. We cannot sleep when this is going on, cannot stop fighting for the good of all people, cannot allow our country to become destroyed by right wing lies, greed, and hate. Stay awake, my friends, stay awake.

Postscript: One Year Later, Still Tossing and Turning, Still Not Knowing What to Do

I knew it was a grave mistake when Trump was voted into office. I knew that he would harm many people; that he would cause considerable damage; that his presidency would be corrupt and immoral. I never imagined, though, that it would be this bad. I knew I wouldn't be able to sleep as long as Trump was in office. I knew political action would be necessary to stop the destruction. I just didn't know what to do, what action to take. I still don't. I never imagined it would be this bad, that our political resistance would have such limited effect. I never imagined how it would take its toll on me.

I never imagined that Trump's guiding policy would be to undermine or overturn anything that President Obama supported, from environmental protections, to healthcare, to immigration policy, to LGBTQ rights, to women's rights, to relationships with foreign governments, to treaties with allies and adversaries, to. . . . The attacks never stop. There are no well-reasoned arguments for disagreements with previous policy, no fact-based logic, no consideration of the consequences in people's lives. Trump's justifications are nothing but flimsy falsehoods disguised as rationale, and then he signs another executive order.

I never felt such dismay that reasoned discourse, that fact-based policy, seems to have no place in this administration, that so many argue on behalf of what they know is false, that known lies gather support. Led by Trump, we have policy driven by vindictiveness, by revenge, by racism. We have policy built on lies. We have policy guided by greed.

I never imagined that Trump would unleash such hate throughout the country; that so many citizens would find his racism, sexism, homophobia, and xenophobia license for their own deplorable behavior; that he would defend Nazis as good people; that he would collect the support of so many Christian leaders who remain blind to Trump's indifference to the suffering of others. I never would have guessed that there were so many in this nation living under the banner of Christianity who were so ready to let Trump's hate, rather than Jesus' love, guide their lives.

I never felt so torn, wanting to reach out to those who align with Trump and wanting to speak out with as much power as I can bring forth about their uninformed, misguided, unethical positions. I want, like so many others, this country to heal. I want generosity, kindness, and love rather than hate to be our path. That's what all the major religions of the world teach.

I never imagined that Trump would so quickly move us toward a fascist state; that he would so embolden his extreme right followers; that he would encourage his disciples to attack with the vilest language, treats, and physical violence anyone who might speak against him; that his Gestapo would march without thought to the beat of his drum.

I never felt so vulnerable after being attacked following the publication of the first part of this essay in *Qualitative Inquiry*. The right wing outlets, *The College Fix* and *Breitbart*, published excerpts from the essay, some out of context, to feed their angry readers. It was like giving them raw meat. I was told I was a snowflake, unmanly and insane; that I should not be allowed to teach; that I should be taken out of my misery. Such attacks, often in much more obscene and threatening language, followed each article. Such attacks were also sent to my email and home mailing address as well as the email addresses of my departmental colleagues, University of Louisiana administration, and the school paper. Intimidation can be a powerful force. I will keep writing, aware that many others have suffered much more vicious attacks than I have, that many others experienced, not just threats, but actual violence for speaking their mind.

I never imagined Trump would convince so many people that mainstream conservative TV news outlets like ABC, NBC, CBS, and CNN are fake news and that the Republican propaganda outlet, FOX, should be trusted; that Trump would call any source that questions his actions fake news; that Trump would hang in his country clubs fake *Time Magazine* covers that praise him; that Trump would refuse to acknowledge the Russian fake information campaign during the election; that Trump would attack the first amendment of our constitution and have so many people say he's right to do so.

I never felt so disappointed in our journalists who continue to grant legitimacy to constant onslaught of lies coming from Trump and his team. They continue to give coverage to deceptive press releases and briefings, to talking heads who spin reality beyond recognition, to campaign speeches feeding falsehoods to Trump followers without naming the lies as lies. Their practices continue to be a violation of journalistic standards. Their coverage continues to be irresponsible and unethical.

I never imagined that the ads I saw before the election warning me that, if elected, Trump would have his finger on the nuclear button would become a daily worry; that Trump's reckless behavior in his dealings with Iran and North Korea, in his "big man" talk that nothing is off the table, in the constant tweets that undermine diplomatic efforts, would put the world at such risk.

I never felt so frightened, so petrified, so close to the edge of annihilation.

I never imagined that Trump's Republican colleagues in the Senate and House would be so complicit; that they would look away when they see the crimes Trump is committing, the harm he is doing, the shame he is bringing to our country; that they would pretend to have the interests of the American people in mind when they allow Trump's withdrawal from the Paris climate accord, when they permit Trump and his family to illegally stuff their pockets and waste taxpayer dollars, when they try to undermine investigations into Russian interference in our elections, when they do his bidding knowing it is wrong.

I never felt so disillusioned, watching them look out for what they see as their own interests, telling lie after lie to please Trump: sycophants all, settled in the swamp, squirming here and there, seeking the blessing of their master who will turn on them without a second thought.

I never imagined that I would not have enough time or space to tell you all the ways Trump's actions are actions I never imagined, like how Trump is filling court seat after court seat with judges who are anti-LGBTQ and anti-choice; how Trump is battering, perhaps beyond repair, our government agencies; how Trump is mistreating Muslim citizens and Muslims around the world; how Trump is putting Hispanic and Black lives at risk; how Trump is weakening, if not destroying, our relationship with other nations; how Trump, after hurricane

Maria struck Puerto Rico, is abandoning the people of Puerto Rico; how Trump is deregulating the banks; how. . . .

I never felt so impatient waiting for Robert Mueller to present his findings.

I never felt so exhausted.

I never felt so helpless.

I never felt so committed, so convinced that we must take action. We still can't sleep, my friends, now that we see what he's doing. We must turn our sleeplessness into strategic acts of resistance. We must not let our exhaustion diminish our diligence. We must figure out what to do that will make a difference. We must find the right strategies. We must stop Trump's destruction.

Note

1   This chapter revisits, updates, and extends arguments first made in Pelias, R. J. (2017). On not being able to sleep: After the 2016 U.S. Presidential Election. *Qualitative Inquiry*, https://doi.org/10.1177/1077800416684773

SECTION II
The Critical Imagination and Pedagogies of Change

9

RESEARCH 4 REVOLUTIONARIES BY #JIMSCHEURICH

James Joseph Scheurich

Much more than an acknowledgement: What follows in this chapter could not exist without four years of conversation and collaboration on numerous projects with the folks of the Kheprw Institute (www.kheprw.org), a Black-led, grassroots, activist community organization that has existed for over 15 years in Indianapolis. These folks—Imhotep Adisa, Paulette Fair, Pambana Uishi, Alvin Sangsuwangul, Diop Adisa, and Rasul Palmer—have impeccable integrity, astute insight, an impressive vision, and total commitment in regards to the loving development of a truly loving society and a loving attitude toward our home, the planet. However, they certainly cannot be held responsible for my viewpoint. We agree on much and disagree on some, but my words are solely my responsibility. Nonetheless, I could not think the thoughts I think or write the words I write without my ongoing relationships with them. I very much love them, and I know they feel the same about me.

Critical research, especially white critical ethnography, has largely failed. It has failed in terms of not just studying and interpreting the world but radically changing it: "The [critical researchers] have only interpreted the world, in various ways. The point, however, is to change it" (Marx, 1845/1970, p. 15). While many critical researchers might blame exogenous reasons, like the entrenched power of the status quo or the lack of support from universities, here I will argue that a primary cause for the failure is actually endogenous to critical research, especially white critical research. I will argue here that its methodology is overwhelmingly colonialist. Indeed, I contend that social science research methodology in general is largely colonialist, whether labeled critical or not. Also, even at its best, the content of critical research is generally limited to critique only, which is important but insufficient *by itself*. Indeed, today, one can be a famous critical scholar and never be a threat to the social status quo. In response, I will provide a critique of critical research (and social science research broadly) and offer one way forward for (mainly white) critical researchers to do research that I will argue is revolutionary, i.e., moves beyond critique to radically changing the world.

To be critical, in my view, means to start with a critique of the dominant U.S. social system, a critique that explicitly concludes that the foundation and the building blocks of this social system are a set of overwhelmingly inhumane and highly destructive assumptions, policies, and practices. That is, it is not that there are aspects of this system that just need some improvement (which is what I would call a "liberal" view). It is that the entire system, including its most basic ontological categories, the categories that create the "real" as we know it today, is overwhelmingly inhumane and highly destructive to human wellbeing and the survival of a world climate that will sustain human life. We call various aspects of this system white racism/white supremacy/whiteness, capitalism (classist), misogynist (sexist), heterosexist/homophobic, ableist, and xenophobic (Christian dominant). Overall, it is a horrid system that hugely privileges the few based on the exploitation, debasement, deprivation, and devastation of the many worldwide.

If you do *not* agree with this "picture" of our social system, this chapter is probably not for you. If you do *not* agree with this picture, I do not have space here to show you the research and information that powerfully supports this view, though the research is overwhelming and has been provided by some of our most outstanding scholars and activists. If you do *not* agree, it also probably means (but does not necessarily mean) you are visually white, financially upper middle class, evidently male, apparently heterosexual, temporarily able, and fundamentally Christian (all of which could be used to describe me), as these are the dominant and thus privileged social constructions or scripts of our social system, though "others" can and often do unfortunately buy into and try to adopt these privileged social constructions or scripts for themselves (see, for example, Bonilla-Silva, 2010). All of this is readily and constantly apparent all around us, though you have to have broken the choke hold of the dominant scripts or master narrative on your mind to be able to "see" it. For instance, being Black or trans* or Muslim can prevent or break the hold of the master narrative just by their experience in the world, while white people, whether critical or not, are generally so privileged and made "comfortable" by the world as to be imprisoned within the status quo mindset (see, for example, Yancy, 2008). (If you do want to start breaking the hold of the dominant script, I would suggest starting with Dunbar-Ortiz's *The Indigenous People's History of the U.S.* (2014) and Joe Feagin's *Racist America* (2014).

Critical Research Methodology and Social Science Research in General are Colonialist

Critical research, for the most part, has taken up social science *methodologies* uncritically. Instead, what most critical research does is have a critical focus in terms of the purpose and content of the research. As Thomas (1993) has said,

"Critical ethnography is conventional ethnography with a political purpose" (p. 4). For example, critical research might use standard qualitative research methods, like coding and thematizing, to illustrate how, say, schoolteachers evidence racism in their treatment of students of color. While the research purpose and content could be argued to be critical, the methodology is standard. The same can be said of critical research that has a quantitative or mixed-method methodology. The research purpose and content may be critical, but the methodology is standard social science methodology.

This point, however, is not a new one. Scholars of color and Indigenous scholars have long been saying various versions of this, at least back to DuBois and probably earlier. For me, though, it started with Freire's *Pedagogy of the Oppressed* in English in 1970 (though it was later when I read it), Anzaldúa's *Borderlands/La Frontera* in 1987, Collins' *Black Feminist Thought* in 1990, and then Tuhiwai Smith's *Decolonizing Methodologies* in 1999 and the emergence in education in the late 1990s of Critical Race Theory. In response to this and other similar work, I published "Toward a white discourse on white racism" in 1993, one of the earliest critical whiteness articles in education, and then "Coloring epistemology" with Michelle Young in 1997. Especially with the latter article, I was trying to communicate that scholars of color were well on their way to an insightful and well argued demolition of the very foundations of (white) social science research epistemologies and methodologies, but white social scientists were largely ignoring this.

Unfortunately, white social scientists, probably not surprisingly given the dominant scripts and the deep connections of white privilege with these scripts, have continued to largely ignore this work by Indigenous scholars and scholars of color, although it has grown substantially in depth and breadth. For example, just in the last few years, Indigenous scholars have published several volumes, including in 2009, Diversi and Moreira's *Betweener Talk: Decolonizing Knowledge Production, Pedagogy, and Praxis*; in 2011, Byrd's *The Transit of Empire: Indigenous Critiques of Colonialism*; in 2013, Battiste's *Decolonizing Education: Nourishing the Learning Spirit*; and in 2015, Tuck and McKenzie's *Place in Research: Theory, Methodology, and Methods* and Strega and Brown's *Research as Resistance: Revisiting Critical, Indigenous, and Anti-Oppressive Approaches*. Also, Critical Race Theory, which now has many hybrids, like LatCrit (www.latcrit.org) and multiracial CRT (Harris, 2016), is rapidly proliferating in numerous directions and education disciplines, while deeply critiquing and replacing white mainstream and critical epistemologies and methodologies. My advice in regards to this work is to read widely.

However, here I am going to provide my take on how (the largely white) mainstream social science in general and even (white) critical research is still colonialist, i.e., performs a colonizing social function and colonizes new researchers to continue to perform this oppressive social function. Let's look then at how social science research "works." Social science researchers are overwhelmingly university based, which itself is an elite social institution deeply interwoven into the larger oppressive social system and substantially focused on the replication and sustenance of that system (e.g., Foucault, 1970; Heller, 2016; Wilder, 2013). This makes social science researchers important agents of the university and of the social system itself. Whether we are critical or not, we are still such agents.

Accordingly, we social science researchers are taught that we as autonomous individuals get to decide what research we want to do. Of course, we are influenced by what is going on around us, especially within our discipline, which is strongly influenced by the dominant narrative. Nonetheless, this is an incredibly powerful position to be in as individuals, an elite colonial agent's position, as social science research often defines and shapes the nature of reality itself as we experience it. For example, if education researchers conclude that certain groups of students, like Black students, are "at-risk," the educational system starts labeling them as at–risk and treating them as if they are at-risk, i.e., at a deficit (see, for example, Valencia, 2010, for a critique of such deficit thinking). Thus, as long as we follow standard social science assumptions, practices, and methodologies, we social science researchers individually get to decide what the research questions are, what data are relevant and appropriate to analyze, what ways we will analyze that data, what the interpretations of the data are relevant and appropriate, and where to publish it. As long as we play by the standard methodological rules, these are all decisions we can make individually.

This is an incredibly powerful, elite position. Even if you take Kuhn's (1962) point that most research is about filling in the details, we researchers are reality builders. We are brick by brick constructing the social ontology or the social "reality" within which we all live. If you mix in the fact that university social science researchers are overwhelmingly visually white, financially upper middle class, evidently male, apparently heterosexual, temporarily able, and fundamentally Christian and hugely influenced by the dominant narrative and its privileging of these positionalities, you get a very potent and toxic mix. You get a contemporary version of a colonizer, a very small, very powerful elite who individually are naming and constructing the social "reality" in which everyone must live.

Within this frame, social science research is what I call an *extraction* methodology, just like a colonizer going in and taking the minerals or vegetation out of a country. I parallel this concept with Freire's idea of education as banking. In *Pedagogy of the oppressed*, Freire (1970) said,

> Education thus becomes an act of *depositing*, in which the students are depositories, and the teacher is the depositor. Instead of communicating, the teacher issues communiques and makes deposits which the students patiently receive, memorize, and repeat. This is the "banking" concept of education, in which the scope of action allowed to the students extends only as far as receiving, filing, and storing the deposits [emphasis added].
>
> (p. 72)

Instead of depositing, social science researchers, just like capitalists, *extract*. Social scientists are free, indeed, required, to take "data," analyze it, interpret it, and distribute it however they want, but without any real decisions by and accountability to those from whom or about whom the data was extracted.[1] Further, these extractions have material value for the social scientists in terms of scholarly respect, fame, professorial positions, and reward/salary, which is directly connected to what Harris (1993) called "whiteness as property." Thus, social science research is property gained through extraction, largely from less powerful people and contexts and largely without their consent.

That the social sciences are like this, though, should not be surprising. The social sciences emerged in the mid to late 1800s as Europe was expanding its power across the globe through colonization.[2] While the early social sciences were certainly imitating the "physical" sciences, they were also deeply entangled with the arrogance of elite white European males who were busy creating a social system—at a deeper "level," a social ontology—that included capitalism and white male supremacy. In their arrogance, the world was theirs to name, define, and control. For example, virtually all of the leading intellectuals, scientists, and business and political leaders were deeply invested in the superiority of white people over all others (Kendi, 2016). They were building an integrated social ontology in which we still largely live (Scheurich, 1997), supported by an epistemology that validated their selected ontology (i.e., reality as experienced by its key categories, like individualism, profit, race, etc., the categories we continue to make meaning with). And the social sciences increasingly became a significant "truth" operation within that ontology (Foucault, 1970).

How, though, did the *critical* social sciences get caught up in this "truth" operation? One major issue is that the critical folks largely took the mainstream social science methodologies as a given. For example, most critical researchers in education doing qualitative work just use typical qualitative methodologies, like categorizing and thematizing, which are both just aspects of the "extractive" process controlled by the elite positioned researcher. They address "critical" issues, like the widespread racial disproportionality in discipline or special education, but they do not problematize the methods themselves. What is on their boats is often radically different from what is on the boats of those who support or only want to modify the status quo, but they are all using the same kinds of boats. For the most part, they have simply not problematized the methodology (the boats they ride in), even though the nature of the boats themselves emerged out of the same elite, white, European male colonial history, out of its ontological and epistemological assumptions.

I know, though, that there will be critical researchers who will agree with me to a significant extent, but argue that there are some exceptions. They will likely talk about action research, which is research by those who are going to use the research (e.g., Reason & Bradbury, 2011). There is PAR, participatory action research (e.g., Whyte, 1990), and YPAR, youth participatory action research (e.g., Cammarota & Fine, 2008). There is what is being called "community-based research" (e.g., Beckman & Long, 2016), though the degree of in-depth community involvement varies considerably. There are even some rare examples of a community of people defining the research, gathering the "data" together, deciding how to analyze it together, interpreting the results together, and deciding collaboratively how the research is to be used. For example, I recently taught a course in which community folks in an urban grassroots organization whom I have worked with for over four years and doctoral students in a class I taught worked collaboratively on the research with the community folks from start to finish. (e.g., Turner, et al., 2017) I enthusiastically applaud this approach to research. These examples move from elite university research to collaborative community research, which is a major point that Indigenous researchers have been making: the research should be of, by, and for the community, not the researcher or the university (e.g., Tuhiwai Smith, 1999). This is definitely a step in the right direction.

However, my question for this relatively small group of critical researchers doing this kind of work is: Are you sure the methodologies themselves are not deeply infected with the oppressive ontological and epistemological assumptions of the colonizer? Even if a critical researcher is working deeply with a community of people, what does it mean to go out into the world and gather data (like minerals or crops) that the researcher or researchers and the community have decided is appropriately "data," interpret it (i.e., refine it, as with minerals, or cook or preserve it, as with crops), publish it (i.e., sell it), and gather the gains (i.e., scholarly respect, fame, professorial positions, and reward/salary, which are like profit or property)? What does it mean to go out into a social world that is deeply racist, classist, sexist, heterosexist, and ableist and divide it into pieces (little chunks of "reality") called data, interpret it (typically without connecting those pieces to the entire system's deeply oppressive nature), and gather the gains, even if it is PAR, YPAR, or some other community engaged collaboration?

Do you see a certain white, masculinist colonial worldview at work here? To know "the world" or "reality" is to divide and isolate it into pieces, called data, whether words or numbers, whether quantitative or qualitative. Thus, these pieces are separated out from the social web in which they already exist in a deep, interwoven relation to other pieces. Next, with quantitative research, we then analyze those pieces, using statistical techniques, for patterns while ignoring that the statistical methods intersect with the data such that the data is refashioned or reshaped into "patterns" that is an amalgam of both data and statistical method. Thus, the patterns are not just data free from the methods; the patterns are data integrated with methods, an artifact of the interaction. And then the patterns are named and interpreted in terms of the colonial worldview that produced them. Thus, pieces of "reality" have been separated from the social whole or social fabric in which they existed (as the colonialist worldview says this atomizing is the way to "know" the world); reshaped, reconstructed, and resurrected, through a statistical process, to form a pattern, a "discovery," a new entity, which is then interpreted to the world as a social science-produced truth. Can you not see that the process itself, the methodology itself, is a colonialist project to create the "world" in its own image, its way of imagining truth?

Unfortunately, qualitative research is no different and no better. To know the world is to collect data from the world, based on words in this case, words that themselves already exist as embedded in social contexts and social meanings, socially interwoven contexts and meanings. For example, qualitative researchers collect the voices of individuals (based on a Western colonialist idea of individualism; Taylor, 1989[3]). These voices are treated as autonomous, separated from the other voices within which they live, separated from the contexts in which people live. Using so-called systematic qualitative analyses methods, like coding and thematizing, these researchers atomistically chunk or divide an interwoven contextual reality into pieces based on university-trained (including all of what that entails) researchers' perceptions, assumptions, inclinations, etc. and the scholarly literature or past research that they have chosen from which to draw. Like the quantitative researchers, they then "find" patterns in their "data," which then through presentation and publication, i.e., dissemination, become a kind of truth that is university branded. Whether quantitative or qualitative, this whole process is a major construction process, an assimilation of life, of the human lifeworld, into a white, masculinist, colonial mindset, with the process itself (so-called research methodology) as colonial and colonizing as the content of the research.

Of course, there are qualitative "researchers" who are working differently. Some autoethnography has essentially become the writing up of creative interactions between the researcher and some context or experience, though the researcher is typically at the center (auto) of the story (see, for example, some of the pieces in Jones, Adams, & Ellis, 2013). Richardson (1997) has elevated fiction as a way to "represent" research results, and Donmoyer and Yennie-Donmoyer (1995) have argued for the use of readers' theater. Others have used poetry in a similar fashion (for one review of such research, see Lahman et al., 2009). Performance ethnography is another relatively open "methodology" (Denzin, 2003: Hamera, 2011). Indeed, I find autoethnography and performance ethnography to be the most promising possibilities as they seem to be vessels that can be filled with just about anything.

I applaud these efforts, too. Nonetheless, I think too many of them are still too caught up in the colonial model, including that autonomous individuals, separate from a community, but who are still part of the university, are privileged to pronounce on the nature of "reality" (see my later discussion of communion and community), as I would suggest that the very idea of an individual artist, scholar, or voice who is individually identified as separate from a community and its needs is a Western colonial project. For example, for many Indigenous societies, someone might be an excellent, respected storyteller, but the story is the community's story and typically a story that has been told over and over by many storytellers. The community's story is the center, not the individual storyteller.

A Somewhat Different Take

Thus, I have made an argument that the social sciences as a whole are a colonial "truth" project that ultimately serves the deeply inequitable status quo and assimilates people and "reality" into that status quo. I have also suggested that (white) "critical" research has failed in its goal to change the world, change the nature of the social reality. Finally, I have argued that not just the content of social science research is colonialist, but that the methods themselves are an integral part of the same project. However, I am unsatisfied. I want to take another cut at these issues, one strongly influenced by Michel Foucault and Judith Butler (though they might complain about my corruption of their views).

The world we experience is a socially constructed ontology (what we call "reality"); we see, feel, hear, make meaning, know the world through a set of socially given, already existing set of ontological categories, like individualism, teacher, race, property, happiness, etc. Together these socially given categories are knitted together into social narratives about the human lifeworld. These social narratives are then linked together into larger discourses about life and the lifeworld. Thus, ontological categories coalesce into narratives, and narratives coalesce into discourses. Taken together, all of this creates the social reality (or social ontology) in which we live.[4]

Other times and places have totally different socially given ontologies. For example, the ancestors of the Apache and Navaho began arriving in the Southwest from the late 1200s to early 1400s (http://nativeamericannetroots.net/diary/tag/Apache%20Indians). Not surprisingly, they lived with an entirely different social ontology with a different set of categories and a different set of narratives connecting these categories. Similarly, the *Tao Te Ching* emerges in China first as an orally transmitted spiritual practice that is a way of experiencing and understanding life extremely differently than the dominant Western ways of knowing. For example, those that follow this practice completely let go of their individual egos, which is virtually the opposite of the West's focus on privileging autonomous individualism. Those living in this Taoist tradition would see, feel, hear, make meaning, know the world through an entirely different set of ontological categories and narratives or discourses (Tzu, 2016).

As mentioned earlier, the socially constructed ontology within which we currently live was predominantly created in the European enlightenment by elite white European males, philosophers, social and political theorists, economists, the wealthy, leaders of governments, etc. like Kant, Descartes, Locke, Smith, Hume, Voltaire, etc., constructing "reality" in a way that would favor, benefit, and privilege them (e.g., Kendi, 2016). It is they who constructed our ontological categories like individualism, capital, race, profit, liberty, progress, etc. and constructed the narratives and discourses that link these categories. Of course, there have been some modifications over time; nothing sits completely still over time. For example, today there is a much stronger antiracist counter-discourse than there was in the time of the Enlightenment, while almost all of the major Enlightenment voices were deeply racist and colonialist (Kendi, 2016). However, that this world making has been and continues to be extremely powerful and determinative can be seen in a one page spread the *New York Times* published on February 16, 2016, called "The faces of American power." On this page are tiny pictures of the American leaders of the most important corporations, of the largest book publishers, of the Ivy League universities, of the main media companies, of the largest music producers, of the largest television publishers, of pro baseball and football and basketball teams and the largest city mayors, military leaders, governors, Supreme Court Justices, Obama and his cabinet, and U.S. senators—i.e., 509 of the uber elite. Forty-three (or 8.4%) are people of color even though they are around 38% of the population, with city mayors and Obama and his cabinet contributing the most to the racial diversity in this group. If the European Enlightenment started in the late 1600s, that is over 300 years ago. Thus, 300 years ago a white male elite provided us with our ontological categories, narratives, and discourses, and that same group is still in the dominant position today 300 years later. That is the power of a dominant social ontology, sometimes called the dominant or master narrative.

Another way to think about this is that social reality (our social ontology) is a house within which we live. Those who built the house, the European white male elite, built their views, their experiences, their desires, their dreams, their assumptions (conscious and unconscious) into every aspect of the house, the floors, walls, ceilings, furniture, water pipes, air we breathe in the house, all of it. They also built who the residents can be, what is their nature, how do they think, feel, know, experience—these are all part of the social ontology; it is not just the "external" world, the social ontology also provides the nature of the "internal" world. We could say that their views, experiences, desires, dreams, assumptions are a fungus or a poison that is built into all aspects of the house, including inside those who live within the house. We cannot escape the poison; it is everywhere around us, and it is inside us.

Accordingly, research and its methods are just additional ontological categories linked to other ontological categories, like property, universities, knowledge, individualism, through various narratives and then larger discourses. Thus, research and its methods are full of the poison. Research is just another feature of the house, deeply interwoven with all other features of the house. Research is just another aspect, like capitalism and its requisite exploitation, gender binaries, and white racism and supremacy, of the colonial project, just another ontological category interwoven with various ontological narratives and the larger discourses. Accordingly, it is not possible to pick up or use pieces of research, like various methods, even if the users are collaborative, community engaged, etc. as these methods are substantially reproductive of the colonial project, of its ontology, of its exploitive ways of thinking and being and relating to the physical world.

This "house" metaphor obviously raises questions about oppressed groups. Following the same metaphor, I would suggest that oppressed groups have, to some degree, developed their own rooms within the house. These rooms are their families, churches, social groups, activist organizations, etc. Within these rooms, it is not as if the oppression is completely gone, but it is to varying degrees reduced. The poison is still there, but its power has been somewhat reduced. As Homi Bhabha (2004) has argued, oppressed groups always reinterpret, reshape, and reconstruct in relation to the lifeworld of the colonialist. For example, in the hands of enslaved and post-slavery Blacks, Christianity largely became a liberation theology that was substantially different than the Christianity of whites (Cone, 2010). Blacks and Latinx often define individuality somewhat differently, a difference that includes more family or social responsibility. Nonetheless, despite all of the reconstruction done by the oppressed, they still must survive within dominant social reality created by elite white males and still ruled by them.

Is the Poisoned House a Totalized Prison, or Where's the Hope?

I know the poisoned house metaphor sounds as if there is no way out of the oppression. However, like many others throughout history, I believe there is. The nature of the material world, which includes we humans, is increasingly understood by the sciences, from biology to physics, to be an interwoven whole from which no part can be separated or isolated. Our bodies are not separate from the physical world in which we live. Indeed, recently it has become known that each of us, breath by breath, breathes out millions of living critters into the air to be consumed by others, and each of us breathes in millions of living critters that have been breathed out by others. "A person's mere presence in a room can add 37 million bacteria to the air every hour—material largely left behind by previous occupants and stirred up from the floor—according to new research" (www.sciencedaily.com/releases/2012/03/120328172255.htm). Our bodies and the physical world, living and not, are in a constant interchange that is so deep and thorough that it becomes much more accurate to say we are all part of the same fabric.

In addition, we now live in a world in which we are all connected electronically through the internet, email, cell phones, and social media. We are interconnected worldwide in a way we have never experienced. In this way, too, we are not separate. We are all already augmented beings, perhaps cyborgs. Our being as humans is interwoven with internet, email, cell phones, and social media, which is all social.

Similarly, our minds, which are not separate from our bodies (another erroneous and oppressive colonial bequeath from the Enlightenment), part of a social fabric of words (categories), narratives, and discourses. None of us are ever autonomous individuals (another Enlightenment oppression embedded in us and our social world); we are all deeply social who live in terms of the categories, narratives, and discourses of our time and place, just like the Apache and Navaho of the 1300s lived theirs and the Chinese in the time of the emergence of the *Tao Te Ching* lived theirs.

In addition, a large range of spiritual views, including some voices within the so-called major religions, such as Christian mystics like Teresa of Avila and Islam's Rumi, support the view that all existence is interwoven into a large fabric. In addition, the Indigenous societies I have been exposed to tend to believe much the same. I would also suggest that despite the various oppressions she addressed so well, Gloria Anzaldúa believed the same. To be a curandera, you must believe in the spirit world. For me, personally, I was raised Christian though I now practice Zen Buddhism. I believe the Jesus teaching that I learned is that we are all interwoven together, which is known as Love. I also believe the Buddhist message is the same, though they tend to use the word "compassion," instead. For example, I was once at a Zen retreat, and the teacher said there were no degrees of difference among all of us. We are all fundamentally inseparable. That recognition or, better, the experience of that is for me Love.

With deep and dreadful consequences, we, instead, have the Western colonial worldview that radically and destructively divides and stratifies the world with its racialized structure, its gendered structure, its capitalist class structure, its sexuality structure, its ableism structure, its culture and language structure. And now we have the rapid destruction of the climate that can sustain the human lifeworld. As Ta-Nehisi Coates in *Between the World and Me* (2015) said, the American Dream is destroying the world. Though the world is too large and complex to reduce to a reductive Manichean perspective, it is not a far reach to say that the Western worldview that emerged out of the European enlightenment and is now mainly carried forward by the U.S., that worldview itself which has largely become the world's social ontology, is the single, largest threat to humankind (Chomsky & Naiman, 2011; Hansen, 2017).

Nonetheless, my view, and that of many others, is that the unitary fabric of existence is always with us. This is true of the physical world. This is true of the social world. This is true of the spiritual world. And, thus, to bring it into play ending the worldwide dominance of the Euro-American colonial world and to develop a better world for all people and all living beings, we need to develop thousands of ways to hear, feel, see, know Love. There are always already such seeds existing in our current world; we must cultivate them.

What is to be Done?

Unfortunately, though many voices have tried to tell us that there is a better way to live together, largely we have not heard them, and we have not tried to construct a world based on principles of Love and communion of and for all people and the planet. A large reason for this is that the colonial oppression is built into us. Even though we want a different world, a better world, a more caring and loving world for all people and the planet, we do not really know how to be the kind of people who could think the kind of thoughts, feel the kind of emotions, be the kind of beings from which we could construct that loving world. In response, I would suggest that we need to take one step based on our best understanding and our best effort to be at one with each other and the planet, in other words, to act out of Love for people and planet.

However, in taking that step we must always keep two understandings at hand. On one hand, we need to be very clear that the current Euro-American social system is entirely, deeply, thoroughly oppressive and corrupt from top to bottom. The poisoned house must be entirely dismantled. No more white supremacy. No more capitalism and its exploitive class structure and its greed-driven disregard of the planet. No more sexism and misogyny. No more hetero-sexism and homophobia. No more deficit-driven disabilities. No more dominance by any group, language, culture, or religion. No more elites of any kind who think they are above, richer, better, smarter, etc. than others. Reforming the current system will simply not work. Reform always reverts to assimilation, leaving the core system in place.

On the other hand, we need to keep strong that where we want to go is a human society based on Love for people and planet.

In between, then, is where we act; *in between is where we create a revolution.* In between, no, to the oppressive system and, yes, to a society based on Love of all people and the planet, we must learn together.

In between, we decide on a step to take and take it. We pay attention. We reflect on the step and its consequences. We talk about it together. We build communion. It could be a creative, generative step, or maybe we find it was a mistake. Whatever we decide it is, doing this together changes us and changes the world.

Step after step we keep doing this, which creates difference in the world and alters us. We try our best to lovingly work with that difference and alteration in preparation to taking another step. Thus, each step, if built out of where we are coming from and where we want to go, reconstructs the world and us as part of it, making a somewhat different world and making us somewhat different. We do not have certainty about the way forward; we only learn it by taking each step, but we do know the nature of oppression, and we do know we can struggle to make people and the planet the beloved community.

Each step is a decision together. Each step requires attention, reflection, sharing, communion, always doing our best to act out of Love for one another and for the planet.

When I say this, though, I do not necessarily mean something sweet and sugary. Love can be in a rage over the damage and destruction of oppression.

Love can be angry at white supremacy's privileging of white people based on the daily subtraction of people of color. Love can be confrontation, protest, resistance. Love is dangerous. Love is a direct threat to the current social order and the benefits the few receive at the expense of the many. Love is revolution, not reform.

While this process needs more discussion and explication, many others have written about it. A really good place to start is Grace Lee Boggs' *The Next American Revolution* (2012).

So What's Research Got to do with All of This?

We have this construct called social science research. It connects to other constructs like truth, the university, professors, etc. to create narratives and discourses that are powerfully oppressive in our world. This construct of research, its epistemologies and methodologies, is a colonial one that continues to colonize. It is directly assisting in the maintenance of the oppressive system.

What I am going to suggest is that those of us interested in "research," those of us who have been involved in conducting it, are going to build a series of new social constructions called research. The reason there has to be a series is that the first one (and we, too) will still be too deeply infected with the poison, as will the second, third, fourth, and so on, but with each new version, I am suggesting that we can eliminate more and more of the poison. However, these new constructions will not be like the old ones.

I am suggesting that the first version of these social constructions will include three interwoven and iterative areas of critical activism: critique, resistance, and community. Critique is working on identifying and understanding the oppressive colonialism and the way it socially constructs are world, our experience, our thinking, our feeling, our "reality" as we know and experience it. However, critique alone is not enough, not sufficient by itself. Resistance is also required. We have to collectively resist within ourselves and among each other. We must resist the colonization in all of its areas, from the educational system and the (in)justice system to the media and employment. *Indeed, we must resist "reality" itself.* We must resist that which is said by the dominant narrative to be true. We must resist that we have to be individualized the way we are taught to be. We must resist that capitalism and its exploitation are necessary. We must resist being gendered in some set way. We must resist white supremacy. We must resist xenophobia. We must resist differences being negatives. We must resist all hierarchical categories of separation. We must resist norms, like those of white supremacy, that privilege some based on damage to others.

This resistance, though, can take many forms. Some resistance will be public demonstrations like that of Black Lives Matter. Some resistance will be collective efforts to disrupt oppressive narratives and discourses, like calling out gentrification. Some resistance will be individuals working on themselves, working on our interior assumptions, beliefs, etc. Our resistance, though, must always have a strong collective or communal orientation. Resistance, like research, should not be an individual decision; it always needs to be a collaborative decision.

However, even critique and resistance are not enough. Community or community building is the most important critical action. We have to stop operating as independent, autonomous individuals. No one has such status (such individuality is a destructive illusion of the Euro-American master colonial and colonizing narrative), and those who can come the closest are only those with the most resources and the most elite status. Instead, we are all social beings, communal beings. Indeed, it is the denial of the human and planetary community that lies at the heart of oppression. Racism is a denial of community. Sexism is a denial of community. Capitalism and its classes are a denial of community. Heterosexism is a denial of community. Ableism is a denial of community. Xenophobia is a denial of community. Exploitation and maltreatment of the earth is a denial of community. All of these are denials that we are always already in communion with all people and the earth. This is what MLK meant by the beloved community. We are always already interwoven into a living fabric of being that includes all people, all other living beings, and the earth itself. To love all people, all other living beings, and the earth itself is to live that communion.

However, the truth of the matter is that, for the most part, we do not know how to do this, yet. We are certainly infected by the poison, but we do have the teachings of Indigenous civilizations. We do have the teachings of wise, loving folks in all traditions, histories, and geographies. We do have individuals who have tried, like Grace Lee Boggs or Frederick Douglass, or are trying to lovingly move us toward this communion. This teaching, this message resonates and echoes throughout all time and space because this communion is the nature of time and space itself. The universe itself is a communion from which we have become separated. Instead, a worldwide society has been created that manages that separation and its attendant destruction for the benefit of a few, whose gain is pitiful when compared to the direct experience of communion.

It is true that I do not know how to live this communion or even accurately describe it. I only know how to dream it. It is true we do not know how to live this communion, but we know how to dream of it. It may even be true that none of us really knows how to build and live this communion. It is also certainly true that we do not know collectively how to get there or, better, build it. We do know that the socially constructed society that dominates the world with its racism, classism, sexism, heterosexism, ableism, and xenophobia is the largest barrier we must overcome. Without knowing how to do so, we must try one step toward communion and see what happens, see what we learn, see our mistakes. Our step may be completely wrong. That is ok. We try again. We try another step. We just keep trying and learning; we just keep taking one step. Sometimes we will go a 100 or a 1000 steps in the wrong direction and have to go back and try a different direction.

That poisoned house that we now live in is not our true home. It is our prison. Our socially constructed world is a colonized and colonizing prison that only exists because we believe in it, reinforce it, participate in continuing its existence. Our prison is a narrative, the master narrative, though this narrative has hugely negative effects on the physical, psychological, and spiritual well being of people. Even the colonizers of today have been colonized into their roles and positions. The colonizers of today did not originate and build the prison, though they sustain it and benefit by it. As Freire (1970) contended, both colonizer and colonized are living in the prison, whereas our real home is communion with all beings and the earth. We want to go home; we need to go home; it is a deep yearning within us as our true nature, the true nature of being, is the interwoven communal fabric of being.

Some people call this Love. Not romantic love. This Love is to live in communion with all that is. This love is to live in harmony and peace with all that is. Right now, though, the question is how do we as a society, not as individuals, but as many societies, as many social groups large and small, dismantle the colonial prison and move into our rightful home.

I am suggesting we start small and start with where we already are. We build community with those already around us. Could be family, work colleagues, neighbors, friends, identity connections. We critique. We must start with the understanding that our socially constructed world is totally corrupt and destructive. It cannot simply be reformed. We must totally dismantle the prison. If we do not start with this systemic critique, we will simply fall for reform once again, which in the end only sustains the prison.

We also start with our currently limited understanding that our ultimate goal is communion, the beloved community, the social enactment of a loving society committed to all people, all other beings, and the earth. It is ok that we do not yet know what this really means or even how to get there. Nonetheless, we need to always keep in mind that we need and want to go back to our true home.

Thus, *on one hand*, we understand and critique the system, the entire system, the entire social arrangement, the colonial prison. We also resist it in a thousand different ways, large and small, tiny to huge. We call out the destruction. We call out the damage. We call out white racism. We call out xenophobia toward Muslims in the U.S. We call out heterosexists. We intervene in oppression. *On the other hand*, we know where we want to go, communion, the beloved community, a loving society. We know where we have to start from, and we have a sense of where we want to go. We just take one step with each other.

Notes

1. For example, in education a very high percentage of social science research is what is called "studying down," studying a population or context that has less power. This is fairly easy in education. It is relatively easy for university researchers to get access to less powerful people and contexts. It is much, much harder to "study up," that is study

those who are more powerful. I have done the latter, and it is excruciatingly difficult. The powerful do not want to be seen and understood. In one case, they would only agree to the most limited exposure, and there were almost as many lawyers in the room as researchers (see Nader, 1972).
2. There existed a social science in the Islamic world far before there was one in Europe. As early as the 1300s, Khaldun was doing social science work, most widely known through his book, the *Muqaddimah*. The role his work played in his civilization at that time is not the focus of this piece. However, it is apropos to point out that the European creators of the social science, in the arrogant fashion of the white male European elite, thought they were the point of origin for the social sciences.
3. Charles Taylor calls his book *Sources of the self: The making of the modern identity* (1989). I would call it the *Sources of the white heterosexual male self*, but he does discuss how this latter self was made in modernity.
4. See the work of Judith Butler for much more discussion of the social constitution of "reality" as we know it. Also, the work of Foucault, which Butler was much influenced by.

References

Anzaldúa, G. (1987). *Borderlands/La Frontera*. San Francisco, CA: Aunt Lute Books.

Battiste, M. (2017). *Decolonizing education: Nourishing the learning spirit*. Saskatoon, SK: Purich.

Beckman, M. & Long, J. F. (Eds.) (2016). *Community-based research: Teaching for impact*. Herndon, VA: Stylus.

Bhabha, H. (2004). *The location of culture*. New York: Routledge.

Boggs, G. L. (2012). *The next American revolution: Sustainable activism or the 21st Century*. Oakland, CA: University of California Press.

Bonilla-Silva, E. (2010). *Racism without racists: Color-blind racism and racial inequality in contemporary America* (3rd ed.). Lanham, MD: Rowman and Littlefield.

Byrd, J. A. (2011). *The transit of empire: Indigenous critiques of colonialism*. Minneapolis, MN: University of Minnesota Press.

Cammarota, J. & Fine, M. (2008). *Revolutionizing education: Youth participatory action research in motion*. New York: Routledge.

Chomsky, N. & Naiman, A. (2011). *How the world works*. Berkeley, CA: Soft Skull Press.

Coates, T.-N. (2015). *Between the world and me*. New York: Random House.

Collins, P. H. (1990). *Black feminist thought*. New York: Routledge.

Cone, J. H. (2010). *A Black theology of liberation* (40th anniversary ed.). Maryknoll, NY: Orbis Books.

Denzin, N. (2003). *Performance ethnography: Critical pedagogy and the politics of culture*. Thousand Oaks, CA: Sage.

Diversi, M. & Moreira, C. (2009). *Betweener talk: Decolonizing knowledge production, pedagogy, and praxis*. New York: Routledge.

Donmoyer, R. & Yennie-Donmoyer, J. (1995). Data as drama: Reflections on the use of readers theater as a mode of qualitative data display. *Qualitative Inquiry, 1*(4), 402–428.

Dunbar-Ortiz, R. (2014). *The Indigenous People's history of the U.S.* Boston, MA: Beacon Press.

Feagin, J. (2014). *Racist America: Roots, current realities, and future reparations* (3rd ed.). New York: Routledge.

Foucault, M. (1970). *The order of things*. New York: Pantheon Books.

Freire, P. (1970). *Pedagogy of the oppressed.* New York: Herder and Herder.

Hamera, J. (2011). Performance ethnography. In N. K. Denzin & Y. S. Lincoln (Eds.), *The Sage handbook of qualitative research* (4th ed.) (pp. 317–329). Thousand Oaks, CA: Sage.

Hansen, S. (2017). *Notes on a a foreign country: An American abroad in a Post-American world.* New York: Farrar, Straus, and Giroux.

Harris, C. I. (1993). Whiteness as property. *Harvard Law Review, 106,* 1710–1791.

Harris, J. C. (2016). Toward a critical multiracial theory in education. *International Journal of Qualitative Studies in Education, 29*(6), 795–813.

Heller, H. (2016). *The capitalist university: The transformations of higher education in the United States since 1945.* London: Pluto Press.

Jones, S. H., Adams, T. E., & Ellis, C. (Eds.) (2013). *Handbook of autoethnography.* Walnut Creek, CA: Left Coast Press.

Kendi, I. X. (2016). *Stamped from the beginning: The definitive history of racist ideas in America.* New York: Nations Books.

Kuhn, T. (1962). *The structure of scientific revolutions.* Chicago, IL: University of Chicago Press.

Lahman, M. K. E., Geist, M. R., Rodriguez, K. L., Graglia, P. E., Richard, V. M., & Schendel, R. K. (2009). Poking around poetically: Research, poetry, and trustworthiness. *Qualitative Inquiry, 16*(1), 39–48.

Marx, K. (1845/1970). Theses on Fuerbach, Thesis 11, in *Marx Engels Selected Works,* Vol. I. Moscow, Russia: Progress.

Nader, L. (1972). Up the anthropologist: Perspectives gained from studying up. In D. H. Hymes, *Reinventing anthropology* (pp. 284–311). New York: Pantheon.

Reason, P. & Bradbury, H. (Eds.) (2011). *The handbook of action research.* Los Angeles, CA: Sage.

Richardson, L. (1997). *Fields of play: Constructing an academic life.* New Brunswick, NJ: Rutgers University Press.

Scheurich, J. J. (1993). Toward a white discourse on white racism. *Educational Researcher, 22*(8), 5–10.

Scheurich, J. J. (1997). *Research method in the postmodern.* London: Routledge.

Scheurich, J. J. & Young, M. D. (1997). Coloring epistemology: Are our epistemologies racially biased?" *Educational Researcher, 26*(4), 4–16.

Science News. With you in the room, bacteria counts spike—by about 37 million bacteria per hour. www.sciencedaily.com/releases/2012/03/120328172255.htm

Strega, S. & Brown, L. (2015). *Research as resistance: Revisiting critical, Indigenous, and anti-oppressive approaches* (2nd ed.). Toronto, ON: Canadian Scholars.

Taylor, C. (1989). *Sources of the self: The making of the modern identity.* Cambridge, MA: Harvard University Press.

Thomas, J. (1993). *Doing critical ethnography.* Newbury Park, CA: Sage.

Tuck, E. & McKenzie, M. (2015). *Place in research: Theory, methodology, and method.* New York: Routledge.

Tuhiwai Smith, L. (1999). *Decolonizing methodologies: Research and Indigenous Peoples.* London: Zed Books.

Turner, J., Patrick, S., Washington, D., Zakem, M., Luis, A., & Fair, P. (2017, April 22). *A critical discussion exploring Indianapolis charter schools (a public forum).* Indianapolis, IN: The Kheprw Institute.

Tzu, L. (2016). *Tao the king.* CreateSpace: An Amazon self-publishing company.

Valencia, R. R. (2010). *Dismantling contemporary deficit thinking*. New York: Routledge.

Whyte, W. F. (Ed.) (1990). *Participatory action research*. Newbury Park, CA: Sage.

Wilder, C. S. (2013). *Ebony and ivy: Race, slavery, and the troubled history of America's universities*. New York: Bloomsbury Press.

Yancy, G. (2008*). Black bodies, white gazes: The continuing significance of* race. Lanham, MD: Rowman and Littlefield.

10

METHOD OL O GIE S . . . THAT ENCOUNTER (SLOWNESS AND) IRREGULAR RHYTHM

Mirka Koro-Ljungberg and Timothy Wells

Meeting and Encountering *Slowness* in Scholarship

In order to find different and more productive methodological places within the social sciences, academia, and qualitative inquiry we, similar to other scholars (e.g., Berg & Seeber, 2016; Ulmer, 2016), trouble the notion of 'speedy' scholarship and rapid methods. We found it productive to pay attention to rhythmic patterns, irregular, and potential slowing forms of inquiry. In the midst of hectic academic life, competition, and ever-increasing neoliberalism we problematize speed as a fueling force for the academic marketplace and competition, and as a central character of the bottomless trap designed to simplify methodological technologies and techniques to produce more, faster, and increasingly efficient knowledge, knowing, and science. This trend towards increased production without the equal consideration of quality, living, and slowly 'maturing' intellectual thought evokes critiques of neoliberal influence on academic culture. This trend also provokes questions about 'slow science' and irregularly patterned scholarship. What might slowness in scholarship produce?

Recently, the question of slowness—as well as rapidity, broadly speaking pace—has gained currency. For instance, Honoré (2004), in his book *In Praise of Slowness*, documented worldwide movements that embrace the very idea of slowing down. Covering topics from schooling to medicine, *In Praise of Slowness* is a manifesto to halt the rapidity of life, to stop and smell roses, to find value in process, and to achieve *Tempo Giusto*—Honoré's term for the perfect rhythm. In the realm of academia, prominent journals, such as *Nature*, have turned their attention to research pace and alternate forms of productivity in documenting five of the slowest, longest-running projects in operation, some of which are lasting hundreds of years, producing a single data point per decade (Owens, 2013). Similarly, researchers in the natural sciences (e.g. Garfield, 1990; Lutz,

2012) have called for a shift away from the rapidity of grant funding cycles and the pace of the tenure track to an academic culture that values longitudinal studies and time-honored tasks. In fact, Berg and Seeber (2016), in their acclaimed book *The Slow Professor*, argued that professors should actively resist the academic 'culture of speed' by deliberately slowing down processes to better reflect and think. These calls for slower life and slow-paced work within and outside of the academy have afforded new space for those critical of institutional trends.

Furthermore, Apple (2005) has argued that neoliberal market principles have infiltrated the public university space. These market principles create endless drives for production and efficiency, spawning audit-based cultures that undermine the democratic function of the university. Rather than educating for a democratic citizenry, Apple warns, the university system is becoming a site for shareholder profit generation and an expanding managerial class with less concern for public interest. Taking up Apple's concerns, scholars have examined the speedy pace of academic culture specifically in relation to neoliberal cultural ideals (Berg & Seeber, 2016; Hartman & Darab, 2012). In one instance, Hartman and Darab (2012) found that the neoliberal shifts towards managerial control objectifies scholars, pacifies workers, and leads to consumer-oriented views of students. In response, they call for slow scholarship to counter the drive towards efficiency-at-all-cost rationality. From these critical perspectives, the audit-based and managerial cultures of academia stifle the patient, careful, innovative, and truly productive possibilities of research.

It is within this context that many social science and qualitative researchers grasp for the concept of slow research. Some of the most widely recognized work on slowness comes from the slow food movement, a movement dedicated to preserving traditional cuisine and regional agriculture. In fact, Honoré's (2004) book specifically praises these slow food movements for the community engagement and environmental benefits that they afford. In a similar light, scholars have explored slow food as a site of social, economic, and environmental resistance, finding that such movements offer alternatives to the environmental destruction caused by industrial agriculture and fast food (Van Bommel & Spicer, 2011). Others have approached slow food from the geographical and political perspectives, finding that slowing down recreates relations and movement (Hayes-Conroy & Martin, 2010), as well as forms of identity and values in geographical place (Knox, 2005). Slow food movement could also been seen as one form of material turn where ecological matter and natural world displaces the centrality of humans. However, the benefits of slowness often fail to permeate neoliberal research practices, which disproportionately value findings and controllable outcomes over the methods and processes of more organic inquiry. As Kuus (2015) cautions, scholars must "avoid the illusion of contingency that privileges events over process" (p. 838). More than anything else, the slow science, slow professor, and slow movement culture embraces slowness as a response to a culture that relentlessly 'eats up' our time and hails for fast dutiful citizens and academics. Responding to the fast-spaced academic culture is far from a simple affair, yet, or perhaps because of this, we would like to explore some methodological possibilities of differently paced scholarly work.

In fact, during the same time that the increasing pace of academia has been critiqued, the notion of slowness as a direction of research—as opposed to an object of study—has crept its way into various methodological spaces. This is most readily found in the post-qualitative inquiry practices, where many researchers return to questions of relation, rhythm, and irregular patterning within the material world as one possible way to intertwine ontological and epistemological knowledge formations (St. Pierre, 2016). This is a shift toward material processes, which is concerned, as Lather (2013) describes, with conceptions of *difference* and *becoming* (in the Deleuzian sense), relationality and entanglement (in the Baradian sense), as some potential ways to move away from representationalism and inquiries based on fixed sameness. These shifts could also stimulate scholars to pay increased attention to the problematics of speed and they might encourage many qualitative researchers to work against simplicity, speed, and unnecessary efficiency (see Koro-Ljungberg, Mazzei, & Cegloswki, 2013). Ultimately, these ontological moves directed towards process, decreased speed, and slowness, prompted also our attention to work through *slowness*, to slow down, experiment with effects and affects of the 'slow', and pay more attention to the variations in the methodologies and rhythms of inquiry.

Following recent propositions to reposition ontologies in relation to qualitative research (de Freitas, 2012; Lentz Taguchi, 2013; MacLure, 2013; St. Pierre, 2016), we wonder what slowness and irregular rhythm might look like as a 'method' or a proxy for a 'method' and how it might shape 'data', inquiry, processes, and practices (see also Koro-Ljungberg, 2016). For if we follow Lather's (2016) suggestion to conceive of subjects less as layered, stable, and inert and more as folded, relational, and (intra-)active, what becomes of 'data', subject, inquiry when their pace, rate, and rhythm are deliberately slowed? Drawing from St. Pierre (2016) who reconsiders empirical research, we also wonder how data are experienced when they are deliberately slowed or slower? Additionally, similar to those who have suggested turning theory into practice with method-based techniques (i.e., Michael's (2012) "lucid action" and "inventive problem-making"), we turn to *slowness* and irregular rhythm as an opportunity to create "differently productive" methodological practices (Ulmer, 2016). In this light, our use of *slowness* and attention to rhythm might surface ontological questions and loosen the constraints of normative epistemological constrains and binary logic (e.g., slow-fast, ineffective–effective, subjective–objective).

Experimenting with (Slowness and) Irregular Rhythm

Some time ago, when we started our work on slow methodologies, we anticipated slowness, slow science, slow movement to be desirable and, simply, a 'good thing.' We thought that normative speediness and rapid methodologies stagger while boredom, contemplation, and concentration actuate deep engagement and relational dialogue between the researchers and their worlds and surroundings. As post-qualitative inquirers, we called for reconceptualization of methodologies that reinvent and transform taken for granted epistemological and ontological practices. It felt important and significant to play with speed, duration, and stillness/nothingness without really knowing where our experimentation would lead. Assuming that our 'being in the world' simultaneously constructs the world, we were curious to know what kind of living assemblage might the act of slowing produce and how difference would become possible in relation to slow movement. In addition, other and becoming methodological implications of slowing down and slowed rhythm intrigued us.

However, as we carried out some 'slow' activities and experimented with slowness from various perspectives, wondered about the relation between slowness and speed, tackled with notions of duration, movement, and rhythm, our initial anticipation towards the 'goodness' or benefits of slowness withered as uncertainty and productive skepticism ensured. We questioned our initial, non-critical commitment to slow science and slowness practices. As a result of this questioning we came to think that slowness itself might not necessarily function as a desirable force or state since in order to recognize something as slow it often needs to be defined and operationalized in relation to speed. In this way slowness is functioning and presenting itself mainly as a part of a vital yet possibly unproductive binary (slow–fast). It is also possible that slow's fundamental connection to speed further perpetuates and promotes the ideals and goals of neoliberal academia such as individualization, deregulation, and the supposed free choice of autonomous subjects. Slow being defined and practiced potentially only in relation to fast/rapid/efficient limits the potentialities of rhythm and the ways in which rhythm could be becoming and emerging. Instead, one might imagine and create variations in speed and intensities situating slowness and rhythm in diverse and shifting ontological planes. While in some contexts slowness might also be interpreted as a (theoretical and pragmatic) resistance and an agentic force responding to neoliberal discourses, we suggest slowness might also be too intimately tied to neoliberalism and its functions and, therefore, making the uncritical acceptance of 'slow and slowness' problematic. Therefore, in our practice and thinking reflection and critique of, or "challenge" to, slowness led us away from uncritical promotion or use of slowness and sensitized us to the varying formations of speed as rhythmic (including movement and duration).

Rhythms in knowledge, inquiry, and methodology themselves offer shifting ontological dimensions and as such could account for space and intensity of thinking-moving without a commitment and direct connection to the binary structure. As Deleuze and Guattari (1988) found, "rhythm is critical; it ties together critical moments; it ties together in passing from one milieu to another" (p. 313). Thus, the following text addresses what might happen to teaching and learning, inquiry and methodology in a classroom context when rhythm, movement, and duration are explicitly attended to? And, when a classroom's rhythm is deliberately altered and when the rhythm and movement of data are similarly disrupted?

Potentiality and What Might Become Possible (with/in/through (Methodological) Rhythms)

Whitehead (1967) conceptualizes rhythm through repetition and as "the conveyance of difference within a framework of repetition" (p. 17). Repetition without difference lacks rhythm. Thus, a metronome could be seen as a guide to a non-differentiated pattern but not rhythm. Rhythm comes from the creative, divergent, and disruptive elements within one's use of pattern. While a musician learns timing and patterns of 'sameness' from the metronome, the production of rhythm emerges through the process of one's own creative endeavor. However, Whitehead cautions against overlooking the role of repetition; for along with difference, it too is a prerequisite of rhythm. Without repetition, difference lacks its particularity as well as its value for use. Whitehead's understanding rings not only of Deleuze and Guattari's ontology difference and attention to repetition, but their conceptions of rhythm which exists "whenever there is a transcoded passage from one milieu to another, a communication of milieus, coordination between heterogeneous space-times" (p. 313). Whitehead (1968) refers to natural pulsation as a rhythm for a process. For Manning and Massumi (2014) "everything has rhythm, and rhythms have a way of coming together. They resonate and accrue" (p. 32). In addition, by visiting in other's (human and non-human) past and then moving to their futures might also produce different rhythms. According to Manning and Massumi, relationality and living changes the tempo, prompting co-compositions of rhythm-becoming-language and rhythm-becoming-movement to happen. When language counterpoints the movement at the limit, it "tweaks into a rhythm with movement" (p. 51), potentially producing polyrhythmic effects that might only be sensed. "Research-creations as we propose to practice it is [sic] a polyrhythmic attuning of mutually composing autonomous activities" (Manning & Massumi, 2014, p. 123) that resist capture and quantification. These components—repetition, movement, difference—serve as provocateurs for our 'experimental classroom' activities, which we explore below.

Example 1: Disrupting Normative Classroom Movement

Scholarship, thinking-doing, and research-creation (see Manning, 2016) in our inquiry contexts and classrooms often disrupt normative classroom activities and regularly patterned movement. For example, with deliberate attempts to disrupt movement, we prompted graduate students in an advanced qualitative research course to attend to rhythm through difference, creativity, and 'thought-in-the-act' (Manning & Massumi, 2014). Offering diverse prompts to disrupt normative movement, we took up the Bergsonian task of dissolving sugar in water to experience movement and duration. Later, we read books at different paces, some fast, some slow, while tracking time without clocks. Additionally, class periods started without beginnings slowly and repeatedly and we asked the class to move slowly throughout the room with recording cameras in hand. For an undisclosed amount of time, we simply wanted them to experience movement, rhythm, and relation.

What happened during our experimentation? How were methodologies, knowledges, bodies and relations between these elements produced? In many ways, we found bodies in diverse relation to others. Bodies, methodologies, thoughts in the act, writings and so on were not singular but always multiple relations affecting and being affected. We found various degrees of collectivity already embedded in our thinking-in-the-act. Clock time no longer structured interactions, instead relational time, duration, parkour time, leg time, and rug time shaped collective experience. Moving a leg over the desk, bringing camera lens closer to carpet, stepping high up above the desks, moving underneath the desks and between the chair legs oriented experimenters to different angles, viewpoints, and perspectives simultaneously generating diverse narrations and unanticipated ways of knowing. Learners constructed themselves in relations and relations constructed them as knowing–doing relationality. Different questions about knowing, senses, bodies, and pedagogies surfaced. Moreover, imaginative and unexpected colors, smells, and sounds were created when differently colored lines of the commercial rug blended with a brown leather bag, water bottles, and the metallic legs of the furniture. Various rhythms were experienced and sensed; rhythms of bodies, colors, intersecting images, shoes, sounds, texts and signs, and intensities between details and blurred boundaries of unrecognizable objects. Moving over and around obstacles intensified some activities and focused viewers' attention. Hands were reaching the roof, the sky, holding phones and touching classroom furniture in shifting yet patterned way. Everything was learning. The angle of recording video produced a rhythm from the floor to the roof, from objects to subjects, from city parkour to classroom parkour and back.

> The degree of slowness is directly proportional to the intensity of memory; the degree of speed is directly proportional to the intensity of forgetting.
>
> (Kundera, 1997)

Beyond connection and immediate vision, perception lost clarity as objects lost stability while extending outside their borders. Tables continued toward bags that reached toward hands and legs which then touched students and moving bodies. Blurriness activated wonder and a continuous sense of becoming and knowing. The multiplicity of connected events functioned as links and joints between toes, carpets, parks, bushes, blurred objects, phones, backpacks, flags, chairs, tables, holes, shoes, T-shirts, bodies, stripes and stars, colors and on and on. Where did the subject/object end or begin? According to Deleuze and Guattari (1988), events are possible activated in between(s): "between night and day, at dusk, twilight or Zwielicht, Haecceity... landing, splashown, takeoff" (p.314). Knowledge and data were collectively yet in unanticipated ways becoming. Knowing, observations, and senses moved to multiple directions at once. In short, when diverse or disruptive flows entered the class students found new rhythms. They experimented, took risks, and expressed with their moving bodies. Equally so, our methodological attention to rhythm provoked experimentation and risk-taking among our data, knowledge, and inquiry processes.

Example 2: Slow and Differently Rhythmic Dialogue

Our inquiry into slowness led us to experiment with interview/dialogical rhythms. It was not our intension to carry out or create interviews or dialogue on the concept of slowness, but interviews and dialogue were practiced in varying rhythms. Both of us having recently read Edward Said's (1996) *Representations of the Intellectual* shaped our conversations. Together and relating with the texts, each other, our past–presents and diverse pre-forms of intellectualism, we explored how a varying rhythm interrupts the normativity of an interview and dialogue.

███ ███ ███

Tim: Mirka ... do .. You . Feel . Like . An . Intellectual .. today?

███ ███

Mirka: Not sure. . . . . What is . Intellectual anyways.

███ ███

Mirka: Is it state? . . . Is it activity? . . Does it have to do with uhm space? . . . Is it . Duty? . . . . Is it a call? . . . . . Is it something that emerges? Or is it always here already?

Tim: Do you say RRRRResponsibility?

Mirka: [quietly] I said duty.

Tim: it's a d-uuuuu-tttt-yyy-y ? . . . .

Mirka: N-n-n-n-n-ot sure . . . . What do you think? . . .

Tim: I'm also .
Tim: Ambivalent .
Tim: Aaaaaaabout . .
Tim: Bbbbbbbbbeing an intellectual. . . .

Tim: do you think . Your work . . Has been intellectual?

Pause (25 seconds)

Mirka: it's interesting because I don't think I have ever thought
AAAAAAbout it.
Mirka: Uh . I have done scholarship for some time but I have never
kind of thought of it as some sort of intellectual activity. It is just an
activity that I do. Or the person(s) that I am . .

■

And am I intellectual or are my activities intellectual?
Mirka: In someways . . I don't know if it matters.
Tim: uh huh]

■   ■

Tim: How do you see your work . . Or what do you see the function
or role of your work? . . . . . .

Mirka: I'm not sure that I can determine that . . .
Mirka: That the impact and influence of my work is somehow always
becoming . . And it is . . Constituted in different times and places and
spaces mostly by other people. And within my interactions with my
environments . .
Mirka: Uhm . . .
Mirka: And I guess ultimately I just do what I like to do . . . . . And
I just put it out there
Mirka: and see what happens . . .

Tim: do you think of your work in the classroom . . . As . The work in the classroom as a teacher in a similar way . . That you think of y-y-y-y-your research? . .

Mirka: I don't think I can separate teaching from thinking. Or other kinds of activities . .

Mirka: It all kind of the same thing. Or kind of one big assemblage in a way-y-y-y-y-y- . . . . . .

Mirka: But where is intellectualism in there? Uhm . . . . I think it is nowhere and everywhere.

Mirka: Uhm . . . Uhm . . . Uhm . . . Uhm . . . Uhm . . . Uhm . . . Uhm . . . Uhm . . .

Mirka: I'm not sure that I able to detect it. But I think I

May

be

doing

it.

What Is Happening?

From our perspective altering the rhythm of dialogue, talk, discourse, words, utterances, expressions, among other things opened up a different space or a variety of spaces; some of which will be discussed and reflected upon in this section of the paper. *In s o m e ways, w e moved away f r o m* an interactive yet predictable dialogical discussion or interview space toward '*wild space*' and space of non-anticipation where doing, roles, actions upon actions, and behaviors became less expected, normative and where ideas and thinking fluctuated and continuously shifted. Pauses and silences stimulated un-patterned diversion and difference. Slowness and slowly paced thought as well as irregular rhythm produced *rr eee llll aaaaat iii ooo n aaa lity*. The dialogical question imposing an answer or question–answer pattern was not guiding our responses or thinking but interactive relationality was prompted by w-h-a-t-e-v-e-r and w-h-e-n-e-v-e-r.

Explanations or even procedural descriptions of the occurred event were and are desperately inaccurate and limited. In many ways, the directionality of the dialogue was released from its normative function and the most frequent direction was un-non-anti-direction and diverse potential embedded in irregularity. Responses were not responses to the questions per se but diverse ways to navigate through one's own thinking-doing. Additionally, the normative communication rhythm became so much disturbed and the question answer pattern so deeply broken that other dialogical spaces, including spaces of silence, fragmentation, and unclarity, became possible and desirable. Occasionally, we did not know if we were answering or posing a question. Words followed each other without particular and predetermined function. Irregular rhythm offered a differentiation gesture or movement into a different direction all at once. In addition, it is possible that the links between diverse thinking-doing were formed organically and potentially but also randomly. Furthermore, the notion of linear time or 'dialogical/interview time' disappeared and became less relevant even as we returned to more regular speaking pattern and rhythm during our (later) interactions. Dialogical differentiation and variation in the rhythm of talking was already established and repetitions continued in their different forms. The irregularity of the question answer pattern sustained its' force and gained dynamism from its organic processes. In some ways, it was beneficial to begin our dialogical relation by somewhat artificial 'slowing talk and slow interactions'. A performance space was created which also stimulated this different and new negotiated rhythm of our dialogue.

Overall, we noted that dialogical and material flows produced relational rhythm which only through forceful analysis could be broken into distinctive and nameable units (of time, data, subjects, material, thinking, question–answer patterns, life). The absence of distinctive analytical and performance units, methods, and material introduces paradoxes and (im)possibilities to method-ological processes. The potential void of methodological stability enables scholars to think-in-the act. In addition, the irregular rhythm functions similar to the irreducible flux or unexpected flow of time. Everything changes and takes place in the movement. Massumi (2002) conceptualizes movement (among other things) by relating it to the reconceptualizations of time, which is "the immediate proximity of before and after . . . nonlinear, moving in two directions at once: out from the actual (as past) into the actual (as future)" (p. 58). In this immediate proximity, movement registers intensities. Movement might not be captured in speed but in intensities; certain events are accentuated, multiplied, maybe over-lived. However, this accentuation is not intentional or planned—it just happens when forces of energy overlap and coincide.

In our experiments, the prompt to slow down first evoked hesitation, a sense not knowing how to proceed when rhythmic structures are disrupted. This hesitation was intensity. It was an encounter of the unknown, suspended momentarily, before deciding how to proceed. Looking around a classroom of students moving in slow motion and irregular rhythm, the tendency to revert to the same movement was lost (at least for most). The carpet floor became a lure, as did the top of desks. Movement in and about the space was consciously creative simply from the proposition for slowness. In the slow conversation, the break between words evoked a different type of intensity. On the one hand, the need to fill conversational space was gone, we sat in silence and considered thoughts while moving. The intensity here was collective, as opposed to individualistic and self-conscious. On the other hand, breaks between words and sentences brought forth the intensity of what might become next. Not knowing how a sentence will end or the next one begins created the intensity around possibility(s). There was sense that any sentence could go in any direction and end at any point: "[rhythm] it changes directions" (Deleuze & Guattari, 1988, p.313). We experienced that movement and sensation (e.g., living–experiencing–documenting–reflecting–producing–knowing–sensing–feeling) were intrinsically connected. For Massumi, connectibility is a rhythm without regularity and readiness to arrive. Affect forms a relation of motion and rest. Intensity is always immanent to matter and events composing them and which they compose. Manning (2016), in turn, discusses the intervals in relation to movement–moving. "Intervals are qualitative holes of movement-moving opened up by inflections. Relational movement generates and is generated by intervals" (p.120). Multiple directionalities at once, complexities of speeds and slowness move more than subjects and individuals.

For Koepnick (2014), slowness does not have to do with speed but it enables confrontation, presentness to encounter different durations and potentialities. Similarly, in our examples, the confrontation of duration in a classroom afforded new relationalities. Students related with the climber of desks and that of rolling pins on the floor. The chairs turned to steps and the carpet greeted faces. Classroom time expanded from quantitative sequence to movement duration. Slowness functioned as "an ever-changing meeting ground of multiple durations and potentialities, of competing tempos and temporalities, of dissimilar narratives and visions." (p. 37). As such, "the wager of aesthetic slowness is not simply to find islands of respite, calm, and stillness somewhere outside the cascades of contemporary speed culture" but instead to "investigate what it means to experience a world of speed, acceleration, and cotemporality." (p. 10). As we see it, it became possible to conceptualize 'methodological slowness' as a sensory-perceptual mode of fluctuating rhythm that enabled new subjectivities and new ways of sensing.

As a result of these experimentations our questions have changed yet again. We no longer wonder what happens when methodologies encounter slowness but what happens when researchers relate movement, duration, and rhythm with thought in the act, intuition and senses. Further, how can rhythm, duration, and movement create potential for knowing and inquiring differently? However, we can only anticipate and speculate these becoming processes since 'slowness', irregular rhythm, movement moves and duration needs to be invented, lived, and sensed. Methodologies such as interview studies, observational inquiries, or living encounters might need to break free from the conventional patterns and habits in order to regenerate themselves differently. They might derail and produce something different. They might take new methodological directions and encounter the strange and different. They might become attentive to difference and tuned to affect. They might produce endless entanglements. They might become singular plural and relational. They might unite just to depart again. They might make/unmake producing immanent critique of humanistic subject and knowledge. They might need to rethink knowledge and scientific progress. They might also leave us (scholars behind) and produce faster than qualitative community and its scholars can follow, understand, and sense. They might do and redo until unrecognition. They might relate, become, and continue speculating and critiquing their speculations. They might.

What if methodologies could produce irregular rhythm
create artificial and virtual speed traps
attend to productive spaces when nothing seems to happen
anticipate   and
p-l-a-y with speed and irregular rhythm

■ ■

Not sure. . . . What is . Intellectual anyways.

■ ■

Not sure. . . . What is . Intellectual anyways.

■ ■

Not sure. . . . What is . Intellectual anyways.

maybe in an attempt
to wonder how a varying rhythm in methodology and philosophy could offer surprises and different forms of unthought in act
maybe through the **intuitive, woolly and creative**,
what Kundera (1997) refers to as a
'wisdom of slowness' . . .

References

Apple, M. W. (2005). Education, markets, and an audit culture. *Critical Quarterly*, 47(1–2), 11–29.

Berg, M. & Seeber, B. (2016). *Slow professor: Challenging the culture of speed in the academy.* Toronto, ON: University of Toronto Press.

de Freitas, E. (2012). The classroom as rhizome: New strategies for diagramming knotted interaction. *Qualitative Inquiry*, 18(7), 557–570.

Deleuze, G. & Guattari, F. (1988). *A thousand plateaus: Capitalism and schizophrenia.* London: Bloomsbury.

Garfield, E. (1990). Fast science vs. slow science, or slow and steady wins the race. *The Scientist*, 4(18), 380–381.

Hartman, Y. & Darab, S. (2012). A call for slow scholarship: A case study on the intensification of academic life and its implications for pedagogy. *Review of Education, Pedagogy, & Cultural Studies*, 34(1), 49–60.

Hayes-Conroy, A. & Martin, D. G. (2010). Mobilising bodies: Visceral identification in the Slow Food movement. *Transactions of the Institute of British Geographers*, 35(2), 269–281.

Honoré, C. (2004). *In praise of slow: How a worldwide movement is challenging the cult of speed.* Toronto, ON: Random House.

Knox, P. L. (2005). Creating ordinary places: Slow cities in a fast world. *Journal of Urban Design, 10*(1), 1–11.

Koepnick, L. (2014) *On slowness: Toward an aesthetic of the contemporary.* New York: Columbia University Press.

Koro-Ljungberg, M. (2016) *Reconceptualizing qualitative research: Methodologies without methodology.* London: Sage.

Koro-Ljungberg, M., Mazzei, L., & Cegloswki, D. (2013). Diverse ways to fore-ground methodological insights about qualitative research. *International Journal of Research & Method in Education, 36*(2), 131–144.

Kundera, M. (1997). *Slowness: A novel.* New York: HarperCollins.

Kuus, M. (2015). For slow research. *International Journal of Urban and Regional Research, 39,* 838–840.

Lather, P. (2013). Methodology-21: What do we do in the afterward? *International Journal of Qualitative Studies in Education, 26*(6), 634–645.

Lather, P. (2016). Top ten+ list (re) thinking ontology in (post) qualitative research. *Cultural Studies-Critical Methodologies, 16*(2), 125–131.

Lenz Taguchi, H. (2013) Images of thinking in feminist materialisms: Ontological divergences and the production of researcher subjectivities. *International Journal of Qualitative Studies in Education, 26*(6), 706–716.

Lutz, J. F. (2012). Slow science. *Nature Chemistry, 4,* 588–589.

MacLure, M. (2013). The wonder of data. *Cultural Studies ⟺ Critical Methodologies, 13*(4), 228–232.

Manning, E. (2016). *The minor gesture.* Durham, NC: Duke University Press.

Manning, E. & Massumi, B. (2014). *Thought in the act: Passages in the ecology of experience.* Minneapolis, MN: University of Minnesota Press.

Massumi, B. (2002). *Parables for the virtual: Movement, affect, sensation.* Durham, NC: Duke University Press.

Michael, M. (2012). De-signing the object of sociology: Toward an 'idiotic' methodology. *The Sociological Review, 60*(S1), 166–183.

Owens, B. (2013). Long-term research: Slow science. *Nature, 495,* 300–303.

Said, E. (1996). *Representations of the intellectual: The 1993 Reith Lectures.* New York: Vintage Books.

St.Pierre, E. A. (2016). The empirical and the new empiricisms. *Cultural Studies ⟺ Critical Methodologies.* doi: 1532708616636147

Ulmer, J. B. (2016). Writing slow ontology. *Qualitative Inquiry,* 1–11. doi:10.1177/1077800416643994

Van Bommel, K. & Spicer, A. (2011). Hail the snail: Hegemonic struggles in the Slow Food movement. *Organization Studies, 32*(12), 1717–1744.

Whitehead, A. N. (1967). *The aims of education, and other essays.* New York: The Free Press.

Whitehead, A. (1968). *Modes of thought.* New York: The Free Press.

11

COLLABORATIVE AUTOETHNOGRAPHY

An Ethical Approach to Inquiry that Makes a Difference[1]

Judith C. Lapadat

With the rise of qualitative inquiry as the dominant paradigm for research in the social sciences, everything about what we understand research to be has changed. In qualitative inquiry, we seek subjectivity over objectivity. We recognize research as a reflexive process. Researchers are embedded within a research context relationally, bodily, cognitively, and emotionally, which influences the conceptualization, processes, and outcomes of the research. Qualitative scholars embrace the complexity of context: meanings are particular, interactive, layered in time, dependent on perspective, and provisional. Research is not value free. Our actions as researchers are inherently political and contribute to the tenor of our world in small, and sometimes large ways.

This chapter focuses on one historical evolution within qualitative inquiry—the rising centrality of ethics—and specifically, the ethics of autoethnography. As scholars in the social sciences, especially those within sociological and ethnographic traditions, sought alternatives to colonial and positivistic research practices, they re-examined their ethical obligations as researchers. They questioned the assumption of cultural superiority underlying studies of others and saw how research engagement with informants could be self-serving, even parasitic. Human relationships were being exploited as a means to an end, and relational ties neglected (Ellis, 2007a, b, 2009b). Research designs concerned with controlling contextual factors and others' behavior in pursuit of formulating generalized laws ensconced the researcher in a position of power and were blind to how subjectivity, positionality, emotions, and intent interacted to shift meanings. What right did researchers have to take people's stories, speak for them, or represent them to the world? These are moral questions, and how researchers act in relation to others as they pursue their scholarship is an ethical matter.

Autoethnographic inquiry as it emerged and matured has existed on the leading edge of this change, pushing the boundaries of how we think about, do, and share research, and more importantly, why. Autoethnography (AE) "recognizes and tries to accommodate procedural, situational, and relational ethics" (Adams, Holman Jones, & Ellis, 2013, p. 673). As an approach to scholarly inquiry, AE has challenged the ethics of doing and evaluating research (Lapadat, 2017).

One reason many scholars first turned to autoethnography is because this approach addresses ethical issues inherent in representing, speaking for, or appropriating the voices of others. In telling their own stories, autoethnographers are both researcher and participant. They speak in their own voices, telling those stories that they have selected, for the purposes that they have chosen. There is no power imbalance as the researcher and participant are one and the same person.

Therefore, autoethnography is rooted in ethical intent. Yet, as it has evolved methodologically, some knotty ethical problems with autoethnography itself have become apparent (Ellis, 2007a, b, 2009b; Tullis, 2013). In this chapter, I contend that some of the ethical issues that confound solo autoethnographers diminish when a more collaborative approach to doing autoethnography is adopted. The focus of this chapter is ethics in autoethnographic inquiry, and specifically in collaborative autoethnography (CAE).

Collaborative autoethnography is a family of multivocal approaches in which two or more researchers work together to share personal stories and interpret the pooled autoethnographic data (Chang, Ngunjiri, & Hernandez, 2013; Lapadat, 2017). Like autoethnography, collaborative autoethnography is motivated by ethical intent. Both AE and CAE locate responsibility for ethical decision-making reflexively with the researcher, and support ethical social change in the interest of making the world a better place. However, CAE extends the reach of AE and offers some ethical and methodological advantages over AE.

Research Ethics

Research ethics now are viewed as a necessary consideration in conducting research with living beings. General ethical guidelines and processes for ethical review were developed decades ago in response to a number of egregious examples of researchers' unethical treatment of humans and animals (Christians, 2011). Universities and medical institutions formalized and enforced research ethics guidelines in order to prevent such ethical violations. Thus, institutional research ethics processes are bureaucratic at their core, arose out of earlier research paradigms,[2] and were implemented to regulate their converse: unethical research practices.

As qualitative inquiry flourished, developing an ever-expanding array of naturalistic research approaches that challenged the epistemological assumptions of rational empiricism and positivism, it became apparent that the ethical review processes and guidelines used by university Institutional Review Boards (IRBs) or Research Ethics Boards (REBs) often were a poor match for qualitative studies (McIntosh & Morse, 2009; Tolich, 2016). Qualitative proposals were being evaluated on the basis of assumptions and procedures drawn from the very methods that the qualitative approaches were designed to replace. Ethics reviews at times were overly restrictive because proposed qualitative studies did not resemble quantitative research designs familiar to the reviewers (Tolich, 2016). As well, the types of ethical dilemmas confronting qualitative researchers simply were not on the radar, so oftentimes the guidelines failed to offer relevant guidance (Denshire, 2014). As an example, there are ethical implications when autoethnographers tell personal stories that implicate intimate others (Ellis 2007a, b), yet many IRBs/REBs exempt autoethnographic studies from research ethics review (Tullis, 2013).

Approaches to research have changed, necessitating changes to how we evaluate the ethical conduct of research. So, too, has thinking about ethics changed as qualitative scholars have grappled with ethical dilemmas in their work. Research ethics are not just a prescriptive regulatory checklist of steps for researchers to take. Rather, ethics are interwoven with research purposes, acts, relationships, and intended outcomes. Ethical inquiry encompasses social values and relationships enacted within community, an ethic of care that does not begin and end at the boundary of the study (Christians, 2011). Cannella and Lincoln (2011) describe ethics as "particularized, infused throughout inquiry, and requiring a continued moral dialogue" (p. 81). Through emotional engagement, a researcher is able "to perceive, judge, and act with a moral attitude . . . thus, moral sensitivity is the basis for moral judgment and action—how we care for the other" (McIntosh & Morse, 2009, p. 100). Research ethics are layered, iterative, and formative, and ethical inquiry is accomplished through the reflexive deliberations of the researchers themselves.

Autoethnography as Ethical Inquiry

When it emerged in its historical moment, autoethnography provided an alternative to research approaches that presumed to represent others (Coffey, 2002); that were racist, appropriative, and exploitive (Lincoln & Denzin, 2005); and that failed to care for and maintain relational ties (Ellis, 2007b). AE is a scholarly approach that emerged in response to ethical, epistemological, and methodological problems within modernist social science research (Holman Jones, Adams, & Ellis, 2013), and holds ethics as central to its practices. For these reasons, I see autoethnography as *fundamentally* ethical in intent.

As an autoethnographer is both subject and researcher, AE reflexively positions the researcher within the study. Reflexive researchers embrace the idea that their account is a partial perspective as seen through their own point of view at a particular place and point in time. Only the teller can speak that particular tale. Researchers turn the lens on themselves rather than on others, thereby avoiding representing, speaking for, or appropriating the voices of others. Autoethnography addresses the ethics of researchers hiding their voices behind a false objectivity, and prevents a power differential between vulnerable participants and an invisible researcher who controls the story.

We are living within the era of the personal story. AE draws on the centrality of narrative in human moral decisions and behavior. Autoethnographers have provided a methodological approach for the scholarly study of personal narratives, means of interpreting the stories within a cultural context, and strategies for deriving insights about culture via the particularities of stories.

By telling their individual stories and theorizing them, researchers democratize research, critique racist and hetero–gender–normative discourses, and disrupt the power politics of corporate interests. A focus on the particular, on valuing each individual story and experience, counters the colonial enterprise of constructing a master narrative. Denzin (2003) tells us that, together, our collection of personal stories presents an alternative to the dominant discourse and a way forward. Writing and performing one's autoethnographic story is a courageous moral act that says: I am singular and unique; I am telling this story so that you can bear witness; each of us is worthy of notice and precious (Lapadat, 2017).

Based on experiences as recounted in personal narratives, autoethnographic method is relational and evocative (Ellis, 2007b). Stories, with their literary qualities, invite readers or listeners to think critically (Richardson, 2000; Richardson & St. Pierre, 2005). People's stories of their own life experiences, told openly and ripe with emotion, engage their audience, thus opening the possibility of human connection. Autoethnographic telling and witnessing fosters trust and solidarity. When we witness, we feel an injustice emotionally as well as understanding it intellectually. We are more likely to connect with the person telling about their experience and come together to work to make a difference.

Autoethnographic inquiry contributes firsthand data, perspectives, and interpretations not available through research framed within previous research paradigms. AE accounts are based on rich data about the self, contextualized in the culture, and history, and experiential lifeworld of the autoethnographer that cannot be accessed otherwise. Many autoethnographers have leaned toward telling about their personal traumas, critical moments, insights, and turning points, thus collectively creating a powerful and evocative literature on human resilience and the personal consequences of many forms of social injustice.

The literary quality of autoethnographic storytelling makes autoethnographic accounts more accessible and interesting to read than technical research reports (Richardson, 2000; Richardson & St. Pierre, 2005). By telling personal narratives situated in the particular, including emotional aspects, and attending to aesthetic qualities of writing and performance, autoethnographers open their research to a wider audience. Scholars are able to share their work outside of their narrow academic sphere.

By expanding concepts of social justice, identifying violations of it, critiquing taken-for-granted norms, and describing actions that support ethical social change, autoethnographers strive to make the world a better place. For all of these reasons, I contend that autoethnography is an ethical approach to inquiry.

Ethical Challenges Facing Autoethnographers

Despite its ethical underpinnings, autoethnography as a research approach faces multiple ethical challenges (Tullis, 2013). Some of the ethical complexities arise from methodological aspects of autoethnography; some from the epistemological stance and positioning of autoethnographic inquiry within an increasingly corporatized and bureaucratic research enterprise; and some are due to the ever-evolving, inventive, and boundary-pushing nature of this blurred genre that resists constraints. Ethical issues derive from the challenges of negotiating relational ethics when publicly performing or publishing personal narratives, from the vulnerable position into which AE places the researcher and relational others, and from a poor match between autoethnographic method and the bureaucratic framework and value-free ethics that typify IRB/REB reviews.

With respect to relational ethics, it is clear that we live in communities connected to family members, friends, colleagues, and others with whom we interact in our daily lives. Autoethnographic stories of our experiences are not wholly our own as they also tell about relational others in our lives. Couser (2004) asks: "Is our freedom to narrate our own lives restricted by the rights of others to privacy? Does the right to commodify one's own life and self entail the right to commodify others' " (p. 7)?

We have ethical obligations to those about whom we write (Couser, 2004; Ellis, 2007b). Yet, because autoethnographers use their own name and acknowledge that they are performing or writing about their own experiences, it is difficult to protect the identities of others who are mentioned in a personal narrative. As a result of this lack of anonymity of the author, an autoethnographic text points directly at the identities of others, especially those family members, colleagues, and community members who play an intimate role in the autoethnographer's life. Even with pseudonyms for names and places, intimate others can be easy to identify, and they certainly can recognize themselves in a written account (Ellis, 2007a, 2009b).

Carolyn Ellis (2004, 2007a, b, 2009a, b; Ellis & Rawicki, 2013) has written extensively on relational ethics in autoethnography. Whereas Tullis (2013) advocates obtaining consent from implicated others "as early in the process as possible" (p. 249) before writing about them, Ellis (2007b) points out that this is not always possible. Often autoethnographies explore difficult life events or turning points. One might not be able to approach individuals for consent in the case of a sexual assault or a teen pregnancy, for example. Sometimes a significant other in the story has died, or does not have the capacity to provide consent (Ellis, 2007b). Ellis says that the ethical complexities will be unique to each particular case as it unfolds over time, and that there is no one simple rule about how to proceed ethically.

Ellis (2009b) proposes that a way to approach ethical quandaries is to openly and repeatedly re-examine and make ethical decisions within each situational context. This ethical strategy, however, is complicated by autoethnographers' personal needs. They must wrestle with competing desires to present an authentic autoethnographic account, protect the wellbeing of others, maintain their ongoing relationships with those about whom they write, meet the publishing requirements of academe, and not stigmatize themselves.

In an autoethnography, things that by social convention normally are kept private are publicly exposed, which can make researchers and related others vulnerable. Muncey (2010) wrote about her own experience with teen pregnancy, presenting a counternarrative to commonly held assumptions about the loose sexual behaviors of teen mothers. As we now know, many teen pregnancies are the result of sexual assault, including incest. Rambo Ronai (1995, 1997) wrote about the abuse she experienced as a child living with her mentally handicapped mother and a father who was a violent sexual predator. Stories such as these shocked complacent academics and social services professionals, but also opened the door to real change. But however courageous the authors are, telling their personal accounts without the protection of anonymity can result in personal and career repercussions that last decades. Considering the possibility of such outcomes and finding ways to mitigate them is an ethical challenge.

What can be said or not said in an autoethnographic narrative must be interrogated for possible future consequences, not only ethical implications in the present. But most ethics committees provide little guidance for ethics in practice or future implications (Tolich, 2016). Knowing the future is an impossible task. Yet the very essence of written text is that it freezes a moment in time. An autoethnographer's point of view and understanding will change over time, but the text persists, static and decontextualized, and tends to be read as an authoritative account. In having the courage to make the private visible, autoethnographers embrace personal vulnerability but cannot know how it will play out as the written material takes on a life of its own.

The greater accessibility of AE leads to unexpected audiences, and therefore potentially creates greater vulnerability for the authors and their relational others. Whereas scholars in the past could be fairly confident that few outside of their academic field would read their highly specialized research reports, AE invites an audience. Literary, engaging, evocative, and providing a firsthand perspective on universal human dilemmas, autoethnographic stories might be read by any-one: your mother, your neighbor, your department chair, the media. Lack of anonymity for the author and the people they write about, the inconsistent inability to obtain consent, the impossibility of anticipating personal and relational consequences over the long term, the risks entailed in making a researcher the sole arbiter of research ethics, and the unpredictably widening audience all present ethical challenges for autoethnographers as they plan, write, interpret, and share their personal narratives.

A number of criticisms have been leveled at autoethnography for reasons of its methodology. Autoethnography, due to its focus on the self, has been criticized as lacking rigor and scope. For example, Charmaz (2006) has suggested that autoethnography lacks means of auditing the data construction or checking the validity of the self-analysis. Because accuracy is expected of researchers (Christians, 2011), one-sided, partial, and emotional autoethnographies might be dismissed as not research, or judged unethical. AE also has been criticized as narcissistic, and for its narrow focus on the lives of academics (Atkinson, 2006). Some decry autoethnographies for exhibiting self-indulgence and sensationalism (Delamont, 2009).[3]

Such methodological concerns have an ethical element. Particularity focused on the self can be seen as constraining the scope of scholarship, leading to questions about whether autoethnographers have anything to say about the wider world. In contrast to ethnographic research, which is broad in scope,[4] AE narrows the potential subjects of study to university-trained researchers and their students in training, who are studying themselves (Lapadat, 2017). Delamont (2009) asks whether autoethnographers have reneged on their responsibility as researchers to use their privileged positions in universities and their research knowledge and training to make a real and positive difference in the world.

When scholars from other paradigms express such criticisms, autoethnographers might dismiss them as revealing a lack of understanding about the nature of autoethnographic inquiry, yet the arguments bear honest examination (Ellis, 2009a). If ethics are central to the purposes and processes of autoethnography, and the goal of autoethnography is to elicit ethical action from the self and others (Denzin, 2014), then we must look to the outcomes of our inquiry to see whether it makes it makes a difference in the world beyond the self.

A final consideration relates to the recent turn in AE toward an ultra-interpretivist stance. Although perhaps controversial, I believe that qualitative inquiry overall has the capacity to embrace a range of approaches and theoretical positions from interpretivism to realism, and in autoethnography, the "spectrum from 'evocative' to 'analytic'" (Anderson & Glass-Coffin, 2013, p. 64).[5] I worry about a turn toward conceptual approaches that are theoretically obscure, and narratives fragmented to the point of incoherence. Whereas autoethnographic writing and performance have opened scholarly inquiry to a wider audience, I believe that this recent extreme interpretivist turn reduces its accessibility. This direction looks inward, not outward, to the wider problems in the world. Such obscurity builds walls to keep others out rather than inviting shared understanding and action. If this is the case, AE is moving away from its ethical core and its potential to make a meaningful difference against oppression and in addressing global issues.

In the next section, I discuss how we might envisage a future moment by drawing upon insights gained from autoethnography: its ethical practices, its commitment to stories, and its methodological advantages, along with its methodological and ethical challenges. Ethics is not only a set of guidelines about what researchers must avoid doing; it is also about what our research positively contributes to the world. Collaborative autoethnography is an approach to inquiry that builds on AE, and I suggest that because of its focus on collective agency, CAE might help bridge us to a workable praxis of social justice.

Collaborative Autoethnography as an Approach to Inquiry

Up to this point, I have discussed autoethnography as a solo practice. I have used the term in the sense of a lone autoethnographer remembering, reflecting upon, interpreting, and writing or performing personal narratives. Yet, just as autoethnography grew out of and concurrently along with the practice of self-reflexivity in participant ethnographies, collaborative autoethnography is an approach to autoethnography involving multiple researchers that emerged concurrently with the solo approach.

Chang et al. (2013) define collaborative autoethnography as an auto-ethnographic research method that combines the autobiographic study of self with ethnographic analysis of the sociocultural milieu within which the researchers are situated, and in which two or more collaborating researchers interact dialogically to analyze and interpret the collection of autobiographic data. Although the label *collaborative autoethnography* is beginning to be used more commonly, in fact a range of multi-voiced collaborative approaches for the study of personal narratives now exist, each with specific theoretical and method-ological elements. These approaches include: autoethnographic conversations, duo-ethnography, co-constructed ethnographies, co-constructed narratives, collaborative autobiography, collaborative writing, collective biography, com-munity autoethnography, ethnographic memoirs, indigenous ethnography, interactive interviews, layered accounts, memory work, performance CAE, and polyvocal texts (Chang et al., 2013; Ellis, Adams, & Bochner, 2011; Lapadat, 2017). I use *collaborative autoethnography* as an umbrella term to refer to the full range of multivocal autoethnographic research approaches.

While offering similar research advantages as autoethnography through direct access to rich, first person stories of experience and because participants have control over how their stories and voice are portrayed, CAE studies address some of the methodological challenges that face AE. Collaborative autoethnography lends itself to greater rigor than AE. In CAE, multiple researchers contribute to data generation, analysis, and writing or performance (Chang et al., 2013). By telling thematically related stories and juxtaposing them, a rich dataset is created. The different disciplinary and experiential perspectives that the team of researchers brings to bear on the research deepen the analytical components.

Using a team approach addresses a weakness of autobiographic data that entails from the researcher being too close to the experience to see it in a holistic or nuanced way, metaphorically the blind spot in the center of the eye (Lapadat et al., 2010). Autobiographic memories do not merely represent facts as they happened, but are constructed by the narrators to tell a coherent story of their lives—a story in which the subject figures as the hero, or victim, or in some other archetypal role. Having a team process for examining or interrogating personal narratives rather than taking them at face value yields a more critical approach to interpretation.

A collaborative team approach is well suited to community-based research. Working with community collaborators broadens the scope of the research beyond the university and the lives of academics (Ellis & Rawicki, 2013). In this way, collaborative autoethnography addresses the concern that autoethnographers have turned away from conducting research responsive to a broad range of social issues, social groups, and subcultures. In this Internet era of proliferating stories of the self, autoethnographers can offer a scholarly approach to interpreting personal narratives within a social, historical, and political context. As researchers share their scholarly expertise and include a range of invested people in studies to define the research focus and add to analytic understandings, CAE is more likely to lead to pragmatic applications and interventions.

Establishing trust among members of the team, along with clear mutual expectations, is necessary for team relationships to gel and for the research to progress effectively. Once team members are confident that they have created a safe place to share their personal stories and meet their intellectual and community goals, collaborative autoethnography becomes a powerful method of team building. It enhances trusting relationships among co-researchers, provides for deep listening or witnessing, promotes creativity and intellectual growth, and offers collegial feedback and mentorship (Chang et al., 2013). These characteristics of CAE also make it an effective method for teaching qualitative research methods (Lapadat, 2009).

Much autoethnographic work has tended to focus on traumas and turning points—those personal and social experiences that have led a person to be marginalized or to feel powerless. Speaking our truths is a starting point for action. However, too often autoethnographers do not venture beyond telling their story in its context to the subsequent steps of bringing people together to work to make a difference in policy and practice. As autoethnographers, we risk trapping ourselves in the margins that we write about so eloquently.

Collaborative autoethnography expands the gaze from the traumas of the self to locate them within categories of experience shared by many. Shared experiences reveal systematic oppression and cultural scripts, which can be better understood through multiple lenses on the individual and shared aspects of those experiences. For all of these reasons, collaborative autoethnography promotes collaborative social action.

The Ethical Advantages of Collaborative Autoethnography

Collaborative autoethnography incorporates AE's ethical praxis while offering some advantages over other qualitative approaches and over solo autoethnography. It seems clear that working together as a team of autoethnographers has ethical advantages over hierarchical ethnographic approaches where individual researchers study the "other." In CAE, everybody involved is a co-researcher, and they all have an equitable voice in the design, research process, and authorship. The method flattens power dynamics because all of the co-researchers contribute their personal stories to the group, and so all of them are equally exposed and vulnerable. All of them choose what to share and how their stories will be portrayed, and all receive credit for the work. Rather than potentially exploiting or misrepresenting the stories of others or constructing an outsider's perspective on a culture or social group, CAE colleagues analyze their own personal experiences. Doing research *with* others rather than research *on* others sidesteps a number of ethical pitfalls.

For these reasons, collaborative autoethnography is not troubled by many of the ethical issues of other approaches to ethnography. But why do I say that collaborative autoethnography offers ethical advantages over solo approaches to autoethnography?

One important reason is that collaborative autoethnography offers more anonymity for researchers. When collaborative autoethnographers publish excerpts from their collection of personal narratives as a group of coauthors, they can use pseudonyms and it will not be obvious to most readers which story elements are connected to which authors. Using pseudonyms for personal and place names can be augmented with other confidentiality strategies such as the use of composite characters, montage, alternative writing genres, fictionalized elements, and omission of unique identifiers (Lapadat et al., 2009). The greater degree of anonymity significantly reduces the level of vulnerability that researchers will be placed in through publicly sharing their private experiences.

Protecting the anonymity of individual coauthors also protects the identities of the relational others who appear in the narratives. The need for considering relational ethics that Ellis (2007a, b, 2009b) has documented so well does not disappear, but the consequences of including relational others in a narrative will be less ethically fraught and reduce the undesired exposure of friends, family members, and associates. With the assurance of a greater degree of anonymity when working in a collaborative team, some autoethnographers might be willing to share personal accounts that they hitherto have kept to themselves in order to protect their own or relational others' privacy, or the identity of their workplace. Such additions will extend and enrich the autoethnographic pool of stories created to date by brave trailblazers who have been less circumspect about revealing all.

Collaborative autoethnography is methodologically more rigorous than AE because it adds a multidisciplinary lens to inquiry, thereby providing a means to interrogate the autobiographic construction of a remembered experience, and also reducing the risk of narcissism or self-indulgence. Although I do not believe that it is possible to attain research accuracy in the realist sense, the checks and balances that team members' insights provide will enhance rigor and trustworthiness.

A team of researchers can provide multiple perspectives to help work through ethical issues such as, for example, the portrayal of significant others. Ethical issues in AE typically are particularized and emergent rather obvious at the outset and as such are outside of the scope of most IRBs/REBs. Researchers must engage in ongoing ethical self-questioning and decision-making. However, autoethnographers are personally invested in their own narrative and motivated by competing needs and desires, so they might find it especially challenging to serve as an axis for reflexive ethical decisions. The team can function as a sounding board and can engage in a moral dialogue, thus mitigating the risk of leaving an individual researcher as sole arbiter of ethical decision-making.

Because of its collaborative nature, CAE provides a structure to support witnessing by building upon autoethnographers' ability to evoke empathy and understanding of another (Ellis & Rawicki, 2013). Opening up and telling one's own story, especially when it is about a traumatic incident or a private personal struggle, can be therapeutic. But the process can be painful and can re-traumatize people as they live through the difficult memories once again. A supportive, trustworthy set of equally vulnerable colleagues can provide invaluable support when the focus of the research is on sensitive or stigmatizing issues. As Chang et al. (2013) point out, the CAE team "offers autoethnographers grappling with such traumatic issues and events an opportunity to enjoy the catharsis of sharing their stories, while at the same time also getting the help they need from the co-researchers" (p. 29), such as knowing when to "put the brakes on" telling certain stories, or when to seek help.

In some academic departments and institutions, there is little awareness of or support for doing autoethnographic work. In such settings, an individual autoethnographer might feel isolated from campus peers or experience stigma. Working on a CAE project with a team that includes members from other departments or institutions provides collegial support, and enhances credibility in the eyes of campus and grant administrators.

Collaborative autoethnography is not without its challenges. Collaborative studies can be logistically difficult to manage, and not all topics lend themselves to CAE. For CAE to be effective and ethical, it is important that participation is fully voluntary, that the focus is mutually agreed upon, and that the sharing context is nonhierarchical and non-coercive. It might not be possible to achieve these conditions with certain pre-existing power dynamics. Just as with AE, researchers must be prepared for iterative ethical decision-making, and attempt to anticipate future consequences.

As an approach, collaborative autoethnography moves beyond description of social issues, witnessing, and personal therapeutic effects to foster joint engagement in social actions. Autoethnographers can use CAE to draw in others from beyond the university, enabling more inclusive research on a less restricted set of individuals, topics, locations, and cultures. Narratives of experiences and problems in the wider community beyond academe enrich the database, and the team processes created in doing the research build relationships within and beyond the university, establishing a means of and stimulus to joint action. Thus, collaborative autoethnography offers the possibility of ethical practical action to address the moral social issues revealed in personal tales.

Conclusion

As qualitative researchers and autoethnographers, we have been motivated to develop aspects of our scholarship in response to research practices that were not ethical. We have resisted and found alternatives to being the invisible authorities, doing research on others, and using our words as instruments of power. Yet despite the ethical core of autoethnography, I believe that many of us still think of research ethics in a way that is too narrow. Influenced by the Enlightenment perspectives that underpin bureaucratic institutional procedures of research ethics, we take those prescriptive, procedural guidelines as our starting point.

I worry that in locating our scholarship primarily within our own personal stories, we have unintentionally wandered into a permanent margin, where we cannot see how to step beyond the self to right the wrongs we tell about. One way forward is to continue to interrogate what we mean by ethics, in the promising directions described by Cannella & Lincoln (2011), Christians (2011), Ellis (2007a, b, 2009a, b), McIntosh & Morse (2009), Tolich (2016), and Tullis (2013). Ethical practice lives within our internal moral reasoning as scholars, our caring and emotional interactions with others, the moment-by-moment decisions we make, and the ways we engage as citizens of the world. In some small way, each of us must be an action researcher, striving for social justice and a better world.

Collaborative approaches to autoethnographic work provide a way to turn our ethical intention toward desired research outcomes. One of the greatest strengths of collaborative autoethnography is that it supports relationship building via shared vulnerability, flattened hierarchies, and the establishment of trust. Collaborators who trust each other begin to see themselves as members of a caring, democratic community, and make the shift from individual to collective agency. When personal experiences are acknowledged, respected, and seen as embedded within workplaces and social structures, people are more likely to work together to change societal practices from the bottom up.

Notes

1. This chapter draws from and extends arguments put forward in Lapadat (2017).
2. Christians (2011) states that research ethics codes were developed to govern biomedical research, as informed by a value-free philosophical stance. Later the scope of Institutional Research Boards was extended from the regulation of laboratory based medical and behavioral research to include interpretive research in naturalistic settings, despite the epistemological and practical incongruence of biomedical ethics with the aims and processes of non-experimental naturalistic research. In the process, ethics committees often stigmatized social science research (Tolich, 2016).
3. Countering the assumption that writing a personal narrative is narcissistic, Melissa Febos (2017) says: "Writing about your personal experiences is not easier than other kinds of writing. . . . The risk of honest self-appraisal requires bravery. To place our flawed selves in the context of this magnificent, broken world is the opposite of narcissism, which is building a self-image that pleases you." Although Febos is talking about writing memoir, I think that her point applies equally to autoethnography.
4. To be sure, ethnographers have been criticized for focusing their research on cultures and social groups that are marginalized, rather than on corporate boardrooms or military leadership, thereby also limiting the breadth of scope of ethnographic studies. Powerful members of society have the capacity to restrict access to researchers, guard against scrutiny, and shape what is said about them, whereas social groups lacking such power are both more accessible for study and more vulnerable to exploitation.
5. I take this more inclusive stance, notwithstanding Denzin's point that in inquiry, "all observation is theory-laden" (2014, p. 71) and understood from the researcher's standpoint, because I believe that defining what counts as autoethnography too narrowly risks exclusivity, or even a kind of research elitism.

References

Adams, T., Holman Jones, S., & Ellis, C. (2013). Conclusion: Where stories take us. In S. Holman Jones, T. E. Adams, & C. Ellis (Eds.), *Handbook of autoethnography* (pp. 669–677). Walnut Creek, CA: Left Coast Press.

Anderson, L. & Glass-Coffin, B. (2013). I learn by going: Autoethnographic modes of inquiry. In S. Holman Jones, T. E. Adams, & C. Ellis (Eds.), *Handbook of autoethnography* (pp. 57–83). Walnut Creek, CA: Left Coast Press.

Atkinson, P. (2006). Rescuing autoethnography. *Journal of Contemporary Ethnography, 35*(4), 400–404.

Cannella, G. S., & Lincoln, Y. S. (2011). Ethics, research regulations, and critical social science. In N. K. Denzin & Y. S. Lincoln (Eds.), *The Sage handbook of qualitative research* (4th ed., pp. 81–89). Thousand Oaks, CA: SAGE.

Chang, H., Ngunjiri, F. W., & Hernandez, K. C. (2013). *Collaborative autoethnography*. Walnut Creek, CA: Left Coast Press.

Charmaz, K. (2006). The power of names. *Journal of Contemporary Ethnography, 35*(4), 396–399.

Christians, C. G. (2011). Ethics and politics in qualitative research. In N. K. Denzin & Y. S. Lincoln (Eds.), *The SAGE handbook of qualitative research* (4th ed., pp. 61–80). Thousand Oaks, CA: SAGE.

Coffey, A. (2002). Ethnography and self: Reflections and representations. In T. May (Ed.), *Qualitative research in action* (pp. 313–331). Thousand Oaks, CA: SAGE.

Couser, G. T. (2004). *Vulnerable subjects: Ethics and life writing.* Ithaca, NY: Cornell University Press.

Delamont, S. (2009). The only honest thing: Autoethnography, reflexivity and small crises in fieldwork. *Ethnography and Education, 4*(1), 51–63.

Denshire, S. (2014). On auto-ethnography. *Current Sociology Review, 62*(6), 831–850.

Denzin, N. K. (2003). Performing [auto] ethnography politically. *Review of Education, Pedagogy, and Cultural Studies, 25*(3), 257–278.

Denzin, N. K. (2014). *Interpretive autoethnography* (2nd ed.). Thousand Oaks, CA: SAGE.

Ellis, C. (2004). *The ethnographic I: A methodological novel about autoethnography.* Walnut Creek, CA: Altamira.

Ellis, C. (2007a). "I just want to tell my story": Mentoring students about relational ethics in writing about intimate others. In N. K. Denzin & M. D. Giardina (Eds.), *Ethical futures in qualitative research: Decolonizing the politics of knowledge* (pp. 209–227). Walnut Creek, CA: Left Coast Press.

Ellis, C. (2007b). Telling secrets, revealing lives: Relational ethics in research with intimate others. *Qualitative Inquiry, 13*(1), 3–29.

Ellis, C. (2009a). Fighting back or moving on: An autoethnographic response to critics. *International Review of Qualitative Research, 2,* 371–378. Retrieved from www.jstor.org/stable/10.1525/irqr.2009.2.3.371

Ellis, C. (2009b). Telling tales on neighbors: Ethics in two voices. *International Review of Qualitative Research, 2*(1), 3–27. Retrieved from www.jstor.org/stable/10.1525/irqr.2009.2.1.3

Ellis, C., Adams, T. E., & Bochner, A. P. (2011). Autoethnography: An overview. *Forum Qualitative Sozialforschung/Forum: Qualitative Social Research, 12*(1), Article 10. Retrieved from http://nbn-resolving.de/urn:nbn:de:0114-fqs1101108

Ellis, C. & Rawicki, J. (2013). Collaborative witnessing of survival during the holocaust: An exemplar of relational autoethnography. *Qualitative Inquiry, 19*(5), 366–380.

Febos, M. (2017) The heart-work: Writing about trauma as a subversive act. *Poets & Writers,* January/February 2017, Special Section. Retrieved from www.pw.org/content/the_heartwork_writing_about_trauma_as_a_subversive_act

Holman Jones, S., Adams, T., & Ellis, C. (2013). Introduction: Coming to know autoethnography as more than a method. In S. Holman Jones, T. E. Adams, & C. Ellis (Eds.), *Handbook of autoethnography* (pp. 17–47). Walnut Creek, CA: Left Coast Press.

Lapadat, J. C. (2009). Writing our way into shared understanding: Collaborative autobiographical writing in the qualitative methods class. *Qualitative Inquiry, 15*(6), 955–979.

Lapadat, J. C. (2017). Ethics in autoethnography and collaborative Autoethnography. *Qualitative Inquiry,* April 26, 2017. doi: 10.1177/1077800417704462

Lapadat, J. C., Black, N. E., Clark, P. G., Gremm, R. M., Karanja, L. W., Mieke, M., & Quinlan, L. (2010). Life challenge memory work: Using collaborative autobiography to understand ourselves. *International Journal of Qualitative Methods, 9*(1), 77–104. Retrieved from http://ejournals.library.ualberta.ca/index.php/IJQM/article/view/1542

Lapadat, J. C., Bryant, L., Burrows, M., Greenlees, S., Hill, A. S., Alexander, J., . . . Sousa, C. (2009). An identity montage using collaborative autobiography: Eighteen ways to bend the light. *International Review of Qualitative Research, 1*, 515–539. Retrieved from www.jstor.org.ezproxy.alu.talonline.ca/stable/10.1525/irqr.2009.1.4.515

Lincoln, Y. S. & Denzin, N. K. (2005). Epilogue: The eighth and ninth moments— qualitative research in/and the fractured future. In N. K. Denzin & Y. S. Lincoln (Eds.), *The SAGE handbook of qualitative research* (3rd ed., pp. 1115–1126). Thousand Oaks, CA: SAGE.

McIntosh, M. J. & Morse, J. M. (2009). Institutional Review Boards and the ethics of emotion. In N. K. Denzin & M. D. Giardina (Eds.), *Qualitative inquiry and social justice* (pp. 81–107). Walnut Creek, CA: Left Coast Press.

Muncey, T. (2010). *Creating autoethnographies.* Thousand Oaks, CA: SAGE.

Rambo Ronai, C. (1995). Multiple reflections of child sex abuse: An argument for a layered account. *Journal of Contemporary Ethnography, 23*(4), 395–426.

Rambo Ronai, C. (1997). On loving and hating my mentally retarded mother. *Mental Retardation, 35*(6), 417–423.

Richardson, L. (2000). Writing: A method of inquiry. In N. K. Denzin & Y. S. Lincoln (Eds.), *The SAGE handbook of qualitative research* (2nd ed., pp. 923–948). Thousand Oaks, CA: SAGE.

Richardson, L. & St. Pierre, E. A. (2005). Writing: A method of inquiry. In N. K. Denzin & Y. S. Lincoln (Eds.), *The SAGE handbook of qualitative research* (3rd ed., pp. 959–978). Thousand Oaks, CA: SAGE.

Tolich, M. (2016). A narrative account of ethics committees and their codes. *New Zealand Sociology, 31*(4), 43–55.

Tullis, J. A. (2013). Self and others: Ethics in autoethnographic research. In S. Holman Jones, T. E. Adams, & C. Ellis (Eds.), *Handbook of autoethnography* (pp. 244–261). Walnut Creek, CA: Left Coast Press.

12

WRITING TO IT

Creative Engagements with Writing Practice in and with the Not Yet Known in Today's Academy[1]

Jonathan Wyatt and Ken Gale

We have developed an approach to collaborative-writing-as-inquiry that we sometimes refer to as 'between the twos' (e.g., Gale & Wyatt, 2009). We have, over the years, sensed they/we were part of the multiplicity of an incessant becoming, becoming something other than what we/they were. In this we sense the emergence of powers to affect and be affected in our collaborative writing practices and to begin to animate a response to Spinoza's fundamental inquiry into what bodies can do.

In working with a 'logic of sense' (Deleuze, 2004), we are working continually to bring concepts to life in event and to transversally give them creative life through extending Richardson's (Richardson & St. Pierre, 2005) practice of writing as method of inquiry through the use of collaborative modalities of practice. Increasingly, we are coming to understand that the only way to continue in this sense-making and affecting is to 'write to it'. Issues, queries, and question arise—in our lives and in our writing—and we say to the other, "let's write to it." Whatever the query or the problem, it is this inducement—'write to it'— that leads to new experimentations and the sensing of the indeterminate rhythms and refrains of the multiple that activates our practice. In this, through making what Barad refers to as "agential cuts" (2007, p. 175) we work intra-actively with productive desiring within and against the traditional representations of research and pedagogic practice in universities.

We are with Massumi when he says "(t)o affect and be affected is to be open to the world, to be active in it and to be patient for its return activity" (2015, p. ix) and so our work offers challenge to the controlling performatives of practice that characterize much of what happens in present day institutions of higher education. We take the view that within the practice of 'writing to it' we are transversally engaging and actively producing, through the animation of a philosophy of the event, what Deleuze and Guattari refer to as 'minor literatures' (Deleuze & Guattari, 1986):

> the notion of linguistic action, whereby we write to and as experiment, where we take on the dominating forces of the 'major literature' that works to produce the canon and the normative force of the privileged practice style and where the living, embodied, performative action of our words and sentences challenges and takes on the coercive and colonising effects of the regulating logic, the traditional grammar and stylistic preferences of the dominant majoritarian form.
>
> (Guttorm et al., 2012, p. 395)

In offering opportunities for bringing non-totalizing modes of sensing to life within Deleuze and Guattari's experimental and creative originations, and in the multiplicity and the vibrant potentialities of always becoming, we make claims for innovative, creatively productive writing practices that might bring new life to research, inquiry and pedagogic practice in the university of the future (see also Sellers & Gough, 2010).

With the intention to bring such claims to life, to animate them rather then only write *about* them, the paper borrows from Wyatt et al. (2010) and Gough & Gough (2016) in taking dialogic play script form: exchanges between the two of us, often written as we travel, the movement an inducement, a prompt; and exchanges between ourselves and those with, to and from whose work we speak. Between us all we see where writing takes us.

Immanent Imperative

J: Writing to it. Present participle, followed by preposition, succeeded by impersonal pronoun. Writing. To. It.

'Writing to it': as if writing had *direction*. As if it were purposeful. Intentional. Instrumental. A goal in mind.

Like a harsh teacher bellowing instructions to cowed children: "Enough messing about. You heard what I said—now put down the guinea pig, get out your pens and start *writing to it*. You horrible lot".

That's how teachers in my school spoke to us. Though I'm not sure what the guinea pig is doing there.

Or like the words of a sergeant-major on the parade ground: "Right! Left! Right! Left! Writing to it!" More of an imaginative stretch, but it possesses a sense of writing as commanded and required.

(I'm on a train north from Manchester on a crowded Friday afternoon. The seats are narrow and privacy is difficult to maintain. I'm at a table, typing. The young woman next to me, whom I haven't yet spoken to, after 90 minutes, has taken a break from her phone to look around. She seems to be looking towards my screen. I can see that her head is turned this way, but I don't want to turn and check. That would seem too wary and I wouldn't want to put her on the defensive. She's reading this text now, I sense. If she is, I want to ask her what she's making of this, whether she'd like me to give her some background. Maybe I could give her a paper to read on this too-slow journey from Carlisle to Lockerbie. 'Here, take a look at Gale and Wyatt, 2013, on assemblage/ethnography. It'll give you the idea.' I suspect she would refuse the offer.

And now I'm thinking if she *is* reading then she will realize that I'm writing about her. Now. Which will seem weird. Creepy, even. Perhaps I should stop.)

The instrumental, line-of-command connotations of 'writing to it' that I've suggested, with their arguable associations with traditional academic writing's commitment to 'transparency' and 'communication', are of course not at all the sense that we intend to convey, nor is it the way that over the years we have used it. In fact, I'm tempted to say it is the opposite of that and anathema to us. When *we* use the phrase 'write to it' we mean exploratory, inquiring, open, hesitant, writing. Writing as flow.' Writing to it' is, as Karen Lee writes:

K: "a gesture of longing" (Lee, 2005, p. 935).

J: Writing that takes us over, writing that becomes.

However, I hesitate in my recoiling. It always pays to be suspicious of binaries. There may be something in the bullying teacher and the barking sergeant-major. Something in their instructions. Something, despite their abhorrence, in the commands issued by those creations that might be offering us something here, something we might find ourselves taking up in this paper. If so it is perhaps this: the sense of compulsion in 'writing to it'. Not an imposed, authoritarian, punitive compulsion, but a compulsion we have found arising in us. A way of coming to understand writing not as something we 'do' but as something that 'does' us. A practice we have *found ourselves* doing. An immanent imperative. Which does not mean that it happens without effort nor that it is unproblematic. It does not happen by magic. Or not by magic alone, anyway.

Writing takes it out of us; and takes us out of ourselves; and out of it. We get out of it by writing. We have to.

Recoiling

K: Yes, I feel something in your recoil. I have never fired a gun but I have a sense of how it might feel when the trigger is pulled and the butt of the rifle thumps into your shoulder hollow forcing you to step back. The suspicion of binaries that you refer to works something like that: we have grown up with them, their discursive effect is insidious, we have grown to be reflexive and wisely warn against them and still we receive an impact, a jolt, when we find ourselves using them again.

So I like the sense in which you carefully step back in your writing to allow space for the imbrication of the different conceptualizations of 'writing to it' to be possible. It is that space, as a territorialization, that opens up for me; it is the little plot of land that offers immediate spatio-temporal emergence. In one sense this resonates with the facilitative pedagogical practice of 'intervention' (see Heron, 2001) in which different practice styles are used to facilitate the pedagogically inclined process. Within the humanistic proclivities of such practices, where interactive strategies—*qua* intentional, directed action between the ontologically separate, the one who does and the other who is done to—are employed to achieve certain learning goals or therapeutic ends, sense is made whereby a 'prescriptive' intervention, say, is categorized as being qualitatively different from a 'cathartic' intervention or a 'catalytic' one. According to such principles, the facilitator or the therapist will act differently as a means of bringing about change in the student or the client. As you seem to suggest in your imbrication of these different possible approaches to 'prescription,' in what you describe as an 'immanent imperative,' where 'writing to it' is not something that we simply do and something that also 'does' us, it is the conceptualization of the term in multiplicity that undoes the dualistic form of thinking that locates it in binary or classificatory forms.

It seems that the interiority that is implicit in your challenge to what I see as the 'hylomorphic' tendencies that manifest in the more obviously prescriptive form of 'writing to it' also opens us up to enactments of affect. Simondon points out and Deleuze and Guattari (1987, p. 268) apply the concept of hylomorphism to describe ways in which external systems are applied to conditions of supposed chaos and/or passivity; it sets in place the attack on the body-without-organs. There is a politics involved in the organizational proclivities of hylomorphism which acts, through processes of territorialization, to impose certain procedures and practices which attempt to control what might be seen as the *dis*organization of the body-without-organs. We can ask, what does this mean for writing to it? Richardson describes how she developed the practice of writing as a method of inquiry as a resistance to what she refers to as "those writing instructions . . . that . . . cohered with mechanistic scientism and quantitative research." She argues that those writing instructions were themselves a "sociohistorical invention of our 19th-century foreparents" and that

> they undercut writing as a dynamic creative process, they undermined the confidence beginning qualitative researchers because their experience of research was inconsistent with the writing model, and they contributed to the flotilla of qualitative writing that was simply not interesting to read because writers wrote in the homogenized voice of 'science'.
> (Richardson & St. Pierre, 2005, p. 960)

Deleuze and Guattari see hylomorphic tendencies of this kind as being agentic in the way that they ac upon and within organizational assemblages to limit experimentation and to promote representation and identification. Therefore, writing to it can be used as a challenge to the use of such codes, tropes and linguistic conventions and the regimes of signification and representation that embody and perpetuate them.

Bennett's (2010) notion of 'agentic assemblages' also evokes the impositional affective productions of hylomorphism that activate limitations upon the body-without-organs. In this respect and echoing Spinoza, Massumi points out that "One always affects and is affected in encounters; which is to say, through events" (2015, p. ix). Therefore, I would argue, it makes qualitatively better sense to think of these hylomorphic affects, à la Barad, and to use the neologism 'intra-vention' as a means of troubling the phenomenological and humanistically inclined proclivities of the signifier 'intervention.' The inference of Barad's use of 'intra-action' here is obvious. In talking about the means by which we can move to understand agency as being distributed through and across human and non human participants, Barad argues that:

J: "Crucially, *agency is a matter of intra-acting; it is an enactment, not something that someone or something has.* It cannot be designated as an attribute of subjects or objects (as they do not preexist as such). It is not an attribute whatsoever. *Agency is 'doing' or 'being' in its intra-activity. It is the enactment of iterative changes to particular practices . . . through the dynamics of intra-activity*" (2007, p. 178, italics in the original).

K: By engaging with Whitehead's use of process to trouble pre-eminent concerns with substance I sense that we find ourselves engaging with the practice of 'writing to it' in affect. The rhythmic transversalities that are at the processual heart of working with Spinoza's view of affect as the capacity of all bodies to affect and be affected suggests an openness and active engagement in, to and with the world. Massumi argues that this process "is the cutting edge of change. It is through it that things-in-the-making cut their transformational teeth" (2015, p. ix).

J: A way of coming to understand writing not as something we 'do' but as something that 'does' us. A practice we have found ourselves doing. An immanent imperative. . . . Writing takes it out of us; and takes us out of ourselves; and out of it. We get out of it by writing. We have to.

K: You refer to writing that takes us over and, in affect, I want to talk about writing taking over. This seems to be the 'immanent imperative', the practice we have found ourselves doing. It is at this point that I sense writing in terms of becoming. Perhaps more than any other methodological phrase that we have uttered and practised is Laurel Richardson's insistence that 'writing is a method of inquiry' (Richardson & St. Pierre, 2005). In ontological terms I sense that we are doing different things with this now than what Laurel intended when she first employed a rhetorical logic to propose this methodology all those years ago, and that's OK. The 'immanent imperative' to which you refer embraces human and non human potentialities; its agentic force is to be found in a coming to terms with the intricate knots and entanglements of materiality and discourse and, therefore, it seems to me that in these movements away from interpretation and representation 'writing to it' animates a becoming that is, in constantly processual ways, essential in its affective world making.

You know that in our writing I have found it exciting and ultimately hugely necessary to engage with the creative nature of Deleuzian philosophical inquiry which is brought to life in the following quotation:

J: "Concepts are not waiting for us ready-made, like heavenly bodies. There is no heaven for concepts. They must be invented, fabricated, or rather, created, and would be nothing without the creator's signature" (Deleuze and Guattari, 1994. p. 5).

K: What is so apposite about this statement in relation to our advocacy of the practice of 'writing to it' is that in living with and through affect this processual practice helps to bring concepts to life. 'Writing to it' is not only part of the creation of concepts it is also about doing something with them, making them work. Deleuze and Guattari propose:

J: 'When one writes, the only question is which other machine the literary machine can be plugged into, must be plugged into in order to work' (Deleuze and Guattari, 1987, p. 4).

K: This is not an easy or straightforward process; as Mazzei and Jackson describe in terms of their own collaborative writing processes,

J: "[W]e had a sense of the ceaseless variations possible in having co-authored texts that relied on a plugging in of ideas, fragments, theory, selves, sensations . . . Plugging in to make something new is a constant, continuous process of making and unmaking . . . it is the process of arranging, organising, fitting together" (2012, p. 1).

K: I would suggest that the way in which they describe the process of writing as a form of 'plugging in' also through the practice of 'writing to it' involves an active territorialisation of time and space. So, for example, in engaging with what they refer to as 'minor literatures' Deleuze and Guattari (1986) also talk about 'stuttering' in the language, not to make reference to some form of impediment of speech or pronunciation, rather to describe, as I've written elsewhere:

J: "a way of speaking and writing in the language that is always emergent, hesitant, and taking new forms . . . offering a 'minor literature' to de-centre and deterritorialize the dominance of 'major literatures' through strategies of experimentation, mistrust of traditional idioms and forms and of nurturing collective action" (Gale, 2015, p. 4).

K: I understand Deleuze and Guattari's use of the concept of 'minor literature' as having something to do with the invocation to 'write to it.' 'Writing to it' is an act; it is about bringing concepts to life, it is about writing within the molar forms of 'major literatures' and the hylomorphic tendencies of dominant and dominating structures and forms to produce difference and in producing difference territorialisation occurs. In such contexts the rhythms that are constitutive of the power to affect and be affected are, as Foucault points out, also infused with institutional forces that work to produce identification with and subjectification to representational modalities of the self. I am with Deleuze when he argues that the smallest unit is the assemblage and so I sense strongly that 'writing to it' will be writing in affective ways that engage with human and non human agency. The molar forms that 'major literatures' produce can be de-territorialised through writing to and with the heterogeneities and contingencies of molecular particularity that live with them. 'Writing to it', in bringing new concepts to life, is agentic; it animates and hence disturbs the distribution of agency and has the potential to bring new vitalities in to play in active processes of world-making.

Clouding

K: Writing to it is an act; it is about bringing concepts to life.

J: We are on the same flight together, you and I, maybe three or four hours into our trip to Illinois for the International Congress of Qualitative Inquiry. Our 12th year. Our 12th such journey. You are a few rows back from me in the middle section. I am at the front of the second-class section. We are both in cattle class, the section of the plane that British Airways euphemises as 'World Traveller.' I'm at the front, where the legroom is more generous, to the right, in the middle seat. (Deleuze would be happy—I'm writing in a middle to you in a middle; and we are in the middle of our flight; and our travel companions are scattered around the plane, so we could say we are in the middle of them or they of us. I'm beginning to write to you in a plethora of middles. Topographic, temporal, geographic.)

I have just re-read your latest writing. It's been in my bag for a couple of weeks since you sent it and I first read it. I am writing to it, unsure—as ever—of where it will take us; not so much a recoiling, because a recoil takes us back whence we came, and away, in a line; and usually in horror. No, not a recoil, more of a spin. In fact, we might want to re-think the phrase 'writing to it' altogether because 'writing to it' hints at direction and goal, and this is what I'm going to work at here.

Do you speak to your neighbours on these flights? I don't. Except when it's you, which we've not managed to arrange this year. I avoid contact at all costs if my neighbours are strangers to me. I like to retreat. I'll pass drinks and empties across, or say excuse me if I need to get past, but I don't want to engage in conversation. I'm not interested in them. After 8 hours of enforced, cramped proximity we will never meet again so I don't feel invested in them at all. I like to see what they're doing though. I like to observe. Ethically, of course. I don't wish to intrude on their privacy, no no.

The man to my left, whom I haven't yet spoken at all to, has started watching the most recent Star Wars film on his tiny black-edged screen. (What a sacrilege it is to watch a film on a screen that size, especially when you have to ram your head back against the seat to gain the distance needed from the screen. And then there's the sound quality. Don't get me started on the sound quality. How you have to turn it down when there's the soundtrack and then up again when characters are speaking.) Anyhow, I've seen this Star Wars film—it's ok, not the best, and I'm not a big fan in general—and I'm glancing over and I see the main character, Rey. She is a scavenger by trade, and we quickly gather she is very competent and experienced despite her youth. When we first meet her, she is plundering whatever booty she can find. She loads it onto her craft, which is some kind of very cool, if scruffy, hover machine—a kind of floating dilapidated motorbike—and—just at the moment of writing this sentence—she is heading back to her home village, if that's what it can be called. She is purposeful. She has direction. She is travelling from wilderness to her home. From, to. She is 'recoiling' herself back home, such as it is.

So I'm not writing 'to' your writing in Rey's sense. I'm not heading from your writing back to somewhere else I know.

K: Writing to it is an act; it is about bringing concepts to life.

J: Of course, what happens next takes Rey on a complicated and dangerous journey a long way from home—on a feisty, incident-packed line of flight—so maybe this Star Wars plot line stands as a better metaphor for 'writing to it' than I'm suggesting.

Maybe, though, we can find a different concept to 'writing to it', one that more readily speaks to how we're thinking of writing not as linear, not as going back and forth from one place to another, but in the sense of the 'immanent imperative' that seeks, as you suggest, to produce difference, engages with human and non human agency, and is agentic in itself. A writing that takes over.

K: Writing to it is an act; it is about bringing concepts to life.

J: I keep needing to repeat this phrase of yours in order to help us in this theorising-in-practice of writing. To help both create and bring concepts to life in the becomings of posthuman education research (Gough & Gough, 2016).

To my other side—I'm in the middle, as I say—my neighbour (a young American woman, is all I know) is asleep. I look out of the window in front of us and see the contours of the wing and a vast, Rolls-Royce engine; through the window just behind I see the level ridges of cloud that themselves must be traveling fast, taking their own lines of flight on and with the wind and weather patterns shaping and moving them.

Which sets me wondering: Maybe we can think of 'writing to it' in terms of the agency of weather. Writing as *clouding*, as a process of gathering and moving and dispersing and travelling, and doing so in response to and "intra-acting" with the winds, currents and forces with/in/into which clouds are embrangled. 'Writing to it' as *clouding* is a way too of suggesting what it does to us as we write: how 'writing to it' does not necessarily clarify but leads us into darkness, into a fog of uncertainty, blurring our senses. It is an 'immanent imperative' that may get us lost, that troubles, that messes up. Clouding as writing take us into what we don't know. In this respect we can think of 'clouding' not as a form of control, as suggested by Sellers and Gough's (2008) practice of 'cloud-sculpting', rather as processes of experimentation, where unforeseen encounters and events might come about.

Clouding as writing may have different powers than we imagine. Like Helen Macdonald's hawk writing might enable us to

K: ". . .see colours [we] cannot, right into the ultraviolet spectrum. [It might] see polarised light, too, watch thermals of warm air rise, roil, and spill into clouds, and trace, too, the magnetic lines of force that stretch across the earth" (2014, p. 98).

J: Clouding suggest a process of writing that holds substance—moisture—but only in passing. No, that's not right: clouding is a writing that does not hold but *becomes* substance, becomes other: making and undoing; making and undoing; and always becoming.

Clouds can give the appearance of uniformity and stability from this height as they stretch into the distance but they are always forming and re-forming. They can appear beautiful and welcoming but we have to be wary. They—like the concepts we play with and create—will not hold all we wish them to. When we are *clouding,* when the writing/clouding takes us over, the ride can be bumpy.

K: Writing to it is an act; it is about bringing concepts to life.

J: . . .even if those concepts don't serve us well or for long. I don't want to make great claims for *clouding,* given my evident meteorological deficiencies. But see where it takes you, takes us.

Meanwhile, I'll stop writing—stop *clouding*—and join one of my neighbours, either in watching something or in closing my eyes. Either way, I'm hoping I'll seem immersed enough for neither of them to try talking to me, though they have seemed as uninterested in me as I am in them.

Clouding (2): Ken's Response

K: I am with you in your flight above the clouds and with you as you consider 'clouding' as part of our creative practice of producing concepts as events. In (y)our flight I am drawn to my seemingly eternally unavoidable return to the Art Institute in Chicago and the pilgrimage I have made now for twelve years to stand in wonder and gaze up at Georgia O' Keefe's epic painting Sky above Clouds, her immense production of infinite skyspace which always takes me on new and different lines of fantasy making and sensing the world differently.

On a canvas that measures an awesome 24 ft by 8 ft and which she painted when she was 77 years old innumerable clouds silently drift into an always receding horizon; the meeting of the clouds and the horizon is indistinct yet luminescent and the title, Sky above Clouds, suggests the possibilities of endlessness. This painting always takes my breath away and leads me to interfere with the ways in which I write; it is as if the clouds are floating off, out, toward and beyond the horizon and I sense a writerly self that wants to engage in the same kinds of journeying. The knowing that infinity is always just around the corner is a huge motivation to start in the middle and write and write again. And so the practice we have called 'writing to it', in multiplicity, energizes those becomings that are always new, encouraging an affective working through the intensities that are always changing and that give us life.

And yes, as I engage with your writing, there is a sense in which recoil can be understood as a reeling back, perhaps, as you suggest, in horror, as something that acts in readiness of another round, a reloading, a retort, a rewinding coiling up process that enables another spring. The annual repetition of engaging with Georgia O'Keefe's painting, of entering the grand coolness of the gallery, of walking up the stairs from the ground floor, of craning my neck and straining my head back to take in the enormity of this powerful image is always different. I sit and absorb, I take pictures and fill my journal with notes and then move on: I coil in and around the intensities that are emergent in the affective immensity of this space; my re-coiling is one of difference, something new is always undone.

J: Clouding is a writing that does not hold but becomes substance, becomes other: making and undoing; making and undoing; and always becoming.

K: Here I sense rhythm and I reel out my emergent understanding of Deleuze's notion of the refrain which Alecia Jackson describes as

J: "repetitious and rhythmic patterns of sound and movement that stake out a territory (that) have a catalytic function to make something new, such as when music takes hold of a refrain and releases into an improvisational creative expression" (Jackson, 2016, p. 1).

K: So it seems to me that engaging in the practice of 'writing to it' we are animating ontological selves and actively producing, through the animation of a philosophy of the event, what Deleuze and Guattari refer to as 'minor literatures.' There is a sense in which the 'it' in this phrase might be seen as signifying some 'thing,' some kind of object that is categorised in difference. That is how I could describe my writing in and around the intensities I sense in relation to O'Keefe's painting: that is not the intention here.

I understand 'writing to it' as involving a writing to, a writing with, a writing to inquire into what might be troubling, what might be emerging in conversation, bringing about laughter, generating pain: 'writing to it' is affective and it is creative in engaging with the constant processual entanglings of materiality and discourse that are involved in bringing concepts to life. The notion of writing to a determinate object is not our intent; indeed in 'writing to it' the determinacy of objects becomes deeply troubled, seriously fractured and ultimately eliminated. So I feel really comfortable with the notion of 'writing as clouding' that you have offered in your last piece of writing, it takes me to the differences in repetition involved in immersions of self in Georgia O'Keeffe's painting and it encourages me to engage in, as you say,

J: "a process of gathering and moving and dispersing and travelling, and doing so in response to and "intra-acting" with the winds, currents and forces with/in/into which clouds are embrangled".

K: When you describe 'clouding as writing' in terms of

J: "[the] 'immanent imperative' that may get us lost, that troubles, that messes up . . . (that) take(s) us into what we don't know."

K: I gain a powerful sense of writing as affect. The immanence of writing (to it) brings us in line with Spinoza's oft quoted and highly rhetorical question, 'What can a body do?' Writing is not simply a practice, a task, an activity that bodies do from time to time and in certain places; in these terms, writing is an affective condition of selves in relationality. As you say,

J: "Clouding is a way . . . of suggesting what it does to us as we write."

K: I see that in our work, 'writing to it' is about desire; it is about always producing new concepts as a means of both dealing with and creating the world: as you say,

J: it "does not necessarily clarify but leads us into darkness, into . . . fog(s) of uncertainty, blurring our senses."

K: . . . and in this it is about world making. Therefore, writing to produce concepts that are always new is the animation of the practice of the encounter. Each new concept that 'writing to it' produces is an event that sets up an encounter with the world: writing does. In making these claims it seems imperative that we draw down Austin's work on performative utterances and work with his view that 'speech acts' and argue that writing acts: writing *does*, it is *performative*, in the sense that Della Pollock claims, "[recognising] its delays and displacements while proceeding as writing toward engaged, embodied, material ends" (Pollock, 1998, p. 96). In making these claims we can make a move away from representational domains of signification and identification and, in so doing, trouble the concerns of the academy that bind pedagogy and inquiry within the entanglements of interpretation, analysis and criticality.

J: *Clouding is a way . . .of suggesting what it does to us as we write.*

K: I want to argue that writing to it is event/ful, it is instigative of generating becomings in worlds of multiplicity, it is about event/uality and involves, in Whitehead's terms, always engaging with process prior to substance: in these respects it is a creative act, it is a writing into the not yet known. I sense that, with time, space is made; I sense its relationality and its potency in terms of movement in moments. I am motivated by Thrift in his promotion of a 'processual sensualism' and wish to employ this in precedence to and in preference of an Enlightenment logic of reason and rationality. In 'writing to it' I sense that we are using what Deleuze referred to as a 'logic of sense' to think with and through affect. It is important to assert that we are not using writing to reflect, to somehow attempt to engage in a mirroring of reality, in collaboratively 'writing to it' we are engaged in concept forming and, with Haraway (1994) and Barad (2007), using writing as a diffractive practice which does not simply reflectively engage with the world but interferes with it, troubles it and, in so doing, makes it different.

J: *Clouding is a writing that does not hold but becomes substance, becomes other: making and undoing; making and undoing; and always becoming.*

K: So 'writing to it' has a political valency: in saying that writing does, it feels to me that we are also saying that writing does in particularity, in different ways. I make sense of what we do when 'writing to it' in terms of what Deleuze and Guattari (1986) refer to as 'minor literatures.' These literatures stutter in the language to create new languages that trouble and disrupt the discursive orthodoxies and traditionalised tropic tendencies of the 'major literatures' that it works within. In this we can animate 'writing to it' as a politics of the event and be constantly attentive to Spinoza's claim to which, in my theorising as practice, I find myself returning again and again, that all bodies, human and non human, have the capacity to affect and be affected.

Again, and also in Spinoza's terms, writing as an engagement with affect is to do with power. As we write collaboratively we are with Deleuze and Guattari when they argue that the smallest unit is the assemblage. In this respect we can work to further animate the shift away from the humanist and Cartesian concerns with the individual; writing is not about individualization, it is about constant processes of becoming in relationality, of individuation. In this respect I understand and want to use the concept of the assemblage in its original form of *agencement* and, in so doing, take cognizance of Bennett's claim that all assemblages are agentic, in heterogeneity and contingency; they do something, they act. The capacity to affect and be affected is a capacity of all things and, as Bennett argues, the vibrancy of matter can be understood in terms of 'thing power'. The vibrancy and vitality of matter is entangled with the writing that is imbricated within it; in these entanglements, writing and materiality co-exist in the affective complexities of intra-action, where place can never be pinned down and located and where space is the constant animation of what Massumi (2015, p. vii) describes as an "invitation to voyage"—

J: [in] a process of gathering and moving and dispersing and travelling . . . intra-acting with the winds, currents and forces . . . [perhaps leading us] into darkness, into a fog of uncertainty, blurring our senses . . .[that] get[s] us lost, that troubles, that messes up. Clouding as writing takes us into what we don't know.

K: 'Writing to it' is a cartographic practice; it is a mapping that is cognitively attuned and sensitively oriented to worlds in the making, to active processes of world making. The processual nature of affecting and being affected creates space (not takes place) in and through events; it involves writing as doing, as encounter. 'Writing to it' works to dissolve those binaries of difference that categorise subject and object, nature and culture, theory and practice by positing transitive modalities of 'what if': What if I plug this little piece of writing into this space? What if I theorise this practice this way instead of that? What if, here and now on these pages, we were to write otherwise, disrupting the 'K' and 'J' that are suggestive of the binaries we're writing against? And so on. And, again, as Massumi says,

J: "affect is only understood as enacted" (2015, p. vii)

K: . . . and, therefore, writing through and with affect is a cartographic tendency which activates constant attention to what a body, our bodies, any body can do.

Another Recoil(ing)

J: Yes, my friend, yes to all of that: 'Writing to it' as event/ful, affect/ful, power/ful; writing to it that *does;* writing as encounter; writing that makes possible. A way of becoming with writing which this paper is proposing, offering, inviting.

The 'where' I am in and of now, this mo(ve)ment, is changing as I write. As we move towards the end of creating this paper I am going to experiment. (And I am going to re-claim 'experiment' as an act of unfolding immanence, not of controlled fixity.) I am going to write without writing about what surrounds me, what is happening nearby, by me, what I can hear, touch, see, pick up, sense, what is being suggested in, by and through what I might loosely call 'my' body. Unlike before. I am not going to write about someone sitting next to me on a train. I am not going to bring my neighbours on a flight onto our page. I will resist. I will try to allow 'writing to it', allow *clouding*, to work differently. Situating yourself, bringing place and space, writing on/with the body, is not something you have done explicitly in your writing this time, though sometimes you do. I am addicted to it, I think. I wonder how our writing habits, our writing familiars, our tics, perhaps limit? Maybe my tendency to think with what is around me is because the rhythm of travel seems to draw me to locate myself, even if only for a moment.

This is my 'writing to it' today, to allow what might at times striate take us into smooth space. Perhaps.

This will be different. It is difficult to not tell you of the heartfelt conversation right by me. A baby boy's cry. The sun on my skin. Being alone and away from home. As you can see, this is difficult. I am trying to start from somewhere else.

But perhaps not so different. These are all present in the act and the affect of this writing now. They can't not be. As yours are present too, however and wherever you write. In your notebook at the pub in Kingsand, standing outside with your pint of Betty Stogs on the convenient wooden shelf, looking out over the settling sea. Or in your study, upstairs at home, the room at the back with the steep steps up to it, the room that catches the evening sun. You will have been writing in places such as these. Writing to it. Catching the affect in the tips of your fingers, as it spreads across the screen, your body changing as you write; your body affected by how the words shape themselves.

In turn, wherever I am—on the train, on a plane, in my office at work, where I have to trek up flights of stairs to the printer, key in a code, and wait, then head downstairs to the School office to find a stapler, before the pages are in my hand, ready to read—there, as I read, your words—you—affect me. I write to it. The clouding begins. And begins. And begins.

Note

1 This chapter was original published as Wyatt, J. & Gale, K. (2017). Writing to it: Creative engagements with writing practice in and with the not yet known in today's academy. *International Journal of Qualitative Studies in Education*, DOI: 10.1080/ 09518398.2017.1349957. It is reprinted here by kind permission of Taylor & Francis and the authors.

References

Barad, K. (2007). *Meeting the universe halfway: Quantum physics and the entanglement of matter and meaning*. Durham, NC and London: Duke University Press.

Bennett, J. (2010). *Vibrant matter: The political ecology of things*. London: Duke University Press.

Deleuze, G. (2004). *The logic of sense*. New York: Columbia University Press.

Deleuze, G. & Guattari, F. (1986). *Kafka: Toward a minor literature*, trans. Dana Polan. Minneapolis, MN: University of Minnesota Press.

Deleuze, G. & Guattari, F. (1987). *A thousand plateaus: Capitalism and schizophrenia*, trans. Brian Massumi. London: Athlone.

Deleuze, G. & Guattari, F. (1994). *What is philosopy?*, trans. Hugh Tomlinson & Graham Burchill/London: Verso.

Deleuze, G. & Parnet, C. (2002). *Dialogues II*, trans. Hugh Tomlinson & Barbara Habberjam. London: Continuum.

Gale, K. (2015). Writing minor literature: working with flows, intensities and the welcome of the unknown. *Qualitative Inquiry*, *22*(5), 301–308.

Gale, K. & Wyatt, J. (2009). *Between the two: A nomadic inquiry into collaborative writing and subjectivity*. Newcastle-upon-Tyne, UK: Cambridge Scholars.

Gough, A. & Gough, N. (2016). Beyond cyborg subjectivities: Becoming-posthumanist educational researchers, *Educational Philosophy and Theory*, DOI: 10.1080/00131857. 2016.1174099

Guttorm, H. E., Hilton, K., Jonsdottir, G. U., Löytönen, T., McKenzie, L., Gale, K., & Wyatt, J. (2012). Encountering Deleuze: Collaborative writing and the politics of stuttering in emergent language. *International Review of Qualitative Research*, *5*(4), 377–398.

Haraway, D. (1994). A game of cat's cradle: Science studies, feminist theory, cultural studies. *Configurations: A Journal of Literature, Science and Technology*, *2*(1), 59–71.

Heron, J. (2001). *Helping the client: A creative practical guide*. London: Sage.

Jackson, A. Y. (2016). An ontology of a backflip. *Cultural Studies(Critical Methodologies*, *16*(2), 183–192.

Lee, K. V. (2005). Neuroticism: End of a doctoral dissertation. *Qualitative Inquiry*, *11*(6), 933–938.

Macdonald, H. (2014). *H is for Hawk*. London: Jonathan Cape.

Massumi, B. (2015). *The politics of affect*. Cambridge, UK: Polity.

Mazzei, L. & Jackson, A. (2012). *Thinking with theory in qualitative research*. London: Routledge.

Pollock, D. (1998). Performing writing, in P. Phelan & J. Lane (Eds.), *The ends of performance* (pp. 73–103). London: New York University Press.

Richardson, L. & St. Pierre, (2005). Writing: A method of inquiry, in N. Denzin & Y. Lincoln (Eds.), *The Sage handbook of qualitative research*, 3rd ed. Thousand Oaks, CA: Sage.

Sellers, W. & Gough, N. (2008). Currere and cloud-sculpting, in J. Knowles, S. Promislow, & A. Cole (Eds.), *Creating scholartistry: Imaging the arts-informed thesis or dissertation* (pp. 223–233). Halifax, NS: Backalong.

Sellers, W. & Gough, N. (2010). Sharing outsider thinking: thinking (differently) with Deleuze in educational philosophy and curriculum inquiry. *International Journal of Qualitative Studies in Education*, *23*(5), 589–614.

Wyatt, J. G. K., Gannon, S, & Davies, B. (2010). Deleuzian thought and collaborative writing: A play in four acts. *Qualitative Inquiry*, *16*(9), 730–741.

13

THE FUTURE OF CRITICAL ARTS-BASED RESEARCH

Creating Aesthetic Spaces for Resistance Politics

Susan Finley

March 16, 2016. Norman Denzin invited me to present one of the Keynote Lectures to open the 2017 Congress of Qualitative Inquiry. My response was one of delightful enthusiasm. By March 28, I had a title and a brief abstract. My plan was to present "The Future of Critical Arts-based Research: Creating Aesthetic Spaces for Resistance Politics." I intended that the talk would address the political and theoretical implications of critical arts-based inquiry. Critical arts-based research is a performative research methodology that is structured on the notion of possibility, the what might be, of a research tradition that is postcolonial, pluralistic, ethical, and transformative in positive ways. Exemplars of social and political resistance to post-09/11/01 neoliberalism and its propaganda would be used to demonstrate theoretical practices and research imaginaries made possible by arts-and-research political action. I promised to address some of the key questions for critical arts-based research: What is the future of arts-based research in a post-qualitative world? What are the implications for resistance politics in bioarts, biopoetics, and ecoaesthetics? What are the practices of imagination in performances of arts, research, and social justice? Norman was aware of my recent radiation surgery in treatment for trigeminal neuralgia at the time he invited me for the presentation, and the surgery had seemingly worked, until the summer of 2016. From summer on, I was in a tailspin dominated by pain, brain scans, and eventually surgery that induced a stroke. Norman gave me an option, told me I could defer and come back to do the lecture another year, but the meeting of the Congress became my goal. I would not miss it. What follows is the talk I gave, May 18, 2017.

Further, for an arts-based researcher to deliver a keynote address, it is seemingly mandatory to include art in the presentation! Poetry was in my head, but couldn't make its way to the paper. Drawing and collage have been my most frequent approaches to arts-based inquiry, but those are not yet among my go-to media, under the circumstances of the stroke. Performance was out—although I did enjoy a moment at the conference when the audience was invited to join the dance—and I did, walker and all. The visual presentation was as important as the words I spoke during the keynote. PechaKucha 20 × 20 presentation style was my inspiration, although I greatly revised the timing element. Typically, a PechaKucha shows 20 images for 20 seconds. The emphasis is on the power of the visual to convey a message. In my use of the methodology for teaching and other presentations, I disassociate the visual narrative from the words I am speaking to allow the visuals to tell their own story. Sometimes, I eliminate words completely and use only visuals. In the instance of the Future of Critical Arts-Based Research keynote, the visuals and the vocals were concurrent, with occasional connection points between the two modes of expression. Due to space limitations, only five of the images are repeated here, while others are described. As a painter and collagist, I have typically created images that I either photograph or scan for use in presentations. Here, I had to flip the process and create the images electronically, because of the physical limitations to my ability to paint and collage. To improve the learning curve and the quality of the visual presentation, I collaborated with Alec Lugo, who is a graphic artist (and sometimes actor and director) and Madeleine Finley, who is a visual artist (and actor). With their help we were able to integrate visuals I had already selected from electronic sources and create new "collages" and graphic illustrations for the visual presentation.

Slide 1: Title Page (2 min 19 sec, or 139 sec)

Hello. Thank you for coming. My comments are intended to be futuristic. To reach. To envision new spaces for resistance politics. First, I want to take a minute to give some background to my talk. To the visuals that accompany the talk. To my approach to this presentation.

I need first to ask for your participation in this event by sharing my own situation and how it has impacted my vision of resistance politics.

I am going to ask for your patience. About six months ago, I experienced a mild stroke, secondary to surgery. My vision is profoundly impacted, and I do not hear in my right ear.

Painting, collage, music and poetry are the essence of my life and of my work as an arts-based researcher. As Norman Denzin says, "You need theater to change the world," so it is with all arts. With Norman, I seek a "radical pedagogy of the heart," a radical pedagogy based in art.

Thus, I am now engaged in a project of adapting new mechanics that allow me to continue to do activist, critical art and arts-based research, differently.

Even so, there is no prosthesis for the fact that I can no longer frown.

Dysarthia and dysphasia
Aphasia and apraxia

I frequently mispronounce words, and sometimes a word won't come out, even when I know the word. I sometimes visualize words and, sometimes, I speak them phonetically. If I pause to search for a word, you are invited to shout it out! Often if I hear it, I can say it. Meanwhile, it'll assure me we're communicating and I'm making sense if you participate with me to deliver this talk. Most interesting will be if you begin to shout words different from what I intend, or different from one another. Improvisational theater comes to CQI.

The visuals during this presentation are not paced exactly with my monologue. They will play out behind me and hopefully, they will document the ideas behind what is being said. Still, I have built in a few voice breaks in which there is audio to accompany the visuals. I'm concerned my pacing won't be perfect and these will sometimes be interruptions—side shows that disrupt the flow. I'm comfortable with that, and I hope you are comfortable as well.

Slide 2: Head in a Vice (10 sec)[1]

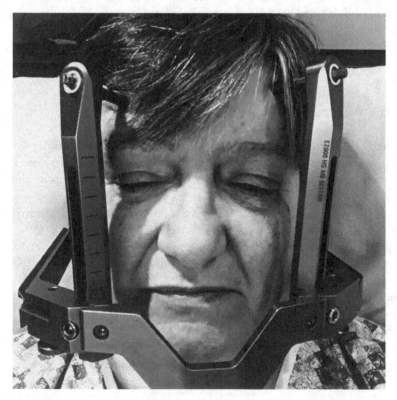

FIGURE 13.1 Head in a vice

Slide 3: The Scar (10 sec)

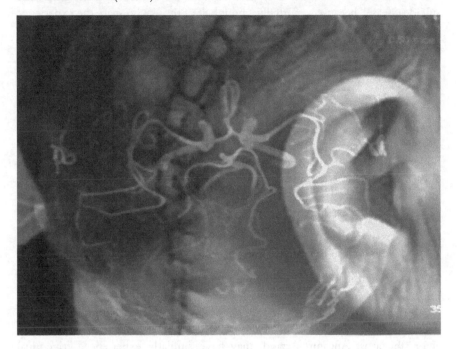

FIGURE 13.2 The scar

Twice in 2016 I had brain surgeries to address trigeminal neuralgia. Nerves and blood vessels in my brain had become twisted together like a knotted ball of yarn. The first surgery was a non-invasive radiation surgery. You can see in the photo that the process is quite medieval.[2] They quite literally place the patient's head in a vice and secure the vice with bolts drilled into the patient's skull. Next, if you undergo this procedure, over the top of your head, over the top of the vice, they place a second device that looks exactly like a kitchen colander. One of the technicians explained to me that initially the colander implement had one hundred holes for radiation to penetrate. It worked well enough, but its performance was greatly improved when someone came upon the idea of using 101 holes. Now, a 101-hole colander is the "gold standard."

Slide 4: Antonin Artaud's "Hanging woman" (33 seconds).

This is a visual I created based on Artaud's drawing of a woman, hanging, in what is presumably the act of suicide.

Radiation surgery provided short-term relief but seemed to ultimately anger the trigeminal nerve.

Suddenly, I knew exactly why another name for trigeminal neuralgia is "the suicide disease" because, reportedly, about half of those who share the experience of trigeminal pain, actually commit suicide due to pain.

Thus, despite the stroke and its numerous complications following a second more invasive, open craniotomy, I continue to celebrate the fact that I had the cranial surgery, as I am now free from trigeminal pain.

Slide 5: Handsome Artaud, my title for a photograph of Artaud before illness dominated his life (4 min 25 sec).

Slide 6: Artaud's Changing Profile, my title for a photograph of Artaud, vastly altered as he became dominated by illness.

Slide 7: Artaud's self-portrait.

Slide 8: Artaud self-portait, abstract.

Slide 9: Artaud final image, my title for a photograph of Artaud, near the end of his life, ravaged by his disease.

During my medical immersion phase, I played at posthumous medical diagnostics and determined to my own satisfaction that playwright, poet, and actor, the artist Antonin Artaud, may have similarly experienced trigeminal neuralgia or some similar neurological malady. It is known, for instance, that he was given opiates beginning in childhood to treat nerve pain resultant from meningitis. He lived to the age of 52.

Further, the faces in Artaud's self-portraits (and his portraits of others) are scarred and marked with lesions. Faces are disembodied or the skin is compressed against the skull. Stuart Kendall (2011) observes profound "discomfort" in Artaud's self-portraits (p. 3). The self-portrait shared here shows a distinct bifurcation of left and right, a feeling I associate with trigeminal neuralgia.

Kendall further observes that, in his self-portraits, Artaud demarcates the features "by forcefully dark lines, cross-hatched and re-drawn in over-emphasis" (p. 9). "Drawn in this way the facial features—the lines of the forehead, of the brow, the bridge of the nose—appear as wounds or scars, as openings in the skin rather than as finely sculpted features" (p. 9). Kendall observes, that in another of Artaud's self-portraits he "includes what appear to be two large pins or needles like those used in acupuncture, one inserted in the nose from below the face to our left, the other into the chin from directly below. The eyes of each of [Artaud's self-images] are over-emphasized, the pupils ringed in black" (p. 9).

My interpretation of Artaud's self-portraiture is that they are expressions of pain. Their expression is as direct as a scream. They *are* pain.

Artaud authored immediacy in all art. In Artaud's mind, "there was to be no distinction between art and life" wrote art critic Michael Kimmelman (1996).

Artaud warned that his drawings should not be regarded as "works of art, works of the esthetic simulation of reality." Instead, Artaud wrote: "My drawings are not drawings but documents. You must look at them and understand what's inside" (Kendall, 2011, p. 10).

Art documentation confronts the question of the relationship between art and life. Artaud sought to perform in what Derrida might call the "dynamis" or others describe as the liminal spaces in which life itself is the object of art and art too becomes life itself.

"Culture" wrote Artaud, "isn't in books, paintings, statues, dances. . . . It's in the nerves and the fluidity of the nerves."[3] Culture is *in the body*.

Embodiment. *"In the body."* Embodiment is the key concept behind Artaud's most enduring creative insight. Artaud recognized *the body* as a space for resistance politics and he remains best known as the creator of the "Theater of Cruelty" mode of theatrical direction.

Artaud conceived the purpose of theater to be universal expressions of life (writ large) through images, human and non-human utterances and through the possibility of performance to shatter expectations and create physical shock among its audiences. That shock, close to pain in its primal capacity for escaping the mediation of conscious analysis, could in turn move the audience to new capacities for recognizing the universal aspects of *being human*.

Audiences' acts of *being human* might create spaces for new myths of what it means to be human such that our responses to the staging of cruelty, or pain (such as rape, murder, even plague) can lead to audience's pleasure as we discover, *empathetically*, the pain in others, or create in ourselves ways to eradicate or supersede our own, human pain. That is, to trump cruelty with empathy and creativity.

Slide 10: Grab 'em. Original slide referencing the "Access Hollywood" tape in which now President Donald Trump describes in lewd terms his privilege of physical, sexual assaults against women. Created by Susan Finley & Alec Lugo

Slide 11: Great leaders. Original slide referencing President Trump's relationships with Russia's President, Vladimir Putin and North Korea's Supreme Leader, Kim Jong-un. Created by Susan Finley & Alec Lugo

Slide 12: Trump's wall. Original slide referencing President Trump's promise/ threat to build a great wall to separate Mexico from the United States.

If "all the world's a stage, and all the men and women are merely players," then we are currently caught up in a profound embodiment of the cruelest of theater performances. Ours is a theatre of cruelty enacted in everyday life by the political and social atmosphere created by the political legacy of a President who is crass and crude, a misogynist and misanthrope in high office. He is a dangerous man who embodies a perilous, nationalistic, power-hungry, and outdated way of being and leading.

Trump's Lament

Environment 90 seconds. This series of slides were set to flip quickly to generate a combined image and feeling, rather than to be seen as discreetly different visuals.

Slide 13: Children/Tree. The image captures a dream Susan had during trigeminal and depicts the children of the world in the branches of a dead tree. Created by Finley & Lugo

Slide 14: Watering hole. The image is adapted from the beautifully illustrated Graeme Base book, *The Water Hole*. Created by Finley & Lugo

Slide 15: Oil bird. Photograph of bird covered in oil spills.

Slide 16: Starving polar bear, melting ice caps. Photograph.

Slide 17: Increasing numbers of children/tree. This returns to the image in Slide 13, but altered to include more children in the tree. Created by Finley & Lugo

Slide 18: Children at the watering hole. This image merges images in Slides 14 and 17. Created by Finley & Lugo

FIGURE 13.3 Children at the watering hole

Trump's first 100 days in office were particularly marked for their cruelty to the world's children, the elderly, to non-human animals and to the Earth itself. Those 100 days will mark the future in what may be irreversible ways. His sins against the environment include the roll back of 23 existing environmental rules and regulations that protect the environment and prevent climate change and extreme weather.

According to Eric Pooley (2017) of the Environmental Defense Fund, the worst action in Trump's first 100 days came down to the appointment of Scott Pruitt to head the U.S. Environmental Protection Agency, compounded by Pruitt's appointment of his pro-industry, anti-environment cronies. Pruitt has formerly made a career of challenging clean air and water rules administered by the agency. His close ties to the fossil fuel industry portend the advancement of corporate gain over public health. Beyond that, this new man against America has introduced a budget that would reduce the EPA by about one-third.

Trump is the villain, but we cannot forget that he has considerable support. It does not matter that he didn't have the popular vote; he's still the President. Slides 19–23 Trauma (30 sec).

This series of slides were set to flip quickly to generate a combined image and feeling, rather than to be seen as discretely different visuals.

If President Trump doesn't cause a straight out nuclear war with his inept foray into world politics, his legacy might still be World War III. It has long been predicted that we run the possibility of a third world war focused on the Earth's diminishing and changing water and the anti-environmental policies of this White House, this Congress, and irresponsible capitalists, still gears us toward a Third World War event.

Slide 19: World War III about water. Graphic word design that includes water drippling from the words World War III. Created by Lugo

Slide 20: Trump's wall. Repeat of Slide 12.

Slide 21: Mechanical suicide. Photo from production of *RUR, Rossum's Universal Robot*, written by Čapek, 1920. Directed by Alec Lugo. Actor in photo, Levi Hudson. Photograph and slide created by Lugo

Slide 22: Kick the dog. Photograph of human kicking a robot dog. www.youtube.com/watch?v=40btf4T6cVs

Slide 23: Resist wall. Graphic arts image of a wall against horizon of sky and grass with the word RESIST in all capitals along the length of the wall. Created by Lugo

We live in an era of technological boom. Donald Trump has taken up one aspect of that technology, the tweet, and has used it to his advantage to create "noise" that distracts from real world administration and decision-making incumbent upon the president, and to use his twitter noise to enlist racist, nationalist, and neo-fandom via twitter technology. I believe his use of twitter has branded him innovative, up-to-date, a part of a modern technological world. He can be characterized as demonstrating his faith in human achievement and human progress through his awareness of advances in communications Technology. This imaging is regardless that closer inspection reveals him to have one technology at his disposal.

That trump holds to a Western notion of optimistic rationalism and blind faith in human exceptionalism plays out in his attitudes about technology and is demonstrated by his appointment of Andy Puzder, the CEO of the fast-food chains Carl's Jr. and Hardee's, who condones the idea of replacing food service workers with robots.

Says Puzder, robots are "always polite, they always upsell, they never take a vacation, they never show up late, there's never a slip-and-fall, or an age, sex, or race discrimination case."

Anti-Nazi Czechoslovakian author and playwright Čapek (1890–1938) first used the term "robot" in the play R.U.R., Rossum's Universal Robots, written in 1920. In the play, in a tale of post-industrial dystopia, whereby the increasing perfection of technology eventually results in the robot as a human "thing," but not person: "Devoid of emotion, personality and thus agency, the robot is introduced to the reader of R.U.R. as an object of technological perversion; man altered to the point of being labor alone, not love or creative intellect. It is humanity without the spark."

The photos here are from a college revival of the play by director and actor Alec Lugo.

In the story, in an effort to make the robots more human the scientist running the project adds to the robots' artificial intelligence the capacity to feel pain—

Pain is considered by many neurological scientists to be at the root of life. Ben Seymour, a researcher in computational and biological learning at Cambridge University, said: "Some people consider pain to be the pinnacle of consciousness. Of course, it's not a pleasant pinnacle of consciousness but it arguably is a time where we feel most human, because we are most in touch with ourselves as mortal human beings."

Moreover, sensing pain and experiencing pain are two very different things, the latter implying *sentience*, or "the ability to have subjective experiences," which requires the presence of a conscience. Yet some neurological scientists agree: "the most searing pains render one incapable of understanding pain or anything else" (Colb and Dorf).

Humans seem to process empathy for pain for both robots and other animal life similarly to their feelings about human pain. In several studies that probed empathetic reactions to beating up robots or kicking robot dogs, people actually refused to "hurt" the robotic form.

Nathan Heller observes that "To the generation now in diapers, carrying on a conversation with an artificial intelligence like Siri is the natural state of the world." He continues: "Addressing other entities as moral peers seems a nonstarter: it's unclear where the boundary of peership begins, and efforts to figure it out snag on our biases and misperceptions. But acting as principled guardians confines other creatures to a lower plane—and the idea that humans are the special masters of the universe, charged with administration of who lives and thrives and dies, seems outdated."

That statement cuts across multiple contexts. It can be applied to performers and audiences—performers do not hold the story as their own, but share its meanings with an audience of peers in the performative experience; we are one with the world and dependent upon its resources and other-than human life. And, when it comes to world politics, American exceptionalism is equally outdated and immoral. It is a fact that "principled guardianship" relegates the non-white, non-majority, non-power-and privilege humans to a similar lower plane.

Slide 24: Hawaiian poet (Voice over; 2 min). Slide is a simple photograph of the Pacific National Monument. Voice over is a reading of the Craig Santos Perez poem, *Detour of the World War II Valor in the Pacific National Monument*.[4]

Poetry reading by Alec Lugo

Academic and poet Craig Santos Perez wrote the poem *Detour of the World War II Valor in the Pacific National Monument* for the National Park Service Centennial event, which commissioned 50 poets to write poems about a park in their state. Perez represented the state of Hawaii.

Sometimes, I am surprised about where I will find the voices of American Democracy. Perez tells us to RESIST. Reframe history, learn to say the names of our neighbors and our students, be one with an-other. My surprise was to find Perez's voice on a governmental website.

The resistance movement may always be known in history as Trump's greatest legacy. Black Lives Matter, the Women's March, and Science Day have all been street performances of great magnitude. With Artaud these protesters have recognized *the body* as a space for resistance politics.

I have asked, how can critical arts-based research disrupt the flow of history, stem the flow of racist, elitist, and nationalist policies? How can critical ABR create new spaces for democratic political action?

Slides 19–23: Resist (30 sec, repeated). This series of slides were set to flip quickly to generate a combined image and feeling, rather than to be seen as discreetly different visuals.

Slide 25: Pussaaay, a photographic image of members of Russia's "Pussy Riot" protest group.

Slide 26: Black Lives Matter. Graphic arts collage from news images. Created by M. Finley

Slide 27: Impeach Trump. Graphic arts collage from news images. Created by M. Finley

Slide 28: Science Day. Graphic arts collage from news images. Created by M. Finley

Stand up! Stand up! Speak out! Resist! Resist! We are *alive* within the THEATER of CRUELTY. Feel the pain! Feel the Bern. You! You are the space for resistance politics! Embody Resistance! Work from within the academy. Take that ultimate place of privilege—the underpaid and underappreciated academic is a ruse. Use that politically embodied space of "the educated" to open doors from within. Cut the elitism. There's no exceptionalism to who we are as educators. We drew a good card. And we kept it.

That card, the one that drapes us in educational privilege comes with a heavy dose of existential responsibility.

We have come to this mecca, we have come home, to commiserate, to learn from one another new approaches to doing research, to rejoice in being with friends and comrades. But when we end this retreat, we need to walk out those doors as members of a resistance coalition ready to RESIST.

FIGURE 13.4 Science Day

"Show me don't tell me," Norman Denzin might suggest.

In order to show, not tell, critical arts-based researchers need to explore new avenues for art documentation. Art documentation of lived events is complex in its processes. Documentations can be creative articulations that shape language, poetics, and musical forms into novel uses of texts and tweets. Deep zoom panoramic photography documents activity and re-conceives environmental spaces. Documentation can transform uses of the Internet and re-conceive photographic methods for sharing life events. Internet documentation revolutionizes communication.

Art activism is not new, history is replete with examples, but critical activism is newly included in definition of the meaning of research. Activist arts-based research is still new in the university. It is new in *research* about human life and human experience.

As artists-researchers we must reach across the aisle to our colleagues in the sciences and bring to them the artists' tools for resistance. Bioart, for instance, has drawn upon the methods of artists who use their bodies as media. Writes Hauser (2010), "Artists are again increasingly attempting to use bodies, including their own, as a battlefield for the confrontation with themes and issues that have arisen in connection with the life sciences" (p. 90). Writes Groys (2008; also quoted by Hauser), Art documentation as an art-form is "defined by the aspiration of today's art to become life itself, not merely to depict life to offer it art products (p. 108)".

Critical arts-based researchers create and perform local performance "events" that embody resistance politics, but we can also be sure to document those events in ways that utilize Internet technology to share the event as an art product, while simultaneously expanding the audience of participants who perceive the re-enacted experience and, in turn, engage with others in conversations about the event as if it is a *happening*.

Groys observes: Today's artistic events cannot be preserved and contemplated like traditional artworks. However, they can be documented, 'covered,' narrated and commented on. Traditional art produced art objects. Contemporary art produces information about art events. That makes contemporary art compatible with the Internet—and . . . Digital archiving, on the contrary, ignores the object and preserves the aura. The object itself is absent. What remains is its metadata— the information about here and now of its original inscription into the material flow: photos, videos, textual testimonies.

Consider the possibilities of "synthetic documentation" as a new method for preservation and dissemination of media art. Its creators describe a "synthetic documentation" as the reproduction of complex multisensory information that a work of media art produces, whereby an "e-Installation" is the analogical equivalent to the "e-Book" as the electronic version of a real book. In an e-Installation, advanced 3D modeling and telepresence technologies with a very high level of immersion allow the virtual re-enactment of works of media art that are ephemeral or geographically restricted.

Arts-based researchers are driven by "egalitarian and democratic" impulses. Traditional means of sharing art, in museums, even in web-based art museums are available to limited audiences. The Internet is much more widely available and so offers unique opportunities for democratizing communications of arts-based research, and most particularly, of documenting performance events.

A democratic and ethical resistance by artist-researchers cannot be elitist. It must involve youths, the primary users of the Internet, and it must involve a creative effort to design new ways to talk to the Trump voter—the man got 65 million votes! It is important that we move outward from self-reflection about personal pain and the pain we share with friends and colleagues to offer aesthetic events of the kind Artaud promoted—events in which we strive to understand the human pain that must be felt by individual voters who supported the election of a bigot in hopes that by his difference, or by his sameness to them, however misconceived, they hoped to find relief from the pain of their own existence.

It is all about the vernacular. About the ability of the arts to speak to and involve a wide and diverse audience in its activities—it is about street performances as protests and about documenting and re-visiting the important moments created in the arts of the streets and TV and internet memes.

Slide 29: Red wheelbarrow (1 min to close). Original drawing of wheelbarrow and chickens. Slide created by M. Finley, voice-over reading of the William Carlos Williams poem, *The Red Wheelbarrow*, read by Lugo, pp. 224–225

> Ultimately,
> so much depends
> upon
> a red wheel
> barrow
> glazed with rain
> water
> beside the white
> chickens.

Notes

1. This photograph was the first of two "selfies" I've taken—the second image is my second "selfie." It's an interesting experience to take a photograph during surgical preparations.
2. Knowing the inexactness of medical science, as I do from the place of my experience—the tale may give rise to a description of science as "magic." The 101-hole solution sounds like superstition to me.
3. In Artaud's day, he would not have received either of the surgical interventions that I experienced. Trigeminal neuralgia sometimes causes its "object" to cry out, to vocalize their immense agony; thus, it was sometimes thought to be a mental disorder. Today, it is recognized and treated as a neurological disorder marked by intense pain.

Early in life Artaud was given opiates to treat pain from meningitis, and so he began a drug regimen that could result in hallucinations, visions, and extraordinary dreams. His treatments resulted in Artaud's incarceration and eventual interment in a mental institution near Rouen where Artaud honed his skills with graphic arts, which included numerous self-portraits as well as other drawings. Almost incidently, Artaud was eventually given heroin and cocaine to combat the physical pain of stomach cancer.
4. Many of the poems in this collection have an audio recording on the website. Sadly, this one did not.

References

Base, G. (2001). *The water hole*. New York: Abrams Books.

Čapek, K. (2017). *RUR, Rossum's Universal Robot*, trans. David Wyllie. Amazon: Create Space Independent Publishing Platform (original published 1920).

Groys, B. (2008). *Art power*. Cambridge, MA: Massachusetts Institute of Technology Press.

Hauser, J. (2010). Observations on an art of growing interest: Toward a phenomenological approach to art involving biotechnology. In B. da Costa & K. Philip (Eds.), *Tactical biopolitics: Art, activism, and technoscience* (pp. 83–104). Cambridge, MA: Massachusetts Institute of Technology Press.

Kendall, S. (2011). Anatomies in action: Artaud's self portraits. http://stuartkendall.com/?p=88

Kimmelman, M. (1996). A gifted man who put his pain on paper. *New York Times*, October 4, 1996.

Perez, C. S. (2016). Detour of the World War II Valor in the Pacific National Monument. Academy of American Poets and National Endowment for the Arts Imagine Your Parks.

Pooley, E. (2017). www.edf.org/blog/2017/04/27/100-days-4-worst-and-1-good-thing-trump-has-done-environment

Williams, W. C. (1991). "The Red Wheelbarrow" from *The Collected Poems of William Carlos Williams, Volume I, 1909–1939* (Ed. C. MacGowan). New York: New Directions (original 1938).

14

MUSICAL CHAIRS

Method, Style, Tradition

James Salvo

The Luminary

> The act of the potentiality to play the piano is certainly, for the pianist, the performance of a piano piece; but what happens to the potentiality not to play when he starts to play? How is a potentiality not to play realized? ... If every potentiality is both potentiality to be and potentiality not to be, the passage to the act can only take place by transferring one's own potentiality-not-to in the act. This means that if the potentiality to play and the potentiality not to play necessarily belong to every pianist, Glenn Gould is, however, the one who is capable of *not* not playing; the one who, directing his potentiality not only to the act but also to his own impotentiality, plays, as it were, with his potentiality not to play.
>
> (Agamben, 2017, pp. 40–41)

What distinguishes a luminary from a mere practitioner? A practitioner can only be a practitioner as such if that practitioner has an ability to practice. Thus, for the practitioner, an ability to practice allows us to think of the practitioner as a practitioner even when not practicing. In other words, just because I'm not at this moment playing the piano doesn't make me no longer a pianist. I'm still a pianist inasmuch as I stop myself from playing, and I can only stop myself from playing if it's given that I'm able to play to begin with. But given that every pianist can do this, what would distinguish a pianist such as Glenn Gould?

What Agamben suggests here is that Gould is distinguished from mere practitioners through his ability to *not* not play, through his ability to play by means of his very potentiality not to play. Though Agamben doesn't use the term luminary, we might apply this to Gould. Though we might have anxiety about never being able to escape the shadow of a luminary, this makes little sense metaphorically if we think of the luminary as the source of light itself. It would be those standing in the light of a luminary casting the shadow. But perhaps to think in terms of a luminary as someone lighting the way is to overlook a much more fitting metaphor. *Lūmen* hasn't only the meaning of light, but of window. It's much more fitting to think of a luminary as someone who's an open window to production, a window open to a bringing forth. The luminary isn't a mere practitioner insofar as the luminary is responsible for opening the ways constituting a tradition.

Thus, for the luminary, even the potentiality to not practice is brought to partake in the act of practicing. In the passage above, this is what Gould brings to his own practice, but might we not extend this to what Gould opens the window to? Might we not say, for instance, that Gould's recording of the Goldberg Variations on piano—a recording that was the first of that work on that particular instrument—opens a window for other artists to record that work, a work originally intended for harpsichord, on the piano also? That Gould is the first to record the Goldberg Variations on piano is significant for the reason that pieces intended for harpsichord haven't any guidelines for dynamics, for how loudly or softly one is to play. Striking a key on a harpsichord results in a plucking. This plucking overcomes the tension between the string and plectrum at a more or less fixed velocity, so striking the keys either harder or softer doesn't produce either a louder or more quiet sound, something that does happen with the hammering action of a piano. Using a different instrument as Gould does opens up the need to interpret the work in one's own way regarding the dynamics of hammered strings. Because these ways aren't given by the piece itself, Gould opens the way of a tradition.

Gould opens this way by not fully exhausting the potential for ways to interpret the Goldberg Variations. Instead, he opens a potential itself by being the first in a series, by creating the need for singular interpretations should we choose to be along the same path that he clears. Gould purposefully leaves room for development. Playing through his potential not to play can be a playing wherein what could be said is deliberately left unspoken. Otherwise, there'd be no clearing. We'd otherwise be enshrouded and overwhelmed by an anxiety producing fullness, and this isn't the aim of a luminary, for the luminary isn't, psychoanalytically speaking, the suffocating mother from whom we must separate to retain our subjectivity. Rather, what's shared by the luminary merges with our partaking in a way without anxiety. Nor is the luminary like the totemic father owning all the women. It isn't the aim of a luminary to own a tradition, but to share it. Further unlike the totemic father—the father we must ritualistically murder and consume—we creatively re-produce and keep the thought of a luminary alive. We do this through our own partaking of a tradition.

Glenn Gould's Chair

> Glenn Gould's chair, a relic from his childhood, became as indispensable to him as his instrument . . . He claimed it had "exactly the right contour" for performing, and he clearly didn't mind the creaking noises it made as he swayed to the music.
>
> (Isacoff, 2011, p. 298)

From the time he started using it, he gave no concerts and made no recordings without it. All the sounds it produced are forever part of the music that we know as Glenn Gould performances. Gould's was a musical chair. But was the chair part of the art of Glenn Gould in another way?

We hear Gould's chair in other ways, hearing, however, only in a manner of speaking. The chair sits much lower to the ground than the standard piano bench. It had formerly been a folding bridge chair. The legs had been sawn down by his father. One might think about the chair as keeping him lower to the ground, but we can also think about it as making the keyboard higher with respect to where Gould's arms would naturally fall. Typically, the pianist's elbows are more or less on the same plane as the keyboard. This is their natural location when sitting on the typical bench. However, as he sways, it seems that Gould's elbows at times dip below the keyboard. That puts him in an almost mantis-like position, a position wherein one wouldn't be so much striking the keys, but pulling down on them. And for the softer pianissimo passages, it appears that he shrugs, shrugging so that his elbows assume a sort of floating position. That seems just about right as it is, but doing the same on a standard bench would've given Gould the wrong leverage, a leverage that would've resulted in a weak sound. *Pianissimo* is a difficult dynamic because it must be soft, but not weak. Gould's was astonishingly solid. So how much of Gould's inimitable tone is the result of that otherwise flimsy-looking piece of furniture? One wonders at this.

Further, the chair would put Gould's ears lower in relation to the strings. One might not think it, but this matters. If one has ever wondered about why Bill Evans seems to be navel gazing—literally—as he plays, this is also why. When one's ears are more at the level of the pinblock, one hears the strings differently. Incidentally, Evans, too, would often play with a chair instead of a bench. His chair didn't seem special, though. As far as I know, it was just a chair. Further, Gould's chair didn't make it necessary to have that same headless-from-the-back posture that Evans often used. Posture can make all the difference.

All this is to say that both according to the artist himself and from what we might observe and speculate about through the hearing and seeing of his performances, the chair was part of Gould's art, a material condition of the art's production, a material condition of its bringing forth. Being a material condition of bringing forth only describes the relation of the chair to the art, however. That leaves the question of: What relationship does the chair have to the artist?

Is it part of Gould's method? Is it part of his style? Or does the essence of the chair's use occupy a place within where method and style become intertwined?

Method and Style Intertwine into Tradition

A method is a way in the sense of a path. The method is never itself the destination, so when we overvalue method as the destination, we fetishize it. Method is valuable insofar as it's useful. A method's value is one of instrumentality. But this is only one part of the meaning of method. Etymologically, to be engaged in method is also to be along with. Thus, the full meaning of method is to be along with on a path. Thus, when we engage in method, we take a path along with others inasmuch as that path is useful. Though we may stop at different points along the way, we all use the path of a given method to arrive at particular places lying along the path. When we think of the method of research, we're stopping along the way at particular truths coming to be revealed. As manners by which, methods are things that bring one to. As regards research, methods are things bringing one to truth.

A style, too, is a way, but not in the sense of being a path. Further, style is also caught up in instrumentality, but it's being caught up differs from that of method inasmuch as style describes what's produced through a particular instrument, literally the pen. A thing produced with a style is indebted to that style. If we're on the way to truth, then style's relation to truth isn't one bringing to or opening a way to a truth, but something giving truth its form. When we say that something is brought forth in a particular style, we're describing the form a thing takes from the way it was brought forth. Style itself is a particular bringing forth. It's herein that we can see how method and style are intertwined.

Method is an instrumental path bringing to, and style is the form resulting from a bringing forth indebted to a particular instrument. While method and style can remain distinct, this isn't so when the instrument used for bringing forth brings forth by bringing to. When this happens, the valued thing lying at the end of instrumentality is what we know as a form. And that our end value is a form isn't to fetishize either the path or the instrument. We still value that which is brought as it's brought. When we seek to arrive at something that's brought as it is, we seek to arrive at something given across. What's given across is precisely what we literally mean when invoking the concept of tradition. Tradition is what's given across inasmuch as what's given to anyone partaking in the tradition is what's been handed down. In tradition, we receive what's brought as it is in the way that it's been handed down along the path opened up by a luminary.

The Essence of a Research Tradition

> What hermeneutics legitimates is something completely different, and it stands in no tension whatever with the strictest ethos of science. No

> productive scientist can really doubt that methodical purity is indispensable
> in science; but what constitutes the essence of research is much less merely
> applying the usual methods than discovering new ones—and underlying
> that, the creative imagination of the scientist.
>
> (Gadamer, 2013, p. 576)

The style of a work does not only depend on the impersonal element, that is, the creative potentiality, but also on what resists and almost enters into conflict with it. However, the potentiality-not-to does not negate potentiality and form, but, through its resistance, somehow exhibits them (Agamben, 2017, pp. 44–45).

The essence of a research tradition isn't the intertwining of method and style, but an intertwining of the essence of method and the essence of style. The essence of a thing isn't the totality of a thing, but a quality of the thing constituting what it is to be that thing. Were it not for the essence, the thing would be otherwise. So to know the 'what' of the essence of a research tradition is to know both the essence of method and the essence of style.

The first quotation above comes from the "Afterword" of *Truth and Method*. In *Truth and Method*, Gadamer, is of course carrying forward the hermeneutic tradition, a way opened by his mentor, Heidegger. As in all relationships of student and mentor, Gadamer had an indebtedness to Heidegger, though this indebtedness doesn't perform a repetition of Heidegger. *Truth and Method* may in some sense be Gadamer's *Being and Time*, but it isn't itself *Being and Time*. Reflecting upon what he had written and responding to criticism, Gadamer asserts that the essence of research is discovering new methods. One might add that the essence of method itself, then, is the potential for development. Because research methods are themselves things never ceasing their bringing to truth, it makes sense that it's essential for these methods to develop when the material conditions wherein we use those methods change. This is important, for material conditions never stay the same; they always only change.

In the second quotation, though Agamben's use of *style* is most proximate to Deleuze's understanding, we can still translate the generic truth of the assertion to what we've been discussing. Style also exhibits potentiality and form for a research tradition. If we reduce the potential of potentiality, we might say, then, that the essence of style is form. To carry forward a style is to think what's impersonal and shared with those handing down in a personal way. If style is that which is brought forth from a particular instrument, what's brought forth through the hands using that particular instrument is shared inasmuch as all the hands use that same instrument. This is what's impersonal. However, the instrument in the hands of a particular handing-down individual bears what's personal to that individual when it comes to the nuances of how that instrument is used. In a manner of speaking, we may all use the same pen, but the things we write with that pen are always in our own hand. When it comes to a research tradition, style is a style of thought. In research, a way of thinking is what brings forth through the bringing to of thought.

The Clearing of the Luminary

A clearing is that into which one enters after walking endlessly in the darkness of a forest when, suddenly, there is an opening in the trees letting in the light of the sun—until one has walked through the clearing as well and the darkness envelops one anew. Certainly not a bad illustration of the finite fate of human beings. When Max Scheler died in 1927, Heidegger gave a speech in his honor during a lecture that ended in the words, "A way of philosophy falls into darkness once again."

(Gadamer, 1994, p. 23)

If method and style intertwine to form tradition, and to know the essence of tradition is to know the intertwining of the essence of method and the essence of style, then the essence of tradition is the intertwining of two potentialities. The essence of tradition is the intertwining of the potential for development and the potential of form. Thus, if a tradition is opened up by a luminary, to follow a tradition isn't merely to follow the luminary down a methodological path, but to enter the clearing opened up by that luminary. The clearing is where we remain faithful to the inner direction of our being, and if we arrive at the clearing opened by the luminary, we arrive not at a particular method and form, but at a potential for development and a potential of form with regard to our ownmost inner direction of being. In other words, to follow a tradition is to arrive at a cleared opening that allows us to find our own way.

Fidelity to the Event of a Luminary

Through all the changes, in ever new beginnings and struggles, he remained faithful to the inner direction of his Being. This fidelity must have been the source of the childlike kindness he sometimes revealed. There is no one seriously engaged in philosophy today who is not indebted to him in an essential way, no one who could replace the living possibility of philosophy which disappeared with him. But this irreplaceability is the sign of his greatness.

(Heidegger, 2017, p. 191)

The above passage is taken from the speech that Heidegger gave honoring Max Scheler, the speech that Gadamer mentions in the section above. To me, it's the last line quoted that stands out the most. I think this is true of any luminary.

Recently, when I was moving from Pennsylvania back to Illinois, I felt compelled to listen to Gould. I didn't have anything on my phone, but I found what I thought was a remaster of the 1955 Goldberg Variations on a streaming service. Something, however, was strangely off-putting about the album, but I couldn't put my finger on it. It almost didn't sound like Gould at all, and I figured the audio engineer had perhaps ruined it through the remastering. The engineering can make all the difference, I thought, much like how the first CD reissues of classic Blue Note records were ruined by whatever nameless engineer, and then subsequently unruined some years later when they contracted Rudy Van Gelder to remaster his own work. However, I was wrong about the version I had listened to being a remaster. It was actually a Zenph re-performance, something with which I was entirely unfamiliar.

Zenph re-performances are recordings marketed toward those who may pass up older recordings because the sound quality doesn't match that of today's. Zenph re-performances aren't remasters, but the results of a technological innovation. The original recording is analyzed by a computer for the exact durations and dynamics of each note played. Then, the data is sent to a Yamaha Disklavier Pro to produce a new recording. Though this is reductive, what Zenph does is to produce a highly sophisticated piano roll, and using state of the art recording techniques and standards, record a digital player piano playing that roll. It's a technological marvel, but at the same time it's empty. While one would think that it faithfully captures both method and style, what Zenph does is to remove the artist from the performance. You can't subtract Glenn Gould from a Glenn Gould performance and expect to end up with the same thing. The performer responds to the particular instrument at hand, and this is what can't be captured, no matter how meticulous the analysis.

If one's ever played a Yamaha grand, one knows that it's a precisely engineered piece of machinery. Every note is perfectly balanced with every other. It's remarkable how a machine whose sound is shaped by as many environmental variables as a piano can have achieved such exactitude. However, the trade-off is character. Steinways, on the other hand, are at the other end of the spectrum. All the notes have a distinct voice, but in any combination, they all blend beautifully. Each interval, each chord on a Steinway is its own thing. For almost half a decade, I had an office in the performing arts building. Less than fifty feet away from that office was where a nine-foot Steinway D lived. Every day at noon, I'd sneak on stage to play it. It wasn't only something to touch keys that Allen Toussaint had once touched—he had given a concert there during my first year—but to play that piano was to direct an 88-member choir. The point is, is that between the two types of instruments, there's a world of difference. Between a Yamaha and a Steinway is the distance between Helvetica and Garamond, between a Mondrian and a Vermeer. The pairs contain similarity only inasmuch as they respectively name pianos, fonts, and paintings. Incidentally, Gould's 1981 recording of the Goldberg Variations was performed on a Yamaha. However, the 1955 recording was performed on a Steinway CD 19.

I think this is why the Zenph re-performance doesn't sound like Gould. Because he was playing a Steinway, Gould would've been responding to the nuances of that instrument. If you transplant robo-Gould onto a Yamaha, you may get all the precise durations and dynamics, but none of what Gould himself was doing as he played the particular instrument he was playing. Could this have been remedied by constructing a Steinway digital player piano? Perhaps, but each individual piano has its own characteristics. The piano's age, the environmental conditions in which it's been housed, the current humidity in which it's now being played, all these things make one's response to the instrument's own response different. Thus, even to have used the original Steinway CD 19 for the Zenph re-performance would've produced something with no fidelity to Gould. Even were the exact environmental conditions to somehow be reproduced, the exact studio, the exact everything, the piano itself would always be of a different time. At any given point after the original performance, the piano can always only be older. There's always at least one thing that can't be the same.

This is yet another reason why luminaries are irreplaceable, their greatness unrepeatable. The luminaries came to be luminaries under specific material conditions that themselves can't be repeated. Thus, not only does even the most faithful imitation fail to be in keeping with the tradition opened up by a luminary, but any attempt to imitate produces the most pronounced infidelity. Repetition in tradition amounts to nothing but a spiritless impersonation. Any repetition will find itself under different material conditions to which the luminary had responded. Thus, fidelity to the event of a luminary must be something other than to repeat.

Two Theses on Feuer-Bach

Hearing Gould's 1955 recording of *Bach: The Goldberg Variations* in its release year must've been like hearing *Nevermind the Bollocks* in 1977. Both have the same fiery intensity of doing something for the first time. Gould's album is incendiary. One can't resist the pun of *Feuer-Bach*!

How does one follow along on such a path? Though one follows along, one can't cover exactly the same ground. To do so can't ever be a faithful repetition of the journey of the luminary, for luminaries themselves aren't ever repeating as they open, as they open by being the first in the series of a tradition. The event of the first can only happen once. Though one is along with on a path, one must find one's own way. Even Gould himself wouldn't cover the same ground in his own 1981 recording of the same material. The 1981 recording, made about a year before his death, is much more exploratory. It's unmistakably Gould, but at the same time it's a very different Gould. And if even luminaries themselves must cover different ground along the opened path, then it must be that others following after must certainly cover different ground. Following along the path of tradition isn't the same as ritualistic repetition.

To cover different ground, it could be that one following develops the method and carries forward the style. One necessarily develops a method as one finds one's own way along the opened path. Take Simone Dinnerstein's recording of the Goldberg Variations. According to Dinnerstein herself, after discovering Gould's recording at the age of thirteen and attempting to play it herself, she put the work aside, for it seemed to her as though she wouldn't have anything to say that Gould hadn't said already. It wouldn't be until she was 30 that she'd revisit the work and try to find her own way. Dinnerstein's interpretation accomplishes the seemingly impossible of being fully aware of Gould, yet covering none of the same ground. Listening to her version is as though to listen to the Goldberg Variations on piano for the first time. For me, both Gould recordings are glimpses of Gould's own thinking: iconoclastic at first, meditative in later years. In both recordings, though, it's as though he himself is the composer of the work. Both recordings are different from anything coming before because Gould entirely subtracts Bach. In a way, he incinerates Bach. Dinnerstein, however, isn't as solipsistic. Not only is there more reverence to the composer, but her interpretation is foremost a sharing with the listener. There's an intimacy to her work that Gould accomplishes in neither recording. Actually, Dinnerstein's is my favorite recording of the Goldberg Variations done in the classical style. It's just right. By way of comparison, a recording one might mention is Beatrice Rana's. It, too, finds its own way. Her version is full of deliberate but, in my opinion, odd hesitations, almost as though she's using *rubato*, something essential for music of the romantic period, though somewhat out of place for baroque. Further, she makes some unusual emphases. Hers is the William Shatner of Goldberg Variations. Not all findings of one's own way work. . . but on second thought, after several careful listens, maybe Rana's version is growing on me. Maybe the brilliance of some findings takes longer to appreciate. Perhaps this means that we ourselves might be open to the ways of various practitioners. Still, these are examples of but one kind of finding.

On the other hand, it could be that one achieves originality by staying proximate to the methodological origin, focusing instead on the finding of one's own way by developing in one's chosen style. Jacques Loussier's version of the Goldberg Variations is another one of my favorites. If Gould's method was to perform the work as though he had composed it himself, this is even more the case for Loussier who's a jazz musician. What is improvisation but instant composition? Loussier's version of the Goldberg Variations is a jazz album, and it remains faithful to that form. Further, improvising is proximate to the baroque method itself. It's well known that the great composers were also great improvisers. Even the written music of that era made room for improvisation by way of *basso continuo*.

★ ★ ★

It was a few months before I'd officially take up my new full-time position helping run the ICQI. I was at dinner with a dear friend after the Congress. I was expressing worry—although perhaps panic is more accurate—about what taking this new job meant. Both of us have at times discussed carrying forward the tradition of our mentor, Norman Denzin. At one point, my dear friend came to me with this conundrum: "How do I write like Norm without writing like Norm?" I never gave her an answer, but reading her work, it seems as though she's figured out how from within the material conditions of her own context. My concern that evening was the impossibility of following in Norm's footsteps. Her answer to me was not to. I knew exactly what she meant.

1. The standpoint of a luminary belongs to the luminary; the standpoint of one following the luminary belongs to the one following.
2. One cannot cover the same ground as a luminary—the point is to find one's own way.

Musical Chairs

There are three chairs in my new office in the Armory. One is the chair that was mine when I was Norman Denzin's graduate assistant, another is Norm's old chair. They've been moved from the office we used to occupy in Gregory Hall. Though I've been away many years, I know they're the same chairs. Mine was broken in a very particular way. It sits lower to the ground than it should. I broke it on purpose. You couldn't adjust the screen angle of our computers back then. They were the famous Bondi blue, late 90s iMac G3s with a static CRT monitor. I broke my chair to make the computer eye-level. Even though the modification is no longer useful, it'd be strange for me to sit anywhere else. The second chair is certainly Norm's chair. It has the same distinctive creak when you lean back in it. Norm liked to lean back when reading. He read a lot. When he was away, I used to apply generous amounts of WD40. That never helped for very long. Did Norm have a paper wastebin ottoman? My memory here is hazy. The third chair is one that I vaguely remember being in James Carey's old office, the downstairs office that Norm inherited when Carey left. I don't know how Carey sat, but the chair is surprisingly stain free. Did he never drink coffee? Perhaps he did, only very carefully. The Carey office chair is a Steelcase knock-off of the Charles Pollock Knoll chair designed in 1963. I know a thing or two about furniture. I've been collecting midcentury modern for the past couple of decades. Once, I even had a booth in an antiques mall, although none of the things I had were anything I'd give the designation *antique*. I feel as though antiques should be at least 100 years old.

That's the thing about furniture. They can become relics of the past long outliving their users. The chairs in this office are sturdy. They'll be the material conditions of much work. When the music stops, others will sit here. My mind sometimes wanders and wonders about how the sitters shall sit when these chairs are properly antiques.

Da Capo

> After many years spent reading, writing, and studying, it happens at times that we understand what is our special way—if there is one—of proceeding in thought and research. In my case, it is a matter of perceiving what Feuerbach called the "capacity for development" contained in the work of the authors I love. The genuinely philosophical element contained by a work—be it an artistic, scientific, or theoretical work—is its capacity to be developed; something that has remained—or has willingly been left— unspoken and that needs to be found and seized. Why does this search for the element liable to be developed fascinate me? Because if we follow this methodological principle all the way, we inevitably end up at a point where it is not possible to distinguish between what is ours and what belongs to the author we are reading . . . In this way, I will endeavor to continue and carry on—obviously, with full responsibility—the thought of an author I love.
>
> (Agamben, 2017, pp. 34–35)

Yup.

References

Agamben, G. (2017). *The Fire and the tale*. Stanford, CT: Stanford UP.

Gadamer, H. G. (1994). *Heidegger's ways* (trans. J. W. Stanley). Albany, NY: SUNY.

Gadamer, H. G. (2013). *Truth and method* (trans. J. Weinsheimer & D. G. Marshall). London: Bloomsbury.

Heidegger, M. (2017). In memory of Max Scheler (1928). In T. Sheenan (Ed.), *Heidegger: The man and the thinker*. London: Routledge.

Isacoff, S. (2011). *A natural history of the piano: The instrument, the music, the musicians—from Mozart to modern jazz and everything in between*. Toronto, ON: Knopf Doubleday.

CODA

Pedagogy, Civil Rights, and the Project of Insurrectional Democracy[1]

Henry Giroux

One of the challenges facing the current generation of educators, students, and cultural workers is the need to reclaim the role that education has historically played in developing critical literacies and civic capacities. There is a need to address its importance in educating students to be critically engaged agents, attentive to addressing vital social issues, and alert to the responsibility of deepening and expanding the meaning and practices of a vibrant democracy. At the heart of such a challenge is the question of what education should accomplish in a democracy. What work must educators do to create the economic, political, and ethical conditions necessary to endow young people with the capacities to think, question, doubt, imagine the unimaginable, and defend education as essential for inspiring and energizing the citizens necessary for the existence of a robust democracy? In a world in which there is an increasing abandonment of egalitarian and democratic impulses, what will it take to educate young people to challenge authority and hold power accountable?

What role might education and critical pedagogy have in a society in which the social has been individualized, emotional life collapses into the therapeutic, and education is reduced to either a private affair or a kind of algorithmic mode of regulation in which everything is reduced to a desired and standardize outcome (Morozov, 2014)? Given the crisis of education, agency, and memory that haunts the current historical conjuncture, educators need a new language for addressing the changing contexts and issues facing a world in which there is an unprecedented convergence of resources—financial, cultural, political, economic, scientific, military, and technological—increasingly used to exercise powerful and diverse forms of control and domination. This is especially true under the Trump administration, which disdains public education, if not critical thought itself. Such a language needs to be political without being dogmatic and needs to recognize that pedagogy is always political because of its connection to the acquisition of and struggle over agency, values, social relations, and some notion of the future. In this instance, making the pedagogical political means being vigilant about "that very moment in which identities are being produced and groups are being constituted, or objects are being created" (Olson & Worsham, 1999). At the same time, it means educators need to be attentive to those practices in which critical modes of agency and particular identities are being denied.

Such a challenge suggests resurrecting a radical democratic project that provides the basis for imagining a life beyond a social order immersed in inequality, toxic assaults on the environment, and that elevates war and militarization to national ideals. Under such circumstances, education becomes more than an obsession with accountability schemes, an audit culture, market values, and an unreflective immersion in the crude empiricism of a data-obsessed, market-driven society. If education is to become insurrectional, it must reject the notion that higher education is simply a site for training students for the workforce and that the culture of higher education is synonymous with the culture of business. In addition, it should challenge the neoliberal assumption that governance should be in the hands of mostly powerful corporate elites who despise the common good. Such elites, as the South African Nobel Prize winner in literature, J. M. Coetzee, points out, "reconceive of themselves as managers of national economies" who want to turn universities into training schools equipping young people with the skills required by a modern economy" (Coetzee, 2013). In opposition to these views is the need for educators to recognize the power of education in creating the formative cultures necessary to both challenge the various threats being mobilized against the ideas of justice and democracy while also fighting for those public spheres, ideals, values, and policies that offer alternative modes of identity, thinking, social relations, and politics.

Crucial to such an analysis is the recognition that pedagogy is central to politics itself because it is about changing the way people see things, recognizing that politics at its core is educative. As the late Pierre Bourdieu reminded us, "the most important forms of domination are not only economic but also intellectual and pedagogical, and lie on the side of belief and persuasion" (Bourdieu & Grass, 2002). Just as I would argue that pedagogy has to be made meaningful to be made critical and transformative, I think it is fair to insist that there is no politics without a pedagogy of identification. This is a mode of learning in which people have to invest something of themselves in how they are addressed or recognize that any mode of education, argument, idea, or pedagogy has to speak to their condition and provide a moment of recognition in which they can locate themselves. Lacking this understanding, pedagogy all too easily becomes a form of symbolic and intellectual violence, one that assaults rather than educates. One can see this in forms of high stakes testing and empirically driven teaching, which numb the mind and produce what might be called dead zones of the imagination. These pedagogical practices are largely disciplinary and repressive. They have little regard for contexts, history, making knowledge meaningful, or expanding what it means for students to be critically engaged agents.

I want to argue for a transformative pedagogy—rooted in what might be called a project of resurgent and insurrectional democracy—one that relentlessly questions the kinds of labor, practices, and forms of production that are enacted in public and higher education. Such a project should be principled, relational, contextual, as well as self-reflective and theoretically rigorous. By relational, I mean that the current crisis of schooling must be understood in relation to the broader assault that is being waged against all aspects of democratic public life. At the same time, any critical comprehension of those wider forces that shape public and higher education must also be supplemented by an attentiveness to the historical and conditional nature of pedagogy itself. This suggests that pedagogy can never be treated as a fixed set of principles and practices that can be applied indiscriminately across a variety of pedagogical sites. Pedagogy is not some recipe that can be imposed on all classrooms. On the contrary, it must always be contextually defined, allowing it to respond specifically to the conditions, formations, and problems that arise in various sites in which education takes place. Such a project suggests recasting pedagogy as a practice that is indeterminate, open to constant revision, and constantly in dialogue with its own assumptions. Understood as a form of militant hope, pedagogy is not an antidote to politics, a nostalgic yearning for a better time, or for some "inconceivably alternative future." Instead, it is an "attempt to find a bridge between the present and future in those forces within the present which are potentially able to transform it" (Eagleton, 2000, p. 22).

At the dawn of the twenty-first century, the notion of the social and the public are not being erased as much as they are being reconstructed under circumstances in which public forums for serious debate, including public education, are being eroded. Under the influence of powerful financial interests, we have witnessed the takeover of public and increasingly higher education by a corporate logic and pedagogy that both numbs the mind and the soul, emphasizing repressive modes of learning that promote winning at all costs, learning how not to question authority, and undermining the hard work of learning how to be thoughtful, critical, and attentive to the power relations that shape everyday life and the larger world. As learning is privatized, depoliticized, and reduced to teaching students how to be good consumers, any viable notions of the social, public values, citizenship, and democracy wither and die. In opposition to dominant modes of education, critical pedagogy is dangerous to many educators and others because it provides the conditions for students to exercise their intellectual capacities, embrace the ethical imagination, hold power accountable, and embrace a sense of social responsibility.

Educators and others must resist views of the university that define its mission in terms that mimic the logic of the market, particularly as market-driven ideology shapes matters governance, teaching, and policy. The questions that should be asked by educators at this crucial time in American history might include how might the mission of the university be understood with respect to safeguarding the interests of young people at a time of violence and war, the rise of a rampant anti-intellectualism, the emerging specter of authoritarianism, and the threat of nuclear and ecological devastation? What might it mean to define the university as a public good and democratic public sphere rather than as an institution that has aligned itself with market values and is more attentive to market fluctuations and investors than educating students to be critically engaged citizens? Or, as Zygmunt Bauman and Leonidas Donskis (2013) wrote, "How will we form the next generation of . . . intellectuals and politicians if young people will never have an opportunity to experience what a non-vulgar, non-pragmatic, non-instrumentalized university is like?" (p. 139).

I want to conclude by insisting that democracy begins to fail and political life becomes impoverished in the absence of those vital public spheres such as public and higher education in which civic values, public scholarship, and social engagement allow for amore imaginative grasp of a future that takes seriously the demands of justice, equity, and civic courage. We may live in the shadow of the authoritarian state, but the future is still open the recognition that education is a civil rights issue is still alive. Democracy should be a way of thinking about education, one that thrives on connecting equity to excellence, learning to ethics, and agency to the imperatives of social responsibility and the public good (Delbanco, 2006). The question regarding what role education should play in democracy becomes all the more urgent at a time when the dark forces of authoritarianism are on the march in the United States. As public values, trust, solidarities, and modes of education are under siege, the discourses of hate, racism, rabid self-interest, and greed are in full bloom, especially with the election of Donald Trump as President of the United States. Democracy is on life support, but rather than being a rationale for cynicism it should create moral and political outrage, a new understanding of politics, and the educational and social formations needed allow American democracy to breathe once again.

Note

1   This chapter was original published as Giroux, H. (2017). Pedagogy, civil rights, and insurrectional democracy. *Howard Journal of Communication, 28*(2), 203–206. It is reprinted here by kind permission of Taylor & Francis and the author.

References

Bauman, Z. & Donskis, L. (2013). *Moral blindness: The loss of sensitivity in liquid modernity.* Cambridge, UK: Polity.

Bourdieu, P. & Grass, G. (2002). The "progressive" Restoration: A Franco-German dialogue. *New Left Review*, 14, 2.

Coetzee, J. M. (2013, November 1). J. M. Coetzee: Universities head for extinction. *Mail & Guardian*. Retrieved from http://mg.co.za/article/2013-11-01-universities-head-forextinction

Delbanco, A. (2006). *College: What it was, is, and should be*. Princeton, NJ: Princeton University Press.

Eagleton, T. (2000). *The idea of culture*. Malden, MA: Basil Blackwell.

Morozov, E. (2014, July 20). The rise of data and the death of politics. *The Guardian*. Retrieved from www.theguardian.com/technology/2014/jul/20/rise-of-data-death-ofpolitics-evgeny-morozov-algorithmic-regulation

Olson, G. & Worsham, L. (1999). Staging the politics of difference: Homi Bhabha's critical literacy. *Journal of Advanced Composition*, 18(3), 3–35.

CONTRIBUTORS

Editor Bios

Norman K. Denzin is Distinguished Emeritus Professor of Communications, College of Communications Scholar, and Research Professor of Communications, Sociology, and Humanities at the University of Illinois at Urbana-Champaign, USA. One of the world's foremost authorities on qualitative research and cultural criticism, he is the author or editor of more than two dozen books, including *The Qualitative Manifesto*; *Qualitative Inquiry Under Fire*; *Reading Race*; *Interpretive Ethnography*; *The Cinematic Society*; *The Voyeur's Gaze*; *The Alcoholic Self*; and a trilogy on the American West. He is past editor of *The Sociological Quarterly*, co-editor (with Yvonna S. Lincoln) of five editions of the landmark *Handbook of Qualitative Research*, co-editor (with Michael D. Giardina) of 12 books on qualitative inquiry, co-editor (with Lincoln) of the methods journal *Qualitative Inquiry*, founding editor of *Cultural Studies ⇔ Critical Methodologies* and *International Review of Qualitative Research*, editor of three book series, and founding director of the International Congress of Qualitative Inquiry.

Michael D. Giardina is Professor of Media, Politics, and Physical Culture in the Department of Sport Management at Florida State University, USA. He is the author or editor of more than 20 books, including *Sport, Spectacle, and NASCAR Nation: Consumption and the Cultural Politics of Neoliberalism* (Palgrave, 2011, with Joshua Newman), *Qualitative Inquiry—Past, Present, & Future: A Critical Reader* (Routledge, 2015; with Norman K. Denzin), and *Physical Culture, Ethnography, & The Body: Theory, Method, & Praxis* (Routledge, 2017; with Michele K. Donnelly). He is Editor of the *Sociology of Sport Journal*, Special Issues Editor of *Cultural Studies ⇔ Critical Methodologies*, editor of three book series with Routledge, and the assistant director of the International Congress of Qualitative Inquiry.

Author Bios

Mitch Allen is President of Scholarly Roadside Service, Research Associate at the University of California-Berkeley Archaeological Research Facility, Research Associate at the National Museum of Natural History-Smithsonian Institution, and Scholar-in-Residence at Mills College, USA. His career in academic publishing spanned 40 years, including 20 years in marketing and acquisitions for Sage and as founder and publisher of Left Coast Press and AltiMira Press. In this capacity, he was responsible for publishing more than 1,500 books in the social sciences and humanities and launching more than 25 scholarly journals. He is the recipient of lifetime achievement awards from the American Anthropological Association, the World Archaeological Congress, the International Congress of Qualitative Inquiry, and the Society for the Study of Symbolic Interaction.

Julianne Cheek is a Professor of Nursing at Ostfold University College, Norway, and the University of South Australia. One of the leading qualitative health researchers in the world, she is the author of *Postmodern and Poststructural Approaches to Nursing Research* (Sage, 2000). She also holds numerous honorary professorships in South Africa and the United Kingdom, and serves on the editorial board of academic journals including *Global Qualitative Nursing Research*, *Qualitative Health Research*, and *International Review for Qualitative Research*.

Susan Finley is Professor of Teacher Education at Washington State University-Vancouver. Her research interests include educational issues associated with economic poverty and homelessness, diversity, and ways of understanding and being in the world. She also researches alternative approaches to curriculum and instruction that improve educational access for all students. Her inquiry takes its forms in arts-based research, life histories, and narratives.

Uwe Flick is Professor of Qualitative Social and Educational Research in the Department of Education and Psychology, Qualitative Social and Education Research, at Freie Universität Berlin, Germany. His main research interests are the further development of qualitative research methods and health and unemployment in the context of migration. He is author of *An Introduction to Qualitative Research*, 5th edition (Sage, 2014), *Introducing Research Methodology— A Beginners' Guide to Doing A Research Project*, 2nd edition (Sage, 2015), *Designing Qualitative Research*, 2nd edition (Sage, 2018), *Managing Quality in Qualitative Research*, 2nd edition (Sage, 2018), *Doing Triangulation and Mixed Methods* (Sage, 2018), and *Doing Grounded Theory* (Sage, 2018). He is editor of *The SAGE Handbook of Qualitative Data Collection* (Sage, 2018), *The SAGE Handbook of Qualitative Data Analysis* (Sage, 2014), and *The SAGE Qualitative Research Kit*, 2nd edition (Sage, 2018—10 Volumes).

Ken Gale is Lecturer in Post-16 Education, Faculty of Arts and Humanities, Institute of Education, University of Plymouth, United Kingdom. Recent books include *Philosophy and Education: An Introduction to Key Questions and Themes* (Routledge, 2014; with Joanna Haynes and Melanie Parker) and *Between the Two: A Nomadic Inquiry into Collaborative Writing and Subjectivity* (Cambridge Scholars, 2010; with Jonathan Wyatt). He has recently edited journal special issues (with Jonathan Wyatt) on collaborative writing for the *International Review of Qualitative Research* and on collaborative writing as a method of inquiry for *Cultural Studies* ⇔ *Critical Methodologies*. He is an associate member of the Higher Education Academy and a member of the International Association of Qualitative Inquiry and the Narrative Inquiry Centre at the University of Bristol, where he is also a visiting fellow. He has three children, Katy, Reuben, and Phoebe and a grandson, Rohan James: He lives, nurtures, and sustains his soul in Cornwall in the United Kingdom.

Henry Giroux is the McMaster University Chair Professor for Scholarship in the Public Interest at McMaster University, Canada. His most recent books are *America's Addiction to Terrorism* (Monthly Review Press, 2016) and *America at War with Itself* (City Lights, 2017). He is also a contributing editor to a number of journals, including *Tikkun*, the *Journal of Wild Culture*, and *Ragazine*, a member of *Truthout*'s Board of Directors, and Editor of *Review of Education, Pedagogy, and Cultural Studies*.

Ping-Chun Hsiung is an Associate Professor in the Department of Social Sciences at the University of Toronto at Scarborough, Canada. She has conducted ethnographic fieldwork, interviews, and archival research to advance knowledge and theory in gender studies and qualitative research at local and international level. She is currently carrying out a project on Mao's Investigative Research during China's Great Leap Forward.

Mirka Koro-Ljungberg is Professor of qualitative research at Arizona State University. Her scholarship operates in the intersection of methodology, philosophy, and socio-cultural critique and her work aims to contribute to methodological knowledge, experimentation, and theoretical development across various traditions associated with qualitative research. She is the author of *Reconceptualizing Qualitative Research: Methodologies without Methodology* (Sage, 2016) and co-editor (with Marek Tesar and Teija Löytőnen) of *Disrupting Data in Qualitative Inquiry: Entanglements with the Post-Critical and Post-Anthropocentric* (Peter Lang, 2017).

Yvonna S. Lincoln is Distinguished Professor of Educational Administration and Human Resource Development and Ruth Harrington Endowed Chair of Higher Education at Texas A&M University, USA. She is co-editor (with Norman K.

Denzin) of all five editions of the landmark *SAGE Handbook of Qualitative Research*, as well as the journal *Qualitative Inquiry*. She has received the lifetime achievement award from the International Congress of Qualitative Inquiry, as well as the Presidential Citation from the American Educational Research Association.

Judith C. Lapadat is an Emeritus Professor, Faculty of Education, at the University of Lethbridge, Canada, where she also served as Associate Vice-President (Students). Her work has been published in wide variety of scholarly journals, including *Qualitative Inquiry, International Journal of Social Research Methodology, Journal of Learning Disabilities*, and *Narrative Inquiry*.

Patrick Lewis is Professor of Early Childhood Education and Chair of the Elementary Program at the University of Regina, Canada. He is the author of *How We Think, But Not in Schools: A Storied Approach to Teaching* (Sense, 2008). His work has also appeared in scholarly journals such as *Qualitative Inquiry, Canadian Children*, and *International Review of Qualitative Research*. He is the Editor of the journal *In Education*.

Silke Migala is a health researcher and doctoral candidate at Freie Universität Berlin, Department of Education and Psychology, Qualitative Social and Education Research. Currently, she is working in the project "Intercultural Concepts of End-of-life care—ambitions and reality from an organizational ethics perspective." The aim of the current study is to reconstruct the significance of cultural diversity of the aging society in scientific and health policy discourses from a critical perspective on power relations. Her main research interests are concepts of interculturality and diversity, End-of-Life care, ethics in organizations and health sciences and the application of qualitative research methods.

Ronald J. Pelias is formerly Professor of Communication Studies at Southern Illinois University, Carbondale (1981–2013). After retiring from there he took a part-time position in the Theatre program at the University of Louisiana, Lafayette. His most recent books exploring qualitative methods are *Performance: An Alphabet of Performative Writing* (2014) and *If the Truth Be Told: Accounts in Literary Forms* (2016).

James Salvo is a Visiting Lecturer at the University of Illinois at Urbana-Champaign and the Associate Director of the International Institute of Qualitative Inquiry. His research interests include continental philosophy, psychoanalysis, and qualitative research. He has never eaten a Twinkie.

James Joseph Scheurich is Professor of Urban Education Studies at Indiana University-Purdue University Indianapolis. He is the author or editor of numerous books, including *Anti-Racist Scholarship: An Advocacy* (SUNY Press, 2002), *Educational Equity and Accountability: Paradigms, Policies, and Politics* (Routledge, 2003; with Linda Skrla), and the *Handbook of Research on Educational Leadership for Equity and Diversity* (Routledge, 2013; with Linda C. Tillman).

Marc Spooner is Professor of Educational Psychology in the Faculty of Education at the University of Regina, Canada. He specializes in qualitative and participatory action research at the intersections of theory and action-on-the-ground. His interests include: homelessness and poverty, "audit culture" and the effects of neoliberalization and corporatization on higher education, and social justice, activism, and participatory democracy. He has published in a variety of venues including peer-reviewed journals, book chapters, government reports, and popularizations. He is recognized by the Canadian Senate as an expert in homelessness and has been the principal investigator for several research studies on homelessness funded by federal and municipal governments. He is the co-editor (with James McNinch) of *Dissident Knowledge in Higher Education* (University of Regina Press, 2018).

Timothy Wells is a doctoral student in the Mary Lou Fulton Teachers College at Arizona State University.

Jonathan Wyatt is a senior lecturer at the University of Edinburgh, Scotland. His article with Beatrice Allegranti, 'Witnessing Loss: A Materialist Feminist Account,' won the 2015 Norman K. Denzin Qualitative Research Award and his recent books include *On (writing) families: Autoethnographies of presence and absence, love and loss*, co-edited with Tony Adams and published by Sense.

INDEX